1981

Y0-BEB-086

3 0301 00055212 1

PETS
AND
HUMAN DEVELOPMENT

PETS
AND
HUMAN DEVELOPMENT

By

BORIS M. LEVINSON, Ph.D.

Professor of Psychology
Ferkauf Graduate School of Humanities and Social Sciences
Yeshiva University
New York, New York
Diplomate in Clinical Psychology
American Board of Examiners in Professional Psychology

CHARLES C THOMAS • PUBLISHER
Springfield • Illinois • U.S.A.

LIBRARY
College of St. Francis
JOLIET, ILL.

Published and Distributed Throughout the World by

CHARLES C THOMAS • PUBLISHER

Bannerstone House

301-327 East Lawrence Avenue, Springfield, Illinois, U.S.A.

This book is protected by copyright. No part of it
may be reproduced in any manner without written
permission from the publisher.

© *1972, by* CHARLES C THOMAS • PUBLISHER

ISBN 0-398-02358-1

Library of Congress Catalog Card Number: 71-187664

*With THOMAS BOOKS careful attention is given to all details of
manufacturing and design. It is the Publisher's desire to present books that are
satisfactory as to their physical qualities and artistic possibilities and
appropriate for their particular use. THOMAS BOOKS will be true to those
laws of quality that assure a good name and good will.*

Printed in the United States of America

R-10

To my wife Ruth

I, a stranger and afraid
In a world I never made.
— A. E. Housman

ACKNOWLEDGMENTS

FIRST and foremost I wish to thank my editor, Mrs. Lucille Oesterweil. Whatever literary merit this book possesses must be attributed to the meticulous care with which she edited this volume. Indeed, her work went far beyond the call of an editor's duty. Thanks are also due to Miss Toby Gang, who prepared the index.

It is a pleasure to acknowledge the interest and cooperation of one's colleagues. Dr. Bluma Weiner and Dr. Beatrice Harris read the final draft. Dr. Arthur Lefford read Chapter II, and Mrs. Ruth Barwicke read the section on folk tales. Professor Beatrice F. Fleisher, Librarian of the Ferkauf Graduate School, was most helpful in securing material not easily available. I wish to acknowledge with thanks the encouragement of Dr. Joseph B. Gittler, Dean of the Ferkauf Graduate School of Humanities and Social Sciences.

I wish to thank Mr. Austin MacCormick, Executive Director of the Osborne Association, for his perceptive reading of the chapter on "The Pet in Correctional Institutions" and for his many valuable suggestions.

I am most grateful to the following students who assisted in the preparation of the questionnaires and in the analysis of the data: Marjorie Badanes, Zita Brandes, Ona Decker, David Gittler, Balla Kohane, Herbert Machovsky, Rena Rosenberg, Bonnie Lee Padrush, Michelle Price, Jason Schwartz, and Claire Sherr.

Thanks are also due to my son David, who assisted with page proof, and to my wife Ruth, who typed the final draft.

The writer wishes to thank the following publishers and authors for permission to quote from the designated writings:

American Veterinary Publications: Animal hospital: Group communication. J. Antelyes: *Modern Veterinary Practice.*

Beacon Press: H. Marcuse: *Eros and Civilization.* E. A. Grollman: *Explaining Death to Children.*

Berkeley Humane Society: L. C. Lowie: *Cats and People.*

Brandt, & Brandt: Louis J. Camuti and Lloyd Alexander: *A Park Avenue Vet.* Copyright (c) 1962 by Louis J. Camuti. Reprinted by permission of Brandt & Brandt.

Cambridge University Press: E. Cook: *The Ordinary and the Fabulous.*

Cowles Book Company, a subsidiary of Henry Regnery Company: V & M Gaddis: *The Strange World of Animals and Pets.* C. Zurhorst: *The Conservation Fraud.*

Delacorte Press: H. Hediger: *Man and Animal in the Zoo.* A Seymour Lawrence/Delacorte Press book.

Dorsey Press: A. M. Des Lauriers and C. E. Carlson: *Your Child is Asleep: Early Infantile Autism.*

Doubleday & Company: R. Dempewolff: *Animal Reveille.*

Dover Publications: H. Hediger: *Wild Animals in Captivity. The Psychology and Behavior of Animals in Zoos and Circuses.* Dover Publications Inc. New York. Reprinted by permission of the publisher.

E. P. Dutton & Co., Inc.: From Axel Munthe: *The Story of San Michele.* Copyright 1929, by E. P. Dutton & Co., Inc.; 1932, by A. Munthe; renewal 1951, by Major Malcom Munthe. Published by E. P. Dutton & Co., Inc., and used with their permission.

Frederick Fell, Inc.: R. Joseph: *A Letter to the Man Who Killed My Dog.*

Harcourt, Brace, and World: K. Lorenz: *On Aggression.*

Harper & Row, Publishers, Inc.: The Joint Commission on Mental Health of Children: *Crisis in Child Mental Health: Challenge for the 1970's.* Table 81, p. 223, "Naming Animals" (Percentages of Responses in Each Class); Table 83, p. 225, "Naming Animals" (Number of Occurrences). Frances L. Ilg and Louise Bates Ames: *School Readiness.* Copyright (c) 1964, 1965, by Gesell Institute of Child Development, Inc. By permission of Harper & Row, Publishers.

Holt, Rinehart and Winston, Inc.: S. Thompson: *The Folktale.*

International Universities Press, Inc.: Bergmann, T., and Freud, A.: *Children in the Hospital.* D. W. Winnicott: *The Maturational Processes and the Facilitating Environment.* G. Roheim: *Psychoanalysis and Anthropology.* A Psychological and Sociophysiological Approach to Aging. A. I. Goldfarb: In Zinberg, N. E., and Kaufmann, I. (Eds.): *Normal Psychology of the Aging Process.* Reprinted from H. F. Searles: *The Nonhuman Environment.* Copyright 1960, by International Universities Press. By permission of International Universities Press, Inc.

Journal of the American Veterinary Medical Association: B. M. Levinson: Pets, child development and mental illness.

Journal of the Long Island Consultation Center: A. Quaytman: Animals as therapeutic aids in child psychotherapy.

The Journal Press: The cat and the child. G. S. Hall and C. E. Browne: In the *Pedagogical Seminary.* Imaginary companions and related phenomena.

Louise Bates Ames and Janet Learned: *Journal of Genetic Psychology,* 69:147-167, 1946.

Alfred A. Knopf, Inc.: On children. Reprinted from *The Prophet* by Kahilil Gibran, with permission of the publisher, Alfred A. Knopf, Inc. Copyright 1923, by Kahlil Gibran Estate and Mary G. Gibran.

McCall Corporation: Redbook's guide to family pets. M. S. Welch: *Redbook.*

MacMillan Company: Jean Gautier: *A Priest and his Dog.* Copyright (c) 1957, by J. P. Kenedy & Sons, New York.

McGraw-Hill Book Company: Desmond Morris: *The Naked Ape.* Copyright 1967, by Desmond Morris.

The National Association for Mental Health: Household pets in residential schools: Their Therapeutic potential: The veterinarian and mental hygiene. B. M. Levinson: *Mental Hygiene.*

The National Humane Review: B. M. Levinson: Nursing home pets: A psychological adventure for the patient.

New Directions Publishing Corporation: Dylan Thomas: *Collected Poems.* Copyright 1952, by Dylan Thomas. Reprinted by permission of New Directions Publishing Corporation.

Oxford University Press: Self, society and culture in phylogenetic perspective. I. A. Hallowell: In Montagu, A. N. F. (Ed.): *Culture: Man's Adaptive Dimension.*

Pemberton Publishing Company, Limited: M. Mitchell: *The Child's Attitude to Death.*

Penguin Books: K. Z. Lorenz: *Man Meets Dog.*

Philippine Journal of Science: R. B. Fox: The Pinatubo negritos: Their useful plants and material culture. *Poet Lore:* E. A. Dietz: Requiem.

Psychological Reports: Levinson, G. M.: Pet psychotherapy: Use of household pets in the treatment of behavior disorders in childhood. *Psychological Reports,* 17:695-698, 1965. Levinson, B. M.: Household pets in training schools serving delinquent children. *Psychological Reports,* 28:475-481, 1971. Reprinted by permission of the publisher.

Random House, Inc.: The age of anxiety. W. H. Auden: *Collected Longer Poems.* Copyright 1946, 1947, by W. H. Auden. J. Henry: *Culture Against Man.* Copyright (c) 1963, by Random House, Inc.

Routledge & Kegan Paul, Ltd: Sylvia Anthony: *The Child's Discovery of Death.* Susan Isaacs: *Intellectual Growth in Young Children.*

Schocken Books, Inc.: Marjorie Editha Mitchell: *Child's Attitude to Death.* Copyright (c) 1966, by Marjorie Editha Mitchell. Reprinted by permission of Schocken Books, Inc.

Simon & Schuster, Inc.: Colin Turnbull: *The Forest People.* (c) 1961, by Colin M. Turnbull. Reprinted by permission of Simon & Schuster.

The University of Chicago Press: Claude Levi-Strauss: *The Savage Mind.* Translated from the French, *La Pensee sauvage.* (c) 1962, by Librairie Plon.

English Translation (c) 1966, by George Weidenfeld and Nicolson, Ltd.

The Viking Press, Inc.: Carmen Bernos de Gasztold: *Prayers from the Ark.*
Translated by Rumer Godden. Copyright (c) 1962, by Rumer Godden.
Reprinted by permission of the Viking Press, Inc. *Voices:* H. Aschaffenberg:
Jackie.

                                                              H.M.M.

155.9
L666

CONTENTS

Page

Acknowledgments ix

Prologue 3

Chapter

    I. Man, Nature, Animal 4

    II. The Pet and Child Development 34

    III. The Pet and the Adult 83

    IV. Pets and Old Age 97

    V. The Pet and Bereavement 113

    VI. Animals and Psychotherapy 136

    VII. The Veterinarian as "Therapist" 161

    VIII. The Pet in Caretaking Institutions 174

    IX. The Pet in Correctional Institutions 207

    X. Epilogue 219

Index 223

97201

PETS
AND
HUMAN DEVELOPMENT

PROLOGUE

IT has by no means been the intention of this writer to indicate that pets are a panacea for all the ills of society or for the pain involved in growing up and growing old. Certainly alienation and isolation result from complex stresses created by a technological society whose values and institutions are in many ways dehumanizing. It will take more than providing children and adults with pets for them to function as productive, happy members of the human family.

However, pets are both an aid to and a sign of the rehumanization of society. They are an aid in that they help to fill needs which are not being met in other, perhaps better ways, because society makes inadequate provision for meeting them. It would undoubtedly be preferable for all children to be brought up in their homes by attentive, loving, understanding parents or parent-surrogates, and for old people to live out their days in their own familiar surroundings, cared for physically and emotionally, and given an honored place in society. It would be better if society were not so mechanized, routinized, and cut off from the vital rhythms of the natural world. But this is not the reality of life, at least in the Western world, and far-reaching improvements will be long in coming. In the meantime, animals can provide some relief, give much pleasure, and remind us of our origins.

Chapter One

MAN, NATURE, ANIMAL,

REQUIEM

Rest sea-gull
  (do I see you breathing?)
Your spotless dress the
  color of night,
  sand for your pillow,
You rode on the seething
  black tide that enticed you
  from circling flight.

Sleep loon,
  Your once buoyant feathers
Are heavy as lead,
  like an ebony shawl.
The once friendly sea
  turned a slick patent leather,
Engulfing your gracefulness,
  ending your call.

Rest sea birds,
  your freedom is over,
  you and your kind
Have bowed once and forever,
  to the highest of mammals –
  the intelligent mind!
  – Florence A. Dietz (15)

MAN'S ESTRANGEMENT FROM THE NATURAL WORLD

TODAY we lead highly planned and structured
lives bereft of the heirlooms of former generations which gave us a
sense of continuity with the past and hope for the future. City
dwellers live alone in high megastructures where we find very little
emotional closeness, where we don't even know our neighbors'
names. There is a loss of kinship with our immediate ancestors and

4

estrangement from the community. Because we do not preserve old neighborhoods, because we keep moving all the time, there is a great hiatus between the current and the older generations; our entire rootless civilization is encouraging alienation and is leading toward chaos. We despair because we cannot recognize the world of our childhood. In an attempt to regain deeper contact with others and assuage our loneliness, we place an ever increasing focus on community reactions, community social systems, and intragroup relations, tending to put into the background the individual and his intrapsychic dynamics. There is widespread identity diffusion and confusion. Outside of our daily planned existence we don't know where we are going; we feel that we cannot steer a safe course and are powerless to avert catastrophe. Life seems like "a tale told by an idiot, full of sound and fury, signifying nothing." We seem to have forgotten the meaning given to individual experience through acts of feeling, perceiving, coping with conflicts, and extolling some experiences and denigrating others. We have come to devalue the fact that each individual is a microcosm having an entire galaxy of experiences with which to contend.

All of our conventional remedies have failed us. The present recourse to sensitivity training, encounter groups, sensory contact exercises, nude therapy, "primal scream" therapy, etc., represents unconsciously motivated attempts to return to our animal origins and to renew our association with the natural world. More direct, more effective solutions must be found.

Part of our difficulty lies in the fact that we fail to see nature and its animals as friends and partners. We were programmed to cooperate with nature and animals.

If we are to meet new and forever changing problems and conditions, we will have to find and incorporate into our lives new relationships between man and his immediate environment, including animals.

Traditional approaches are no longer adequate. We must examine man in his total relationship to his total environment. Man is going through a period of detachment, even estrangement, from nature following his conquests over natural forces. The machine dominates man's thinking and life space (20, 26, 69).

One of the chief reasons for man's present difficulties is his inability to come to terms with his inner self and to harmonize his culture with his membership in the world of nature. Rational man has become alienated from himself by refusing to face his irrational self, his own past as personified by animals. This difficulty is compounded by the fact that the two agencies which have held out hope for man's liberating himself — science and religion — have largely failed him.

Science, by and large, no longer serves the needs of modern man, but actually perverts these needs, while religion denies the hopes for progress and for work toward "an order of peace and love on earth" (64, p. 70), which it once inspired, instead permitting man to have "a good conscience in the face of suffering and guilt" (64, p. 72). Religion has thus decidedly given up its role of helping man to liberate himself.

Man now feels that the world is impersonal and that he no longer controls his destiny. He wants to assert himself and be the master of his soul and of his fate, turning for assistance in this enterprise to technology. However even here he is defeated, for technology, the handmaiden of science, has created an almost insuperable barrier between man and the rest of nature, including members of the animal kingdom. As Marcuse has so well expressed it, "The better living is offset by the all pervasive control over living" (64, p. 100).

As a result of our technological orientation, we see nature as a gigantic, inexhaustible mine of riches or, more destructively, as a whore to be exploited at leisure and then cast out. Man fails to realize that he has survived till now precisely because he has cooperated to some extent, not only with his fellow human beings but also with animals. A symbiotic relationship evolved in the past between man and other animal species, but this relationship is almost completely lacking today. When man is forced to live and work deprived of contact with nature, he loses much emotional strength.

MAN'S RELATIONSHIP TO THE ANIMAL KINGDOM

In order to understand the history of man's current predicament, we must consider his evolution, his relationship with other animals, and the way in which he differs from them. Unlike subhuman members of the animal kingdom, man is a slow-maturing creature.

Approximately a quarter of his life span occurs prior to maturity, whereas in animals this period ranges from an eighth to a twelfth of the total years of life (46, p. 1). At birth man is helpless, and his need for nurture is greater than that of any other animal. This period of immaturity lasts so long among humans that they have a need for protection by caretaking agencies such as the family, which also provides an environment in which the child leanrs an established culture that in turn he transmits to his own offspring (31).

Play

During the early years of this lengthy period of maturation and to a lesser extent later on, play is an important factor in development. This is because play is a free and temporary activity with rules all its own. While play is necessary for life (16), it is not concerned with the satisfaction of life's needs. It takes place within certain limitations of time and space, and it maintains and imposes order with the aim to end a certain tension (44).

Play offers the child an opportunity to get relief from inner anxieties and concerns. Play offers a child "an opportunity to elaborate upon experiences he has had, perhaps permitting him to rearrange elements in them and place them in different contexts" (18, p. 181).

Animals play too, but the play of the human child is different in two respects from that of his animal counterpart and immediate cousin, the primate. First, his emotional ties to his mother are maintained during the play years, even though siblings may be born; and second, he can change peer groups and thus vary his play experiences (18).

Culture

Perhaps the most important difference between man and animals is the fact that wherever man has lived, he has evolved a culture permitting him to transmit what he has learned. Man has the ability to stand on his hind legs which frees his forelimbs to fashion tools. He has an opposable thumb which makes the hand a good grasping device. His stereoscopic vision is helpful in judging distances precisely. As a liability, man has retained physiological features such as hormonal and metabolic responses (19) which served an adaptive purpose in the development of the race, but became less and less suitable as his culture evolved and are no longer helpful in the modern world.

Man also has developed a form of language which not only communicates immediate concerns and warns of dangers, as may be true for animal language, but also expresses complex thoughts and orients attention to historical occurrences as well as to potential future events. In a word, man can respond and communicate through symbols of his own creation. When human beings learned to symbolize, man qua man was born.

Because he can symbolize, man can transmit his knowledge about the world to his heirs, who can start where he left off. There has developed in man during his long history a species-specific drive to acquire knowledge for it own sake. Animals on the other hand must start learning de novo with each new generation.

As this culture-creating being began to develop and grow away from his animal forebears, he found it necessary to repress his longing for and veneration of nature (which he was destroying). To further this repression he applied the term "animalistic" to the basic needs such as hunger and sex, which he still shared with animals, thereby implying that these were contemptible or at least of no account. To reinforce this separation man proclaimed that he alone possessed a soul.

As man moved away from nature to an artificially created world, his language was transformed to correspond to the new reality. Many words associated with feelings of unity with and love for nature became lost through disuse. Only poets occasionally continued to speak in glowing terms about nature's gifts:

> I am a part of all you see
> In Nature: part of all you feel:
> I am the impact of the bee
> Upon the blossom; in the tree
> I am the sap — that shall reveal
> The leaf, the bloom — that flows and flutes
> Up from the darkness through its roots (9 p. 21).

Some of this loss of contact occurred not only in the area of language, i.e. symbolic communication and interaction, but in the ability to communicate through olfactory and tactile means — to be sensitive on a "gut" level to the feelings and aspirations of our fellow homo sapiens.

We have lost the ability to actively wrest our "information from the environment, rather than simply reacting to environmental changes, which is characteristic of all higher modes of animal adaptation" (6, p. 578).

This partial loss of reactivity to certain natural phenomena has been furthered by our technology, which has lulled us into a false sense of security.

Today therefore, many phenomena whose occurrence and meaning were obvious to primitive man are neither noted by us or even thought about, because we have lost both our tactile and olfactory sensitivity and the words by which to describe feelings and thoughts in these old, forgotten domains. Thus now that man has built civilization to his heart's desire and has more than enough means to meet his material needs, he has a tremendous longing, a passion, a love for his primitive origins, for he finds that he cannot survive without them.

He has lost the semantic symbols as well as the sensitivity and empathy by which to understand and assimilate the as yet unverbalized emotions stirring within him, which call for unity with nature. He is becoming aware that nature served him as a "transitional object," helping to "mediate between the known terrors of outer reality and the unknown terrors of the inner world" (56, p. xviii), but he is at a loss to recover his previous balance.

We are in many ways sensorily deprived. Our language is deficient and screens out the recognition of many life-giving sensations and emotions. This is possibly why our age is known as "the age of anxiety." It is imperative to modify our language, to discover new forms by which to express vividly and accurately the inchoate feelings stirring within us which we now characterize as "free-floating anxiety."

All human cultures prior to our technological age were fundamentally the same since they had to meet common human needs through association with animals. Man's culture would be entirely different if there were no animals.

Within broad subcultural limits the range of differences in ways of handling physical, social, and psychological problems has not been great. No matter where and when man has lived, he has been perplexed by fundamental and existential problems: What is the meaning of life? What happens to us when we die? How can we propitiate God or the gods?

> It seems as though thinking men, as yet at a low level of culture, were deeply impressed by two groups of biological problems. In the first place, what is it that makes the difference between a living body and a dead one; what causes waking, sleep, trance, disease, death? In the second place, what are those human shapes that appear in dreams and visions? (82, p. 418)

The earliest evidence we have found about the existence of primitive man involves his attempts to solve these problems. Witness the very early burial mounds indicating the development of complex rituals and beliefs connected with death.

Lévi-Strauss (57) points out that the discovery and transformation of weeds into useful plants as well as the fashioning of clay into pottery required considerable observation of nature. "Animals and plants are not known as a result of their usefulness; they are deemed to be useful and interesting because they are first of all known" (57, p. 9). He concludes from this that "neolithic, or early historical, man was therefore the heir of a long scientific tradition" (57, p. 15).

Thus in the dim prehistoric past as man evolved, there was a process of mutual adaptation and cooperation between him and nature. Man survived because he was a cooperator; otherwise he would have disappeared (66, 67). One of the elements of nature with which he cooperated was subhuman animals. "The myth of the 'ferocity' of wild animals constitutes one of Western man's supreme rationalizations" (68, p. 5).

This adaptation between man and his natural surroundings did not occur by design but by mere chance.

> Adaptations are not originated in the surroundings in which they are found and also are not caused by whatever action of these surroundings; adaptive characters appear as chance mutations without any relation to their adaptational value as pre-variations (73, p. 405).

Some of these mutations were beneficial and promoted the survival and propagation of the mutant members of a given species. The demands of the environment thus helped bring about the evolution and stabilization of certain structures and led to the disappearance of other less useful ones. The need for associating with animals became fixed in our genes and brought about species specific behaviors. "Without our built-in behaviors, we, as species, simply could not have managed to survive for a million years" (42, p. 32).

> If, in the Greylag Goose and in man, highly complex norms of behavior, such as falling in love, strife for ranking order, jealousy, grieving, etc., are not only similar but down to the most absurd details the same, we can be sure that every one of these instincts has a very special survival value, in each case almost or quite the same in the Greylag and in man. Only in this way can the conformity of behavior have developed (61, p. 218).

Throughout his long history man has associated with animals. There was a relationship between the nature of primitive man, his behavior, and the environment in which he had to find food and shelter. For almost all of his life on this planet, man has had to subsist on hunting (66, p. 103). The individual survived who, through mutation, developed structures which helped him to get along better in associating with and hunting animals.

In order to hunt animals, man has to learn about their habits, behavior, mating seasons, and migrations. He has to learn to understand something of their motivation and to integrate this knowledge into his own culture and behavior. In the course of evolution man began to use his intelligence to an ever greater extent, and the human who had greater intelligence or greater ability to adapt to adverse circumstances survived. Man began to use tools in order to make tools for hunting and this further enhanced his powers. Because of the kinship primitive man felt for nature and its animals, he adopted all kinds of animals as pets. We find for example, that among South American forest Indians, animals such as monkeys and parrots were kept not for utilitarian but for other motives (50).

The adoption of pets was in a certain sense a mental hygiene measure helping primitive man to abort mental illness (56). Primitive man could relate to domesticated animals which helped him in his labors, and he could develop a feeling of kinship and respect for them. Now that these animals are spatially removed from modern man, he feels that they are of no emotional import to him.

Primitive man formed a strong alliance with the dog, as it would otherwise have been very difficult for him to hunt other animals since he could not scent them (14). As has been pointed out by Leach, "If any outstanding thing emerges from this survey it is the so called 'savage's' awareness of the ancient intelligence of the dog, his sense of unity with the dog, and recognition of the mystery of his spirit" (52).

We do not know exactly when man first domesticated animals. This writer believes that as soon as man was man, he began to associate with animals and domesticate them. On the basis of current anthropological data, the domestication of the dog occurred around 6300 B.C. (85). However, much human history must have taken place before any records were made of events. Surely man was living with dogs and other animals for hundreds of thousands of years prior to that date. We know for example that fertility rites in which both men and his domestic animals participated antedate recorded history. As a matter of fact, the first gods of men were animals. They represented and symbolized the elemental forces of nature, such as water, fire, the earth, the stars, the sun, and the moon. A question often arises as to who really benefited from domestication. "Was the sequel the adoption of man by cat or capture of cat by man?" (51, p. 46). The association between animal and man was undoubtedly beneficial to both. Probably certain tribes or individuals were not able to adjust to this relationship with animals and died out, whereas others could and survived. In the course of this relationship man's nature changed, as did that of the animal. Thus the domestic animal has lost approximately 20 percent of its brain weight as compared with its wild progenitor (72).

We should be aware of the fact that primitive man did not consider himself to be the lord of creation. As a matter of fact, he knew that he was inferior in many respects to the animals with which he associated, and he therefore made gods of them.

The nature of man's association with nature, his feeling that it protects him, provides for him, and expresses his essence, may be understood in the way the pygmies of the Ituri Forest Speak about their natural home:

> "The forest is a father and mother to us," he said, "and like a father or mother it gives us everything we need — food, clothing, shelter, warmth . . . and affection. Normally everything goes well, because the forest is good to its children, but when things go wrong there must be a reason.
>
> "Normally everything goes well in our world. But at night when we are sleeping, sometimes things go wrong, because we are not awake to stop them from going wrong. Army ants invade the camp; leopards may come in and steal a hunting dog or even a child. If we were awake these things would not happen. So when something big goes wrong, like illness or bad hunting or death, it must be because the forest is sleeping and not looking after its children. So what do we do? We wake it up. We wake it up by singing to it, and we do this because we want it to awaken happy. Then everything will be well and good again. So when our world is going well then also we sing to the forest because we want it to share our happiness" (81, p. 92).

Similarly, the pygmies of the Philippines have become a part of their natural environment. They have developed an intimate knowledge of the interrelationship between the animals and the plants which surround them and on which they depend for survival.

In discussing the quality of Negrito life, Fox (22) spoke of

> . . . a characteristic which strikingly demarcates them from the surrounding Christian lowlanders is their inexhaustible knowledge of the plant and animal kingdoms. This lore includes not only a specific recognition of a phenomenal number of plants, birds, animals, and insects, but also includes a knowledge of the habits and behavior of each. This inclusive knowledge of nature is, of course, a product of their way of life; continual hunting, mobility, depending upon vegetation, as well as a survival of their historical associations. The Negrito is an intrinsic part of his environment, and what is still more important, continually studies his surroundings. Many times I have seen a Negrito, who, when not being certain of the identification of a particular plant, will taste the fruit, smell the leaves, break and examine the stem, comment upon its habitat, and only after all of this pronounce whether he did or did not know the plant. In addition, the intimate familiarity of Negrito with nature is the result of a thorough and sensitive ecological awareness (22, p. 187).

Preliterate man, still to be found at the present time in some areas of the world, lives with animals all his life. In order to survive he must develop expert knowledge of the habits of these animals and of the properties of plants. He has therefore developed a very intricate and exact vocabulary by which to describe their behavior and characteristics.

The attitude of primitive man was similar to that which still exists among civilized men who live in close proximity to animals (57). Lévi-Strauss believes that objective knowledge can also be endowed with sentiment.

We may note Hediger's feelings on first meeting a dolphin:

> I had the good fortune to be allowed to visit Flippy in his private practice tank. He dashed over to me and could not have enough stroking and scratching, especially on his light-coloured throat. The confidence of this legendary sea creature, its exaggerated human eyes, its strange breathing hole, the torpedo shape and colour of its body, the completely smooth and waxy texture of its skin and not least its four impressive rows of equally sharp teeth in its beak-like mouth, made the deepest impression on me. Up till then I had only seen such creatures as stiff, remote figures curling along the walls of museum entrance halls, or caught a glimpse of them from the deck of a liner as they approached in great schools, leaping fish-like over the waves. But Flippy was no fish, and when he looked at you with twinkling eyes from a distance of less than two feet, you had to stifle the question as to whether it was in fact an animal. So new, strange and extremely weird was this creature, that one was tempted to consider it as some kind of bewitched being. But the zoologist's brain kept on associating it with the cold fact, painful in this connection, that it was known to science by the dull name, *Tursiops truncatus* (40, p. 138).

Modern man may feel a similar awe and bewilderment in the presence of even such a natural object as a tree (63). Hardy describes the impact of a tall elm in *The Woodlanders:*

> The shape of it seems to haunt him like an evil spirit. He says that it is exactly his own age, that it has got human sense, and sprouted up when he was born on purpose to rule him, and keep him as its slave. Others have been like it afore in Hintock (36).

ANIMAL SYMBOLISM IN HUMAN CULTURE

Man has not changed essentially over the last million years, and is the same the world over (54, 55, 84). Most men have a need to associate with animals. Some of my readers may question this statement. They know that people differ in race, color, sex, and culture, so that if we are concerned with the peculiarly parochial aspects of the human being, we will find numerous differences among individuals. However if we are concerned with the universals of the human psyche, we will find no differences. We can see this universality in man's dreams, folk tales, drawings, and relationships with animals. According to psychoanalytic theory, the vestiges which we carry of our physical and psychological past break through into consciousness at unguarded moments and are expressed in our symbols and myths.

In order to understand our inner world, we must understand the meaning of the animal in our unconscious and conscious minds and also the bearing these meanings have had on the development of the race. Understanding this will give us a Rosetta stone for interpreting other phenomena and ideas.

There is a plethora of animal symbolism in anthropology, art, mythology, religion, and psychoanalysis (5, 11, 24, 37, 48, 53, 57, 59, 65, 82, 85). However, due to lack of space we can only give some brief consideration to the role of animals in dreams, fairy tales, symbols, and prehistoric art.

Dreams

The animal is a universal dream symbol par excellence. People in every clime and culture dream about animals, and they are at times transformed into animals in their dreams. Dream animals may either help or harm human figures. "Records of the dream life of the child suggest that normally he first dreams of animals, later of adults, and finally of other children" (3, p. 161).

On the basis of clinical evidence we have come to the conclusion that many dreams and dream symbols are not provoked or precipitated by current or past happenings in the life of the individual, but are innate. These dreams, in our opinion, are an expression of the unconscious affinity between man and animal, and they may often serve as a key to the understanding of the inner unconscious drives and motives of an individual.

I am quite aware of the storm of criticism the above statements will provoke. I am not ignorant of the overwhelming body of "scientific" knowledge which seems to contradict this point of view. However we must bear in mind that if one does not accept the possibility that a given phenomenon exists, one will not investigate it. If, on the other hand we assume that such a phenomenon possibly exists, we may find confirmatory evidence for our tentative hypothesis.

Dreams of individuals who come from different and distinct cultures very often have the same symbolic content (73). Some dream symbols are practically universal, and quite likely they functioned in primitive culture the same way they do now. As Roheim (73, p. 413) points out:

> Myths of the dream age, wistful yearnings for the glories of childhood, ritual representations of rebirth, and our dreams do prove that regression is a universal emotion. Yearning for the past is a universal emotion. Daydreams when analyzed always show their roots in the pa⌐ᵗ.

Animals n.ay portray brutal forces (33). Wild beasts particularly may represent passions and sadistic trends (77). Animals may also symbolize specific sex activities or sex organs. We find for example that the following animals represent the phallus: snakes, squirrels, rats, mice, fish, birds, horses, and bulls, while the female organ is represented by shells, oysters, and kittens (33). Animals may also symbolize preoedipal or oedipal conflicts (73).

> Do we really need a "cultural context" to understand the following dream of a little six-year-old girl? "I wandered away from home and met a wildcat. It turned into father and said to me, 'Why do you leave home? Why are you afraid of me?' " Another little girl, age three, always dreams about wolves when her father is at home for the weekend; she screams until her father comes into her room, and then she asks him why he always sleeps with mummy – why not with her?
>
> The first child is a Navaho; the second lives in Manhattan. We could just as easily reverse these dreams – they would still fit the psychology of either child (73, p. 16).

When we inquire why children and sometimes even adults are afraid of the dark, we may discover that they have an unconscious fear of its being replete with ferocious animals. The existence of such a fear is not even suspected by the subject. I believe that these fears are replicas of those of primitive man who, in his effort to preserve himself, very often thought of himself as a victim rather than as an aggressor. Thus a study by Ames (2) indicates that until the age of seven the child-dreamer is not angry at animals and does not attack them but rather is attacked by them, wolves, bears, foxes, and snakes being the chief dangers. While the child is at all times the most important figure in such a dream, he is being acted upon rather than acting. In the study of dreams however, it is very difficult to decide what really precipitated any given dream. Certain patterns are reported at various ages: At 4 1/2 the child dreams of animals with particular emphasis on wolves. At five he has frequent nightmares in which animals — particularly wolves and bears — play a major role, chasing after the child and awakening him. At 5 1/2, while still perturbed by his dreams, the child can tolerate them more easily.

Wild animals such as wolves, bears, and foxes continue to chase after him or bite him, but occasionally even domestic animals, especially the child's own dog, may attack him. Sometimes the 5 1/2-year-old fears that wild animals have crept into his room (2). Lewis (59) has analyzed 176 animal dreams selected at random, and has found that domestic pets such as dogs and cats were mentioned more often than any other animal. Dogs appeared in 35 of the dreams (19.89%), cats in 28 (15.91%), and horses in 16 (9.09%).

ANIMAL SYMBOLISM

We have very few scientific studies in the area of animal symbolism. Most of the experimental evidence we have about the symbolic meaning of animals for children and adults comes indirectly from a study of protocols for such projective tests as drawings (35), the Children's Apperception Test (38), and the Rorschach (4). We should therefore keep in mind the cautionary note sounded by Levy and Levy (58) that in trying to decipher the symbolic meaning of an animal, one must consider the "generic meaning" of animals in general, the "generic" meaning of the animal in question, and its specific meaning to the individual.

A study by Hartley and Shames (37) which was based on a small unrepresentative sampling of Great Dane and Chihuahua owners, disclosed that the "Great Dane may serve as a symbol of masculinity, power, strength, dominance, virility; and the Chihuahua may serve as a symbol of femininity and attributes popularly related to the sex" (37, p. 7).

Goldfarb (28) tested children on the "Animal Association Test," and learned that adults tended to be associated with large animals. The subjects frequently associated aggressive animals with cruel adults and domestic animals with kind adults.

Buss and Durkee (28) secured (a) animal associations to a list of 18 familiar figures, and (b) associations between six parental figures and 24 animals from two different groupings of psychiatric patients and controls. While there was not much systematic relationship between parental figures and animals, they found that cows and deer were associated with a kind, loving mother; bulls with a domineering father; and small animals with children. Phillips and Smith (70) found that the projection of a particular animal figure on the Rorschach reflected underlying personality traits. Goldfried (29) confirmed some of Phillips and Smith's findings, indicating however that some allowance must be made for the age of the individual and for his cultural background. Animals are usually seen as males rather than as females (27).

Van Krevelen (83) stressed that "any person may be characterized by assigning to him the traits of some animal". The same animal, however, may symbolize different wishes or drives for different individuals (83). David (12), by the use of the projective question, attempted to learn directly what kind of animal a person would most or least like to be if he were not a human being. It is hypothesized that by this choice of a certain animal the subject unwittingly discloses some of his underlying psychological strengths and weaknesses (12, 13, 49).

Schwartz and Rosenberg (74) warn that any animal may symbolize two or more ideas and that a particular symbol may be expressed by more than one animal. On the basis of a study of animal drawings (74), they came to the following tentative conclusions: A person who draws rabbits probably has characterological difficulties and is an insecure individual who is always concerned with how he impresses others. He is also trying to escape his obsessive thoughts regarding sex and procreation. Drawing birds may symbolize fear of desertion and a desire to escape from current problems. An individual who draws nonflying birds such as chickens seems to indicate that he, like these animals cannot move about freely, i.e. while the individual is aware of his problem, he is unable either to resolve it or to leave it alone. Drawing water fowl such as ducks and geese indicates that the individual is very much concerned with having a warm, pleasant home. The cow represents the mother in a primary relationship. Pigs, mice, and rats symbolize doubts about one's own worth, which may be based upon feelings of guilt. Dogs and cats are frequently drawn by individuals who wish to appear normal but are somewhat aware that they may not be so. Individuals who draw elephants indicate oedipal problems, while those who draw horses have stronger than average homosexual components in their sexual makeup. Mules are drawn by those who are afraid of sexual impotence.

Folk Tales

We sometimes find that a myth gives rise to a folk tale. Thus Leo Tolstoy's folk tale, "The Grass Snake", has Masha, the peasant heroine, marry a big grass snake which becomes the father of her children.

These tales are seen by some anthropologists as a remnant of earlier totem worship. The totem animals were gods, but when man lost his fear of these gods, he turned them back into animals and created these stories.

In myths and folk tales from different parts of the world and different cultural levels we find a recurrence of the same animal themes (43, 62, 79).

Heuscher remarks for example that "Allegedly there are some 354 variants of the 'Cinderella' story found among the fairy tales from Egypt, India, all parts of Europe, and even the North American Indians" (43, p. 6).

Throughout the world, a belief exists that animals and even inanimate objects can change their shape into various forms whenever they wish to do so (62). In connection with this, Wilhelm Grimm noted over a century ago:

> Fragments of a belief dating back to the most ancient times, in which spiritual things are expressed in a figurative manner, are common to all stories. The mythic element resembles small pieces of a shattered jewel which are lying strewn on the ground all overgrown

with grass and flowers, and can only be discovered by the most far-seeing eye. Their significance has long been lost, but it is still felt and imparts value to the story, while satisfying the natural pleasure in the wonderful. They are never the iridescence of an empty fancy. The farther we go back, the more the mythical element expands: indeed it seems to have formed the only subject of the oldest fictions (quoted in 45, p. 576).

This identity of themes arises from the fact that all human beings, no matter where or when they live, go through the same psychological processes. There are universal psychological mechanisms underlying these fairy tales, of which we can here mention only a few. One of the most important of these involves sexual activity and identity.

"Animals owe a good deal of their importance in myths and fairy tales to the openness with which they display their genitalia and their sexual functions to the inquisitive little human child" (23, p. 9).

No matter where man lives, he finds a desire for self fulfillment through sex activity. In some societies sexual activities are unconsciously identified with successful hunting (71), sexual intercourse being an unconscious equivalent of killing an animal. This attitude indicates that there has always existed rivalry and hostility between man and woman. Notice that even in modern societies the same sex act, depending upon the circumstances under which it is performed, may be considered benign sexual love or criminal rape.

Thus we find various versions of folk tales such as the one of the hero hunting a fawn which later becomes a beautiful maiden (73). Because such themes are timeless and of universal interest, we find that usually they appear in great poetic works. "The best stories are like extended lyrical images of unchanging human predicaments and strong, unchanging hopes and fears, loves and hatreds" (10, p.2).

> The loathy lady, the Frog Prince and the prince in "Beauty and the Beast" are creatures who are both familiar and foul and remind us of any people or things that awaken love and hatred at one and the same time; and it may not be accidental that the theme of the breaking of a spell that has turned fair into foul is nearly always linked with the theme of keeping of promises (10, p. 44).

Man has had a checkered history in his relationship with animals. As was pointed out above, animals played a great role in the development of the human race. It should not surprise us, therefore to find animal themes occurring over and over again in fairy tales. It is sometimes very difficult to tell whether "the actor is really a human being or an animal" (79, p. 217). Furthermore, in these tales many humans learn to speak and to understand the language of animals and the animals have human habits and act and think like human beings (43). From a psychoanalytic point of view, we might say that animals in fairy tales represent man's unconscious drives, and that the oedipal situation reigns supreme in the fairy tale. In "Red Riding Hood" (43, p. 79), for example:

> The oedipal theme can be seen reflected throughout the narrative: the girl rebels against mother and meets the seductive wolf who points to exclusively sensory pleasure; but doing this is dangerous, as the great-mother or grandmother, the one who can carry human beings in her abdomen, appears with the wolf's characteristics. For a while, it is true, the woman, the early-mother figure, appears more powerful than the libidinous male. Only later, when the man appears in the shape of a human being, considerate, forceful, and helpful, this threatening aspect of mother is destroyed and the grandmother, the child and the huntsman-father form a happy threesome. The huntsman who carries off the wolf's skin, combines now the human and sexual aspects of the male without being threatening. He shows that he has control over his animal drives. Instead of using the all destructive gun, which would also have harmed Red Cap and the grandmother, to kill the wolf, he uses his ability to be aggressive wisely and selectively by opening the wolf's abdomen with a pair of scissors (43, p. 79).

Thompson remarks (79, p. 141):

> One famous story coming from Greek drama keeps being repeated as an oral tale, the myth of Oedipus. The essential points always remembered are the prophecy that the youth shall kill his father and marry his mother. He is saved after exposure and reared by another king. The prophecy is fulfilled with tragic results. The fact that it is still told as a traditional story testifies to the close affinity of this old myth with real folk tradition (79, p. 141).

In fairy tales we usually find that the youngest son or daughter is helped by grateful animals who have previously been helped by our heroes, much to the discomfiture of the nasty older brothers or haughty older sisters. Occasionally the gratitude of the animals goes so far as to permit the hero or heroine to transform himself or herself into a part of the animal's body and thus rescue himself or herself or possibly perform some heroic deed (79).

Very often the horse (which is universally known as a male symbol) plays the role of the grateful animal. The animals act in accordance with the symbolic values ascribed to them by folk tradition. Thus the bear is stupid, the fox is sly, and the rabbit swift (79).

We can thus see how the oedipus myth is mirrored in folk lore. We see, too, how common folk have identified themselves with the youngest, weakest, ugliest, most unpromising child who through magic is able to overcome impossible odds.

Primitive Art

We find that primitive man was moved by the same passions and had the same desires as we. When we examine his paintings we note that they reveal extraordinary artistic ability. Surely such highly developed ability did not spring full-fledged from the heads of the artists in their caves. We are merely looking at the existing record. It is likely that there were other records which time has destroyed or which may yet be discovered. Primitive man undoubtedly went through thousands of years of learning how to draw, the accumulated knowledge being transferred from master to student for countless generations until it reached the advanced stages we see in the cave paintings.

Primitive art was doubtless as meaningful to primitive man as our art is to modern man. The primitive artist did not attempt to be obscure or symbolic, but concrete and conventional. His audience, steeped in the same culture as he, understood and appreciated his efforts (53).

The art of primitive man served many purposes; it expressed the artistic aspirations of the artist; it propitiated the spirits of the animals depicted in the paintings; it asserted primitive man's sense of mastery over animals and his ability to harm these at will; it was an object lesson for other members of the tribe, teaching them how a successful hunt was to be conducted; and it possibly consecrated a place of worship.

Hallowell (34) comments that these drawings indicate the

capacity of the primitive mind to handle complex symbolic processes, through the use of which he was able to change and enlarge his environment.

Clinical experience has repeatedly shown that what is uppermost in a child's mind appears in his drawings (16, 35). Thus for example in the depiction of a family, the size of the persons drawn would indicate their importance in the child's eyes; e.g. if the mother played a very important role in the family constellation, she would be taller and heavier than the father. Similarly in the drawings of ancient Egyptians we find that the size of the person represented depends upon his status. The pharaoh is the largest, followed by his queen, and then by members of the nobility. Slaves are much smaller, and animals smaller still.

Primitive man followed this same principle. He drew what he thought was most important to him, namely animals. While many of these were realistic depictions we also find "synthetic images of fabulous creatures, animal-like or human-like, which were not objects of ordinary perceptual experience. These belong, rather, to the world of creative imagination" (34, p. 234).

These paintings symbolized both human and animal characteristics. Further, the figure of the "Sorcerer" (the Sorcerer of Lourdes is an Upper Paleolithic cave painting showing a man disguised as a deer) in the Cave of the Trois Frères is now believed to be a representation of a spirit that masterminded the multiplication of animals and the success of hunting expeditions (34). This art then reflects a system of beliefs equivalent to the myths of more recent nonliterate peoples. "While the iconic type of symbolization employed required some abstraction, there is relatively close correspondence in form between the object seen, the memory image, and the graphic symbolization" (34, p. 233). Yet these drawings are not mere realistic portrayals of what the primitive man saw, but reveal "imaginative functioning and conceptual creativity" similar to those of modern peoples (34, p. 234). The existence of these drawings is thus further indication that man was able to engage in "extrinsic symbolization."

NAMING PETS

Throughout the centuries since man began to domesticate

animals for his use or pleasure, the names given to these animals have reflected the important aspects of various cultures and the psychodynamics of the animal owners.

Lévi-Strauss (57), for example, describes as follows the naming of a pedigreed dog in modern Western society:

> Suppose I buy a pedigree dog. If I determine to preserve his value and prestige and to transmit them to his descendants, then I shall have scrupulously to observe certain rules in the choice of his name, these rules being mandatory in the society of pedigree dog owners to which I aspire to belong. Usually the dog will in any case already have been given a name on the initiative and responsibility of the kennels where he was born, and when I acquire him he will already have been registered with the authorized dog-breeders' association. The name will begin with an initial which by convention corresponds to the animal's year of birth and it will sometimes be completed by a prefix or affix connoting its breeding, much in the manner of a patronymic name. I am, of course, at liberty to address my dog differently. It still remains the case that this miniature poodle to which, for the purpose of calling him, his master has given the name "Bow-wow," bears the name of "Top-Hill Silver Spray" in the registers of the British Kennel Club, this name being composed of two terms, the first connoting a particular kennel and the second representing an available name. Only the choice of a term of address is therefore left to the owner's initiative. The term of reference is stereotyped and since it connotes both a date of birth and membership of a group it is, as we shall see later, identical with the product of the combination of what ethnologists call a clan name and an ordinal name.
>
> I may, on the other hand, regard myself as free to name my dog according to my own tastes. But if I select "Medor" I shall be classed as commonplace; if I select "Monsieur" or "Lucien," as eccentric and provocative; and if I select "Pelleas" as an aesthete. Moreover, the name selected must also be a member of the class of dog-names which is conceivable in the civilization to which I belong and one which is available, if not absolutely, then at least relatively, that is, not chosen already by my neighbour. My dog's name will therefore be the product of the intersection of three domains: it is a member of a class, a member of the sub-class of the names vacant within the class, and a member of the class formed by my own wishes and tastes (57, pp. 181-182).

At various times and in various corners of the globe, the choosing of animal names has been based on widely different rationales. In Egypt during the eighteenth dynasty, names for dogs such as "Ebony," "Cooking Pot," and "Grabber" were quite popular (85, p. 108). The Romans on the other hand, gave their dogs names expressive of their owners' great regard and appreciation. Some dogs were named after favorite friends. Others were named according to their function or characteristics; for example, Aeon (Listener), Cerberus (Watcher), and Hylactor (Barker) were appropriate for watchdogs. Favorite greyhounds might be called Aello (Whirlwind) or Lailaps (Tempest), while Agriodus (Sharkstooth), Cainon (Killer), or Marsipias ("Sic him") were suitable for boarhounds.

The Romans, in naming their race horses, considered their markings or color, speed, general comeliness, strength, appearance (manes and beards), appetite, and psychological characteristics (Hotspur, Ready, Willing, Cunning). Sometimes the names were terms of endearment (Beloved, Much Beloved, Dandy, Lovely). Sometimes they reflected a martial preoccupation (Victory, or names for different weapons). Horses were also named after gods and goddesses, places, other animals, and human professions and occupations (80).

Bucke (7) found that children, in naming their dogs, paid little attention to famous names in dog history or legend. Chosen names fell into several categories reflecting salient qualities of a real or idealized nature: heroism (Colonel, Hero), dignity and poise (Noble, Judge, Queen), fighting qualities (Lion, Bounce), protectiveness (Guard, Safety), temperament (Boozy, Bum, Tramp), esthetic qualities (Beauty, Blacky, Diamond, Pearl), and size (Baby, Midget).

Children may name cats after well-known persons or after individuals to whom they think the cat bears some resemblance. Occasionally the cat's color or physical characteristics inspire a particular name, and sometimes a name is chosen just because the child likes its sound.

Names given to animals reflect to a certain degree the owner's self concept, level of maturity, orientation to the world, age, socioeconomic background, and culture. The operation of many psychological mechanisms may be noted in the naming of a pet. Several of these mechanisms follow.

Enhancement of self. The owner gives his pet the name by which he himself would like to have been called. He identifies with

LIBRARY
College of St. Francis
JOLIET, ILL.
97201

this name and with the pet that bears it. If his friends like the name, this will tend to enhance his self esteem. If the person himself bears a name disliked by others, he may come to terms with this situation by giving his pet a name esteemed by the group. Unlike his own name, his animal's name can be readily changed to please important peers.

Acceptance of self. A pet's name may serve as a bridge from the old to the new. A foreigner wishing to be accepted as an American may give his pet a high-sounding Anglo-Saxon name which reflects the owner's identification with his adopted culture.

Denial or rejection of self. On the other hand, the foreigner who gives his pet an Anglo-Saxon name may be indicating a rejection of self through a denial of his origins. Such a situation is perceptively described in Louis Adamic's story, "A Man and His Dog" (1), in which neither the human nor the animal can come to terms with themselves until they forsake their Americanized names — Cabot and Buster — and resume their true identities as Kabotchnik and Nurmi.

People who reject their background and education may also be repudiating their own families. Giving a pet a wished-for name may be tantamount to assigning oneself a new identity (see Erikson's "negative identity" (21), thus reflecting a death wish against one's parents.

Aggression. Sometimes a name is chosen which is obnoxious to relatives or friends. Names with political overtones may produce such reactions.

Sex confusion. When a woman gives a bitch a male name, this may indicate that she wishes she were a male.

Values. An animal's name may reflect his owners values. When we name a member of our own family, we are restricted by certain conventions — family customs and ethnic and religious practices. No such restrictions need apply when we name a pet, so the animal may be given the name we wish we could give our baby.

Identification. Sometimes people identify with their animals and name them for the characteristics they believe themselves to possess.

ANIMALS IN MODERN LIFE

Important as animals have been to man's development and

civilization, there are now certain threats to animal life which if not corrected may forever destroy the partnership of man and animal. One of these is the population explosion which continually creates pressure for the development or redevelopment of new land areas, thus driving animals out of their natural preserves.

The widespread pollution of our environment, which is poisoning our soil, air, and water is also indirectly destroying wild species. As a result of the use of insecticides, some preferred foods are not available to birds and they die or breed nonviable offspring (the shell of their eggs being too soft).

The introduction of domesticated animals into a region may bring with it certain illnesses to which these animals are immune but not the wild stock.

We know very little about the habits and life cycles of certain wild animals. Therefore our best efforts to save them may come to naught or be counterproductive. We need more research stations for the study of wild life.

Modern man is making attempts both individually and in groups to preserve areas of wilderness and wild life. An individual may spend some time in the wilderness and come back refreshed, with a better knowledge both of himself and of nature.

> I lived with moose, deer, and bear — on their terms. I experienced the thrill of soundless nights of solitude, staring at stars through an atmosphere so clear they looked as though they could be gathered in the palm of a hand. And I gloried in the primitive thrill of canoeing on a lake so clean, so pure, that a cupful could be scooped up and sipped while travelling (86, p. ix).

Man has always adopted wild animals as pets. Witness the large collection of animals kept by ancient potentates in Mexico, Egypt, Persia, and Greece. However, this desire for animal contact may be based on mixed motives. The animal may, for example, be used as a status symbol. Since such animals are rare, usually "exotic cats and monkeys" (25), the owner probably knows very little about their physical needs, so that he provides inadequate accommodations and care. As a result these animals undergo needless suffering and frequently die.

Further, when modern man adopts these wild animals as pets he endangers entire species — particularly the cheetah, ocelot, margay, and monkey. Usually hunters seek out females with cubs, shoot the mother, and ship the babies to distant points. These cubs may suffer psychological shock on being captured, from which they never recover. Approximately 80 percent of these cubs die before they arrive at their new homes. Moreover, after the novelty wears off for the owner and he finds that he can no longer care for the animal because of its size or behavior, he donates it to a zoo. Zoos however no longer have room for these animals, and they are therefore killed (25).

All over the world, efforts are being made today to reserve vast areas of virgin land as sanctuaries for wild animals. The important zoos of the world are also trying to improve the lot of wild animals in captivity (40). An attempt is being made to preserve the natural animal family groupings and to make the zoo habitat similar to what the animal has in the free state. Under such conditions a zoo can also become a refuge for animals which are otherwise in danger of extinction.

Children's zoos, if well-organized and run by a properly trained supervisory staff, present their animals in a manner which shows consideration for the animals while at the same time educates and gives pleasure to the child visitors. "Good and conscientiously run children's zoos are centres where valuable contact can be established between man and animals, encouraging a healthy love for animals and true animal protection" (41, p.109).

This concern for animal welfare is a counterpart to man's growing concern about improving manmade environments to satisfy human needs more adequately. Thus studies are now being made as to how the physical environment affects human behavior. Much information has been derived about such aspects as suitable population densities from observing animals in their natural habitats.

SUMMARY

Part of the alienation from themselves and society which men are experiencing today derives from the fact that we have withdrawn from contact with animal life and nature. We have been destroying the living tree on whose branches we sit. We have forgotten the language of elemental emotions and thus feel a yawning chasm within.

Wherever we turn we find that our past is with us. The reactions of our body remind us that it was designed to deal with different types of stresses from those to which we are now exposed. We were programmed to live in mutual adaptation with animals. Our dreams remind us of a past we personally may not have experienced but which is probably a symbolic residue of the travails of our ancestors. When we turn to literature, music and art, we find reflections of epochs lost in the twilight of our prehistory. In a word, we find that we have a demon which we have not conquered and which shows itself at the most inopportune moments.

We have longings but we cannot tell for what or for whom. We become instinctively horrified when we learn that our environment, the cradle of human life, is being destroyed or polluted. It is not the change in environment per se that disturbs us. Animals, too, modify nature. Beavers build dams; birds build nests to protect themselves against inclement weather; trees modify the local climate, the soil, and the temperature. It is the fact that the environment is being changed for the worse that alarms us.

We need animals as allies to reinforce our inner selves. We must revive our intimate associations with nature and its animals if we are to survive as the dominant species on earth. It is of course possible that man can survive without animals, but we would surely be a depleted race, shorn of most of our emotional strength.

Feeble attempts are being made to reinstate the ancient pact between primitive man and the animal world. Attempts are being made to roll evolution backwards, unpromising as the outcome appears to be at this point. It is doubtful whether crossbreeding can retrace evolutionary steps to resurrect species that became extinct a long time ago.

The number of well-kept zoos is also on the increase. Less fortunately, the number of wild animals adopted into American homes is also increasing. Apparently troubled civilized man is instinctively looking for surcease from his anxieties by associating with remnants of his past. If these straws in the wind definitely indicate a growing force to learn about and associate with the natural world, modern man may yet feel the thrill of renewing old friendships with the animal kingdom and discovering a new world.

REFERENCES

1. Adamic, L.: What's Your Name. New York, Harper & Brothers, 1942.
2. Ames, L. B.: Sleep and dreams in childhood. In Harms, E. (Ed.): Problems of Sleep and Dreams in Childhood. New York, Macmillan, 1964, pp. 6-29.
3. Ames, L. B., and Learned, J.: Imaginary companions and related phenomena. J Gen Psychol, 69:147-167, 1946.
4. Ames, L. B., Métraux, R. W., and Walker, R. N.: Adolescent Rorschach Responses, rev. ed. New York, Brunner/Mazel, 1971.
5. Aymar, B. (Ed.): Treasury of Snake Lore. New York, Greenberg, 1956.
6. Bastian, J.: Psychological perspectives. In Sebeck, T. (Ed.): Animal Communication. Bloomington, Indiana University, 1968, pp. 572-591.
7. Bucke, W. F.:Cyno-psychoses: Children's thoughts, reactions, and feelings toward pet dogs. Pedagog Semin, 10:459-513, 1903.
8. Buss, A. H., and Durkee, A.: The association of animals with familial figures. J Pro Tech, 21:366-371, 1957.
9. Cawein, M. J.: Penetralia. Poems by Madison Cawein, New York, Macmillan, 1911.
10. Cook, E.: The Ordinary and the Fabulous. Cambridge U.P., 1969.
11. Dale-Green, P.: Cult of the Cat. London, Heinemann, 1963.
12. David, H. P.: Brief unstructured items: The projective question. J Pro Tech, 19:292-300, 1955.
13. David, H. P., and Leach, W. W.: The projective question: Further exploratory studies. J Pro Tech, 21:3-9, 1957.
14. Dembeck, N. H.: Animals and Men. Garden City, N. Y., Natural History Press, 1965.
15. Dietz, A.: Requiem. Poet Lore, 66:31-32, 1971.
16. Di Leo, J. H.: Young Children and Their Drawings. New York, Brunner/Mazel, 1970.
17. Dobzhansky, T., Hecht, M. K., and Steere, W. C.(Eds.): Evolutionary Biology. New York, Appleton-Century-Crofts, 1967, Vol. I.
18. Dolnihow, P. J., and Bishop, N.: The development of motor skills and social relationships among primates. In Hill, J. P. (Ed.): Minnesota Symposia on Child Psychology. Minneapolis, University of Minnesota, 1970, Vol. 4.
19. Dubos, R. J.: Man Adapting. New Haven, Yale, 1965.
20. Ellul, J.: La Technique; ou, L'enjeu du Siècle. Paris, A. Colin, Collection Sciences Politiques, 1954.
21. Erikson, E. H.: Identity, Youth and Crisis. New York, Norton, 1968.
22. Fox, R. B.: The Pinatubo Negritos: Their useful plants and material culture. Philippine J Sci, 81 (3-4): 173-414, 1952.
23. Freud, S.: Analysis of a phobia in a five-year-old boy. In Collected

Works, standard ed. Edited and translated by James Strachey. London, Hogarth Press, 1964, Vol. 10, pp. 3-152.

24. Fromm, E.: The Forgotten Language. New York, Holt, Rinehart and Winston, 1960.
25. Fry, F. L., and Cucuel, J. P. E.: The case against wild animals as pets. Vet Med Small Anim Clin, 64:474, 1969.
26. Galbraith, K.: The Affluent Society, 2nd rev. ed. Boston, Houghton-Mifflin, 1969.
27. Gill, W. S.: Animal content in the Rorschach. J Pro Tech, 31:49-56, 1967.
28. Goldfarb, W.: The animal symbol in the Rorschach test and animal association test. Rorschach Res Exch, 9:8-22, 1945.
29. Goldfried, M. R.: The connotative meaning of some animal symbols for college students. J Proj Tech, 27:60-67, 1963.
30. Goldfried, M. R., and Kissell, S.: Age as a variable in the connotative perception of some animal symbols. J Pro Tech, 27:171-180, 1963.
31. Goldsmith, W.: The biological constant. In Hammond, P. B. (Ed.): Cultural and Social Anthropology. New York, Macmillan, 1968, pp. 2-9.
32. Grimm, W.: Kinder und Hausmarchen. Leipzig, Reklam, 1856. Quoted in Thompson, S.: The Folktale. New York, Holt, Rinehart and Winston, 1946.
33. Gutheil, E. A.: The Language of the Dream. New York, Macmillan, 1939.
34. Hallowell, A. I.: Self, society and culture in phylogenetic perspective. In Montagu, A. M. F. (Ed.): Culture: Man's Adaptive Dimension. New York, Oxford U. P., 1968, pp. 197-261.
35. Hammer, E. F. (Ed.): The Clinical Application of Projective Drawings. Springfield, Thomas, 1967.
36. Hardy, T.: The Woodlanders. New York, Harper & Brothers, 1920. (Reprinted from 1887).
37. Hartley, E. L., and Shames, C.: Man and dog: Psychological analysis. Ninth Gaines Veterinary Symposium. New York, 1959, pp. 4-7.
38. Haworth, M. R.: The cat: Facts about Fantasy. New York, Grune & Stratton, 1966.
39. Hays, H. R.: In the Beginnings: Early Man and His Gods. New York, Putnam's Sons, 1963.
40. Hediger, H.: The Psychology and Behaviour of Animals in Zoos and Circuses. New York, Dover, 1968.
41. Hediger, H.: Man and Animal in the Zoo. New York, Seymour Lawrence, 1969.
42. Hess, E. H.: Ethology and developmental psychology. In Mussen, P. H. (Ed.): Carmichael's Manual of Child Psychology, 3rd ed. New York, Wiley, 1970, Vol. I, pp. 1-38.
43. Heuscher, J. E.: A Psychiatric Study of Fairy Tales. Springfield, Thomas, 1963.
44. Huizinga, J.: Homo Ludens: A Study of the Play-Element in Culture. Boston, Beacon Press, 1969.

45. Hunt, M.: Grimm's Household Tales. London, G. Bell & Sons, 1884.
46. Huxley, J.: Man Stands Alone. New York, Harper & Brothers, 1941.
47. Iles, G: My Home in the Zoo. Garden City, N. Y., Doubleday, 1961.
48. Jayne, A. W.: The Healing Gods of Ancient Civilizations. New Hyde Park, N. Y., University Books, 1962. (Original copyright, Yale, 1925.)
49. Kaplan, H. K., and Calden, G.: An elaboration of the "Projective Question" – the animal test. J Clin Psychol, 23:204, 1967.
50. Kroeber, A. L.: Anthropology, Race, Language, Culture, Psychology, Prehistory, rev. ed. New York, Harcourt Brace, 1948.
51. Langdon, S. H.: The Mythology of all Races. New York, Cooper Square, 1931, Vol. V.
52. Leach, M.: God had a Dog: Folklore of the Dog. New Brunswick, N. J., Rutgers, 1961.
53. Leach, R. E.: Art in cultural context. In Hammond, P. B. (Ed.): Cultural and Social Anthropology. New York, Macmillan, 1968, pp. 344-361.
54. Leakey, L. S. B., Curtis, G. H., and Evernden, J. F.: Age of basalt underlying Bed I, Olduvai. Nature, 194:610-612, 1962.
55. Leakey, L. S. B, and Goodal, V. M.: Unveiling Man's Origins. Cambridge, Mass., Scheneman, 1968.
56. Levinson, B. M.: Pet-Oriented Child Psychotherapy. Springfield, Thomas, 1969.
57. Lévi-Strauss, C.: The Savage Mind. Chicago, University of Chicago, 1966.
58. Levy, S., and Levy, R. A.: Symbolism in animal drawings. In Hammer, E. F. (Ed.): The Clinical Application of Projective Drawings. Springfield, Thomas, 1967, pp. 309-343.
59. Lewis, N. D. C.: Some theriomorphic symbolisms and mechanisms in ancient literature and dreams. Psychoanal Rev, 50:5-26, 1963-64.
60. Lorenz, K.: Evolution and Modification of Behavior. Chicago, University of Chicago, 1965.
61. Lorenz, K.: On Aggression. New York, Harcourt, Brace and World, 1966.
62. McCulloch, J. A.: The Childhood of Fiction. New York, Dutton, 1905.
63. McDowell, A. S.: Nature and Man. New York, Frederick A. Stokes, 1923.
64. Marcuse, H.: Eros and Civilization. Boston, Beacon Press, 1966.
65. May, R.: Symbolism in Religion and Literature. New York, Braziller, 1960.
66. Montagu, A. M. F.: Darwin, Competition, and Cooperation. New York, Schuman, 1952.
67. Montagu, A. M. F.: The Human Revolution. New York, Bantam, 1967.
68. Montagu, A. M. F.: The new litany of "inner depravity", or original sin revisited. In Montagu, A. M. F. (Ed.): Man and Aggression. New York, Oxford U. P., 1968, pp. 3-18.
69. Mumford, L.: The Myth of the Machine. Technics and Human Development. New York, Harcourt, Brace & World, 1966.

70. Phillips, L., and Smith, J. G.: Rorschach Interpretation: Advanced Technique. New York, Grune & Stratton, 1953.
71. Reichel-Dolmatoff, G.: Amazonian Cosmos. The Sexual and Religious Symbolism of the Tukano Indians. Chicago, University of Chicago, 1970.
72. Rensch, B.: The evolution of brain achievements. In Dobzhansky, T., Hecht, M. K., and Steere, W. C. (Eds.): Evolutionary Biology. New York, Appleton-Century-Crofts, 1967, pp. 26-28, Vol. I.
73. Roheim, G.: Psychoanalysis and Anthropology. New York, International Universities Press, 1950.
74. Schwartz, A. A., and Rosenberg, I. H.: Observations on the significance of animal drawings. Am J Orthopsychiatry, 25:729-746, 1955.
75. Sebeck, T. (Ed.): Animal Communication. Bloomington, Indiana U. P., 1968.
76. Smith, F. J., Jelliffe, S. E., and Brink, L.: The role of animals in the unconscious with some remarks on the theriomorphic symbolism as seen in Ovid. Psychoanal Rev, 4:253-271, 1917.
77. Steckel, W.: The Interpretation of Dreams. New York, Liveright, 1943.
78. Thomas, L. J. (Ed.): Man's Role in Changing the Face of the Earth. Chicago, University of Chicago, 1956.
79. Thompson, S.: The Folktale. New York, Holt, Rinehart and Winston, 1946.
80. Toynbee, J. M. C.: Beasts and their names in the Roman Empire. Papers of the British School at Rome (new series, vol. III), 16:24-37, 1948.
81. Turnbull, C.: The Forest People. Garden City, N. Y., Doubleday, 1962.
82. Tylor, E. B.: Primitive Culture. New York, Harper, 1958, Vol. I.
83. Van Krevelen, D. A.: The use of Pigem's test with children. J Pro Tech, 20:235-242, 1956.
84. Winnicott, D. W.: The Maturational Processes and the Facilitating Environment. New York, International Universities Press, 1965.
85. Zeuner, F. E.: A History of Domesticated Animals. New York, Harper & Row, 1963.
86. Zurhorst, C.: The Conservation Fraud. New York, Cowles, 1970.

Chapter Two

THE PET AND CHILD DEVELOPMENT

Your children are not your children,
They are the sons and daughters of life's longing for itself:
They come through you but not from you.
And though they are with you yet they belong not to you.
You may give them your love but not your thoughts,
For they have their own thoughts.
You may house their bodies but not their souls,
For their souls dwell in the house of tomorrow, which you
    cannot visit, not even in your dreams.
You may strive to be like them, but seek not to make them
    like you.
For life goes not backward nor tarries with yesterday (29, p.17).

T HE urban crisis which American society is now undergoing is taking a heavy toll in emotional distress. We are witnessing major population shifts from rural to large metropolitan areas and from the South to the Northeast. Many families have no firm ties to the transitional community in which they live. Both husband and wife may be working. Children are often left without any supervision and may even be considered a liability by the parents. Widespread alienation is coupled with extreme cruelty. Thus we find the incidence of battered children constantly on the increase (37).

In contrast, past generations of parents and children lived circumscribed lives, had the same parochial point of view on life, engaged in the same activities, listened to the same fairy tales. The child, who was considered a little man, was exposed to some of the same fare as his parents.

The home was an economic unit with everyone participating in the family enterprises. Life and death were out in the open, to be observed freely and remarked on by the children.

Today the economic function of the home has largely disappeared (5). The home is no longer a producing but a consuming unit. Due to the use of labor-saving devices in the home, the need for children's contributions toward the physical upkeep of the home has diminished, if not totally disappeared. Yet children need something to be responsible for which is also of vital importance to them.

Today, therefore, in many families, the pet may be the only common interest uniting parents and children. Caring for the pet may be the only activity in which they are equals and about which they see eye to eye.

In times past, much more attention was paid to the irrational, intuitive, emotional aspects of living, whether through religious practice or superstition. Hardly anyone worried about the scientific justification for his actions as long as these satisfied inner needs. Today in our efforts to behave in a scientifc fashion, we tend to sterilize our emotions and become like rabbits who, when they lose their intestinal bacterial flora through the ingestion of antibiotic drugs, can no longer digest their food.

Furthermore, today there is an emphasis on the collective rather than on the individual or on the development of a harmonious balance between the two. Instead there has developed a tremendous proliferation of knowledge about the external, impersonal world.

As a result, our scientific ways of helping people who are drained of emotion are becoming less and less effective. Introducing a love object in the form of a pet may help restore the inner balance of such individuals. As a matter of fact, in certain families a pet is no longer a luxury but a necessity.

Although it is as true as ever that children are the nation's future, many of today's children feel left out; they feel they do not belong either to their family or to the adult world with its all-encompassing culture. It should not surprise us therefore that an estimated "10,000,000 under the age of twenty-five are in need of help from mental health workers" (57, p.2). "Using the most conservative estimates from various school surveys, the National Institute of Mental Health estimates that 1,400,000 children under the age of eighteeen needed psychiatric care in 1966" (57, p. 5).

These children need a niche of their own, their own subculture. Through a pet they may be able to create one. When one child meets another member of the pet fraternity while out walking his dog, he may smile a smile of recognition, knowing that he belongs to a group and is no longer alone.

Today society would like to see children develop their potentialities as far as they are capable of doing so, without undue hindrance or restraints by their parents or their peers. At the same time society would like them to become responsible adults. With the aid of pets we can more easily approximate these goals.

We no longer consider mental health or illness to be the outcome of individual bouts with fate. Rather we view them as arising out of conditions prevailing in our society. Social solutions to these problems are slow and difficult to achieve, and under the circumstances conventional methods of psychotherapy are woefully deficient. Morever, the magnitude of the problem is now so great that within the foreseeable future it will be impossible to meet these needs through existing psychiatric channels. Some new resources must be found to alleviate distress, even if only temporarily. One such resource is the use of pets of all kinds, both as therapeutic agents and as aids to normal child development.

On an epidemiological basis, clinical observation has found that families with pets have fewer problems than those without pets, and the problems which do exist are not as severe. Pets obviously represent a mental hygiene resource of vast importance in our technological society, even as they did in the society of primitive man, who domesticated animals not only for his economic but for his emotional needs as well. We must therefore view pets as a community asset.

A pet can serve as an aid to a child in mastering his developmental tasks. A developmental task has been defined by Havighurst (33) as

> . . . as task which arises at or about a certain period in the life of the individual, successful achievement of which leads to his happiness and success with later tasks, while failure leads to unhappiness in the individual, disapproval by society, and difficulty with later tasks (33, p. 2).

When we speak of child development and of developmental task, we do not wish to imply that as one period ends another comes into view. Actually one period blends into another, the new carrying within itself relics of the old. Developmental tasks are conditioned by the child's culture and family status. Meeting these tasks satisfactorily on the appropriate level helps the child to move on to a higher level.

Before a child can meet and resolve the developmental tasks of any period, the basic needs and drives such as hunger and thirst must first be satisfied. In human beings these drives cannot express themselves as simply as they do in animals, but are constantly conditioned by cultural requirements.

Developmental Tasks at Birth

At birth the child begins to interact with his environment in a manner which lays the groundwork for later good or poor mental health. There is a need for love which, if satisfied, can later develop into a need to love (30).

At birth the infant has genetically acquired structures, i.e. "innately fixed behavior patterns" (39, p. 1) which cause him to respond positively to a soft, pliant, warm object. He needs consistent, affectionate nurturing and stimulating experiences which his mother is biologically prepared to give him. Studies have indicated (13, 38, 40) that women usually prefer pictures of babies, whether animal or human, to pictures of adults of the same species. This would indicate that babyishness may release a biological mechanism in adults which leads them to care for infants, thus ensuring the latter's survival (39). Similarly, the display of nurturant behavior towards an animal may act as a releaser of the animal's emotions and elicit a favorable attitude toward human beings.

The child orients himself physically toward his mother so as to be stimulated and fed by her. There is thus an ongoing, active searching and body communication between mother and child. Maternal deprivation represents more than a lack of love. It also represents a lack of sensory stimulation. "The development of the nervous system and even mental health depend upon a constant exposure to sensory stimulation and to new experiences" (21, p. 23).

> This communication between mother and child is concretistic and physical. It is truly a language of the body; of its mass; its weight, dimensions, and extensions; and its appearance and external qualities.

This is truly the "silent language"... . Thus physical conditions of communication appear to be necessary and present from the very first contacts between child and mother soon after birth (17, p. 8).

This phase has been likened to the imprinting period undergone by many animals. These physical contacts help to strengthen the attachment between infant and mother. They are a continuation of the stimulation received by the foetus as his mother worked, walked, sat, slept, and changed her position a hundred times a day.

The infant who has been exposed to many and varied stimulating experiences will learn to respond more effectively and appropriately to new sensations and stimulations than one who has not had such exposure (16, 35, 59). Various studies have indicated that infants stimulated by toys did not fuss while under observation, whereas those who had no toys showed fussing behavior; Rheingold and Samuels (58) considered this to be an infantile response to diminished sensory stimulation. Similarly, premature infants whose neck, back, and arms were gently rubbed by a nurse for five minutes every hour developed much more rapidly than premature infants who did not have this handling (65). Hasselmeyer (32) found that stimulated premature infants cried less than nonstimulated ones, while Freedman *et al.* (25) showed that rocked premature infants gained weight more rapidly than their twin controls. On the other hand, neonates who are inappropriately stimulated by their mothers may, when they mature, either be unable or unwilling to accept or express affection in physical form.

The crucial period for the later development of emotional disorders occurs during the first two years of life, when the child may undergo traumatic events without being able to understand their cause or to verbalize his fears, so that he endows the events with his own unrealistic explanations. Yet it is during this period that millions of children do not "receive consistent emotionally satisfying care" (57, p. 4).

During the first six months of a child's life, he is completely helpless and dependent upon his mother for food, warmth, comfort, and contact sensations. If there is enough pleasurable contact comfort, the child will eventually experience himself as an individual separate from his mother and will develop an adequate body image. At this time he learns to associate contact with something warm and soft, with the life-giving aspects of his mother. Even though he cannot yet recognize his mother, this immature organism needs a constant "someone" who is there to support him in times of stress (45). The infant learns from these experiences either to "trust" or "mistrust" the world (22).

Emotional development is fostered by this interaction between mother and child. Later on as the child grows, other individuals satisfy this need for physical contact. This mode of communication will remain with him throughout his lifetime, and he will normally be able to express his deeply intimate thoughts most effectively and satisfyingly not through words but through touch.

We know very little about the total communicative range between two persons. We know even less about the communicative interaction between people and animals, particularly in the area of tactile communication, nor do we know how a child and his pet interchange their experiences.

A child must identify himself with a living creature before he can begin to wish to live in this world. The child learns how to relate through body activity. When this activity meets no response, retardation of the psychological and physiological functions occurs (9, 10).

The child's ability to think of himself and identify himself as a human being develops very gradually. At first the child "sees" himself and the world as an undifferentiated whole. Later on comes the ability to differentiate himself first from the inanimate, then from the nonhuman animate, and finally from other humans. This finding is confirmed in studies of the Rorschach test with very young children, who tend to interpret the plates as representing inanimate objects such as leaves and trees and give very few animal or human interpretations. As the children mature, their inanimate responses decrease in favor of animal responses, to which are gradually added human responses (1, 15, 20).

Modern civilization, by providing for bottle feeding and commercially prepared baby foods, has decreased, mechanized, and routinized the contact between the child's and mother's bodies. Yet research indicates that each child at birth is an individual and has his own idiosyncratic needs, including those for more or less body contact (70), which may differ from those of other neonates and which must be accepted and met by his parents. Some parents are unaware of the infant's need for extensive body contact or are unwilling to provide it.

What the child requires is some agent that will be soft, cuddly, succorant, yielding, and always present. Unless these conditions are met, the child may later develop social problems, i.e. he will have difficulty in relating to people on a mature level. A specially trained pet can fill this need when adequate human contact is not forthcoming.

It is obvious that preventive measures are most effective in the very early years of the child's development. As an infant the child can project parts of his undifferentiated self onto his pet until such time as "his ego is sufficiently strong to integrate them into his developing sense of self" (64, p.80). Having such a pet around when there is a constant shifting in caretakers helps the child to establish a feeling of self.

If we provide the infant with specially trained, sensitive, "seeing heart" dogs, these would be able to adapt to each child's ways of reacting and give the child an opportunity for a variety of enriching experiences at various developmental levels. Clinical observations of thumb sucking among "pet-reared" children show less intense activity of this kind than among "petless" children. Apparently "pet-reared" children find their environment more comforting and have less need to turn to their own body for gratification.

During the second six months of his life, the child becomes able to distinguish among individual people, thus recognizing his mother and developing a fear of strangers. The child dimly recognizes that there is a world outside of himself that is also important. This is psychologically devastating and the child feels insecure. He needs to develop a trust in the environment so that he can develop trust in himself (23).

He needs a safe bridge between himself and the outside world. Frequently a blanket or an old soft doll becomes this bridge, which Winnicott (72) has called a "transitional object." It is preferable however in cases of early childhood maternal deprivation for this bridge to be in the form of a soft, cuddly pet which will help the child to resolve his problem of security. Normally the child cries when his mother, the source of security and food, goes away from him, and he is happy when she comes back. If during this period the child is taken care of by constantly changing, indifferent people, he will be most unhappy, and when he becomes an adult he may develop severe depressions (9, 10, 11). To abort such an undesirable developmental course a pet may be introduced — to serve as the child's constant companion, lessening his anxiety by providing for that otherwise unavailable continuity which is so important in the development of trust in the world and in one's self.

Developmental Tasks of Early Childhood

Between one and two years of age not many demands are made on the child, from the adult point of view. His parents are quite happy with him as long as he develops in accordance with their culturally acceptable norms. He is expected to give up his bottle and to eat solid food. Weaning introduces him to the expectations of the outside world and to the "reality principle" which will gradually replace the "pleasure principle" as the regulator of his actions.

The child during this period also learns how to walk. Having an active pet to follow around encourages the child's crawling, increases the use of fine muscles, and makes the process of learning to walk easier and even more pleasurable.

However as the child begins to enjoy his explorations, they take him into forbidden territory where he touches and occasionally breaks "taboo" objects, so that a battle of wills ensues between him and his parents. As the child begins to learn more about his environment and encounters some of its dangers, a pet can serve as protector as well as companion, so that the child can become more assertive and independent. He will probably also be strengthened in his negativistic, self-assertive, "no"-saying behavior with his parents, so characteristic of the period when the child is learning that he is a person in his own right.

Around the end of the second year, the child has to start learning to control his bladder and regulate his bowels. If the child meets his mother's expectations, he is praised and feels that all is well. Anxiety develops on those occasions when he has failed to meet his mother's expectations. At this point the pet may begin to play the role of a nonjudgmental, acceptant friend who will help to lessen the child's anxiety and thus avoid any incipient emotional difficulty. On various occasions, having his trusty pet with him will make Mother's unavoidable disappearance for shopping, etc., more tolerable.

From two to approximately seven years of age (all of these periods overlap), the child enters into what Piaget (54, 55) calls the preoperational (egocentric) period of cognitive development. He believes the world revolves around him, that he is the only one who counts in the universe, and that everyone knows what he is thinking. His view of the world is an animistic one. He believes that everything in the world is alive and has feelings akin to his. Furthermore, everything has a cause which is motivational in nature. The wind blows and howls because it wants to.

The child believes in magic and thinks that a wish is equivalent to an act. When he is angry at his pet, he may tell his pet to go away, but simultaneously fear his destructive impulses. However, the pet does not go away. By staying with the child, he may allay the child's anxieties by demonstrating that a wish does not imply a deed and that one can exercise some assertiveness and even hostility without necessarily incurring punishment.

Depending upon the child's age, he may find it difficult to distinguish his dreams from reality. During this period, believing that rules are endowed with magic properties, children stick rigidly by them and are able to think only in absolutes. Only love and hate can exist, with no gradations in between. However when the child observes that his parents continue to accept a pet after it has had an "accident," his fears of rejection may be allayed despite parental scoldings and punishments. The child can learn to accept ambivalence as part of all human relationships.

The child believes that if anything happens to him — if, for instance, he has an accident or falls ill — this occurrence is punishment for misbehavior. Very often the sick child wonders what crime he has committed. "But Mommy, I was a good boy, why am I sick?" He further feels that his mother has magic powers and that she could have prevented his becoming ill if she had wanted to do so. Apparently she wanted to punish him. If a pet becomes ill or requires some kind of medical treatment, however, it is easier for him to see that no connection exists between the pet's behavior and his physical condition, so that the fortuitous nature of illness or injury becomes clearer.

The Pet as an Object of Fantasy

Frequently, as the young child plays with his pet, he makes up stories and fairy tales about himself and his animal friend similar to those which are found in folk literature (14). This occurs even when the child has never been told or read fairy tales

These stories strengthen the child's ties to reality by giving him opportunities to work out in fantasy the problems of day-to-day living, to test out in advance the verity of his conclusions, subsequently applying his newly acquired insights to reality problems. It thus appears advisable to provide opportunities for children to play out their fantasies with and about pets. The fairy tales made up by the child about the pet and the hero of the story further help him to identify with the active representative of goodness, freedom, and justice, who fights against evil forces and often carries the day. This helps the child to develop the human quality of empathy, enabling him to feel sorry for another's misfortune and happy for another's success. It gives him the occasion vicariously to live through emotional experiences (14). This enhances the child's estimate of his self-worth and promotes the development of an adequate self-concept.

The Animal as an Imaginary Companion

We thus find that throughout this period, the child gradually and almost imperceptibly begins to acquire a concept of self. He will now be curious to learn what his self is like and will engage in various games of make-believe (27). Among these is the creation of imaginary animal companions. According to Schaeffer (61), the imaginary companion is a normal one and is related to creativity. Some very young children (ages 2 1/2 to 5 or 6) who play with imaginary animal companions (1) have more than one such companion. The creation of these is very helpful to the child during this developmental period, as in a sense the activity provides a shock absorber to ease the impact of unpleasant occurrences in everyday life (8).

That this imaginative play is a normal phenomenon is "seen in the fact that not only does the child play first with imaginary animals, then with imaginary adults, and then with imaginary children, but that this same sequence appears in the dream life"(1).

We find that children use their imaginary animal playmates as substitutes for siblings or for authority figures, and that frequently they project their fears, anxieties, and expectations onto such companions, which can also be used as a "defense against overprotection" (66, p. 252). Further, these companions give the child the "illusion of freedom" which is so important to mental health (66, p. 258).

Some children create or impersonate imaginary animal companions out of unmet emotional needs. As soon as these needs are fulfilled, these imaginary companions are relinquished. This occurs when the child enters school and interacts with his peers, a situation which produces more rigorous reality demands.

Ames & Learned (1) studied the fantasy companions of 210 children at the Gesell Institute of Child Development at Yale University. The data were gathered either during parent interviews or by direct observation of the children while they were playing. Forty-five children (which Ames and Learned consider an underestimate) had imaginary playmates. Of these 45 children, 11 (or 24%) had imaginary animal companions. Only two of these children feared the animals. As a rule these imaginary animals had first appeared at night, some of them hiding or sleeping under or in the child's bed.

Some children who had imaginary companions seemed to have social, i.e. interpersonal, adjustment difficulties. As seen in this light, the animals substituted for either unsatisfactory or unobtainable human associates (1). The imaginary animals that these children played with were "snakes, roosters, owls, foxes, birds, bears, kitty, tiger, worms, pig, chipmunk, dig-a-dig chicken, cat, dog, wolf" (1, p. 152).

Boy RJ, high average intelligence, an only child. From 30 to 48 months he had an imaginary playmate, "dig-a-dig chicken." This chicken was as big as daddy or so tiny you could put him in tiny places. RJ talked a good deal about his chicken and played with him. He built him a house which he wouldn't allow anyone to knock down. "Dig's" last name was the same as the child's own. Dig had a little boy. Whenever the family went anywhere, RJ asked if he could bring Dig along. Whenever he did anything wrong himself, he blamed it on Dig (1, p. 153).

Boy MC, very superior, second of two children. He and his older sister had two bears, a mother and a father bear. These bears were very real to the children who were fond of them. The bears were for the most part friendly, though sometimes they became dangerous. In this case, the children controlled them by rolling marbles at them along the carpet.

Finally one day the older sister told MC that the bears were dead. She had killed them with a large marble. He was horrified and cried, believing implicitly that the bears were dead.

The source of these bears was a poem, recited by MC's father, a poem about "Algy met a bear." The bears were killed when MC was about six. He did not see the bears eidetically but they were very real to him and he saw them in his mind. The children did not tell their parents about the bears because they couldn't, owing to the fact that they played with the bears in a secret language. The bears were more real to them and more important than their father and mother. Perhaps the bears were in a way a mother and father who were very kind to the children and granted all their wishes, yet who could be kept in hand and sent away whenever the children wished (1, p. 153).

An example of an imaginary companion in an older child (who was not a member of Ames and Learned's study population but who had social adjustment problems) has been described as follows:

Paul was about the most difficult boy in the third grade — if not in the whole school. His favorite expression was "I'll give you a fat lip." Every day he was sent down to the assistant principal's office (where I was working) for fighting. His teacher could not control him. He was aggressive, pugnacious, athletic and very intelligent. At times, he would just run through exercise books, readers and converse meaningfully. One morning — the first day we met — I had to hold his hands for over an hour to prevent him from assaulting the other children in the room. He enjoyed and needed the physical contact. He could have bitten my fingers but contented himself with licking them. He talked continually. After seeing that I really meant him no harm and that he couldn't break my grip, he just relaxed on the floor.

While on the floor he invoked the name of his deity — his dog King. "King-King take care of this guy, make him get off." He talked about how he took care of King, what he fed him, the walks they took together, etc. The Assistant Principal told me that Paul's mother could not wait to throw him out of the house. At lunch hour he would go home and often come back without having lunch. He was always alone. His cousin, who was in the 6th grade, told me that Paul didn't have a dog (52).

Some children in the Ames and Learned group who impersonated animals appeared to be highly active, imaginative, and emotionally dependent upon their mothers. Some of these children may have been destructive, having little awareness of the motivation or the presence of other children and unconsciously trying to learn something about themselves through playing animal roles. The animals impersonated by the children were dogs, cats, a horse, a pig, a mouse, and a hen. One child impersonated a "great big grizzly bear" (1, p. 154). Some children alternately impersonated a dog and a cat.

> *Boy BT, superior, older of two children by 3 years.* At 24 months of age he visited his grandmother, who had a kitten. When he got home, he became a kitten and this continued quite consistently till he was 36 months old. He went around on all fours "meowing"; lapped up milk. At 30 months he took on, briefly, an additional role, that of his best friend's dog. In this role he went around on all fours and bit people (1, p. 154).

Assumption of Responsibility for the Pet

Responsibility for the care of a pet should be introduced early and gradually. The child's age, capacity for making decisions, and ability to perform the necessary tasks should be considered. In this connection, the tasks that interest children should be used as incentives to encourage caring for the pet and the self. In the beginning instructions should be specific, later becoming more and more general. With maturity the child should be given increasing leeway in making decisions. When pet care is introduced in this fashion, the child will learn that there is a certain satisfaction in doing a job well. Moreover, by becoming an authoritative figure in his own right, the child will learn to accept authority more easily and graciously.

Taking care of a pet is the beginning of assuming responsibility for someone other than oneself. Children need this type of training if they are to become mature adults. A child who receives a wished-for pet as a birthday gift cannot expect his parents to assume complete responsibility for the pet, but on the other hand, parents must also bear in mind that there will be periods in the life of even a conscientious child when he feels that continuing to take care of the pet is too much for him. In this case, the parent or some other member of the family must assume the responsibility and allow the child a respite for a few days or weeks. When he returns to his task he may do even better than before.

The child at this age has a need to explore the environment. When he is accompanied by his trusted animal friend, he will not be afraid to try his skill and to compete with his peers. In this way he will begin to shed some of his dependence on adults and broaden his social skills.

By the age of six, the child is already beginning to leave the family orbit and to associate with his peers in the classroom, playground, and community. Under these circumstances he may meet with rebuffs which make him feel insecure and anxious. However, when this happens the child can retrieve the situation by associating with his pet.

> There was a summer resort that my family owned and operated. The guests were old, there were few children my age, the language spoken by the people was foreign. I was alone. Down the parking road there was a clearing and then a brook — surrounded by lush, wild country. Many hours were spent sitting on a stone or on a log gazing at the trout, watching the frogs, snakes, and small mammals and listening to the birds. Where there was nobody — here there was something. At the hotel I was a little boy — here I was big, here there were small creatures that needed my protection. Fish put on an aquacade — my personal giant fishtank. The insects demonstrated what a complex civilization they had — a miniature world. The smells of the flowers, the taste of the fruit and leaves — this was my world. I often tried to bring people down there on a guided tour to share my beautiful world with them. Often a huge dog would invite himself along — for our protection (52).

A child who is foiled or rebuffed in his attempt to make friends with his peers can find acceptance from his pet. The pet will not disappoint him or make excessive demands on him. The child is in no way vulnerable when he exposes himself to a pet. He can be by himself without being questioned or having to account to anyone for his activities. By receiving this emotional support the child is better able to disregard temporary hurts and make new attempts to relate to his peers.

In working with his pet and trying to teach him new skills, the child may develop confidence in his abilities. He may learn to persevere and to find great pleasure in small accomplishments, especially if he wins recognition from others for the outcome of his efforts. His self-image may thus change from loser to achiever. Observing the reactions of the pet to his small master's good or bad treatment may further the development of a conscience and encourage identification with benevolent authority figures. Such changes in outlook facilitate the learning process both in and out of school.

For children who are uncertain of their relationship with the grown-ups around them, the presence of a pet whose constant companionship can be counted upon is priceless. This is particularly true for out-of-wedlock children whose mothers resent them, for foster children who are not looked upon as members of the family, and for children in multiproblem families where the parental figures are unstable and undependable. For the minority child who may have very little status among his majority-culture associates, a pet which is the envy of the neighborhood will provide status as well as companionship.

Starting to School

Frequently even normal children have separation anxieties when they start to school. Having a pet accompany them to the schoolhouse door minimizes the effects of separation even from anxious parents. The nursery rhyme "Mary had a little lamb" illustrates this point.

Sundaran (69, pp. 1-2) describes how her dog helped her to deal with separation anxiety:

> When first starting elementary school it was her dog, Black Beauty, that helped her overcome the anxiety of separation from her family. School was frightening and for some reason at that time the writer was rather shy and not adjusting well to this new experience. The writer can remember actually crying on the way to school several

mornings. She was fortunate to have a pet dog, to which the writer meant as much as the dog did to the writer. Beauty began walking to school with her in the morning as far as the school yard and would always be waiting when it was time for school to let out. This not only provided a certain amount of security, but pride in Beauty gave the writer something very special to tell the other children. One very exciting day the teacher allowed Beauty to come into school and be shared with the rest of the children. Somehow, that experience seemed to break the ice as the writer was able to share that very important part of her life with the other children and suddenly feel like part of the group.

The Pet During the Latency Period

The boy from about six to twelve years and the girl from about six to ten years have the following important developmental tasks to accomplish, among others: acquiring a sense of "identity," accepting the self as male or female, becoming an acceptable, responsible, and even admirable member of a group, becoming a good learner, and developing consideration for others.

Developing a Sense of Identity

The process of "identity" formation is mostly an unconscious one, based largely on interaction with one's peers and significant adults. "Identity formation is dependent upon the opportunity to interact and to learn. Play and constructive leisure activities are one essential element in this needed interaction" (57, p. 87). An aspect of "identity" formation which to this author's knowledge has not been dealt with in the literature of child development is interaction with one's pet.

When a child has a pet with which he works and toward which he expresses a wide range of feelings, he can get a better understanding of what he is like and what his strengths and limitations are. In a sense, his handling of the pet is a reflection of himself, which a perceptive child cannot fail to notice. Is he cruel or kind? His handling of the pet will bring these qualities into bold relief. To some extent the pet is helpless, a piece of clay to be molded by the child. The pet cannot berate the child (outside of an occasional bite) or underscore the child's kindness or cruelty.

Neither can the child excuse his behavior by claiming lack of responsibility for his actions.

The child also learns that there are limits inherent in what he can do and accomplish either with himself or with his pets. Acceptance of these limitations will enhance his sense of reality and strengthen his ego. The child's realization and acceptance of the negative sides of his personality, of the fact that occasionally he is unaccountably cruel or mean to his pet, will also facilitate the acceptance of the negative aspects of other individuals and the development of empathy toward people as well as animals.

On the other hand, the child learns that this creature which he considers his possession has its own needs that must be taken into account, and that animals, like people, cannot be treated as objects to do with what one will. Hediger (36), in discussing children's zoos, points out that children should be taught "to approach animals with respect and the greatest possible understanding", which means learning their characteristics and their needs. Excessive petting can be extremely bothersome even to a contact animal, while it can be intolerable to a distance animal (more likely to be found in a zoo than as a pet in the home). "Friendship between animal and man, in a sense of intimate positive relations," writes Hediger, "can only be achieved by unforced, voluntary approach on the part of the animal, and not through the irresistible force of contact . . . By love of animals we mean a healthy delight in the animal, but with the greatest possible consideration for its biological situation" (36, p. 165).

Developing Independence

Many parents, particularly middle-class ones, tightly schedule their children's activities and rigorously supervise them since these activities are considered important. Fortunately however, parents usually do not consider play with a pet as an important contributor to their child's social and cultural development and are therefore not inclined to regulate it. The child, left alone in this area, has some time to explore his environment and develop some affinity between himself and the animal world.

Sometimes even well-meaning parents do not approve of what

their children are doing, even though the activities may be socially acceptable. Other parents, because of the intense unconscious dislike they have for their children, either overprotect or reject them. (This situation can occur for many complex reasons which we cannot discuss here.) In either case the child is in trouble. When he is overprotected and his parents try to do as much for him as they can, he will find it difficult to grow into an emotionally mature adult who can take care of himself. The child needs certain areas in which he can be independent, his own boss. When he has a pet of which he is the acknowledged master, the child can assume responsibility for feeding, grooming, and teaching the animal and judging when it needs veterinary care.

In a case of undisguised rejection by the parents, the pet will provide acceptance and love which may permit the child to grow up relatively unscathed.

Abreaction of Guilt Feelings

Animals play an important part in helping children to abreact their guilt feelings in fantasy.

> Thus living things which can be killed with impunity are animals, and if you have wished someone dead, and it was a human being, you are guilty, but if it was an animal you are innocent and safe. Those against whom we have death wishes which we cannot admit without shame and guilt are represented in our fantasies as animals (6, pp. 119-120).

Pets as Symbols of Life's Continuity

Sometimes a family must move to a distant city or even a foreign country. Acquiring a desired pet some time before the family moves can lessen the shock for the child of losing old friends. The pet can give the child some measure of security and show him that some stability still exists in this world. It will provide a sense of continuity with the past until such time as he is able to find new friends.

The Pet as a Love Object

It is a truism that everyone needs love and affection. However, the meaning of love differs for the child and the adult. Love has to be palatable and digestible. What may be good for the adult or the parent may not be good for the child. When the adult fondles a child, he may be merely satisfying his own needs rather than those of the child he "loves."

Where his pet is concerned, the child initiates the "loving" and is not merely a submissive recipient. He is an active seeker and doer who in turn receives love from the object of his affections. The pet is not too busy or preoccupied to receive the child's expressions of love, and when the animal expresses its own affection this is done without mixed motives.

Each person loves a pet in a different way. Generally speaking, love for a pet may be the crucible which turns out a better human being, because loving a pet also involves the assumption of responsibilities which can at times be onerous, such as taking the pet out in inclement weather, etc. This teaches the child the need to sacrifice or undergo inconvenience for the sake of a loved one. This is one of the most important lessons he will have to learn if he is to relate to human beings in a loving way.

In ascertaining the meaning of a child's love for a pet, one must consider both the child's needs and the qualities of the pet. Some children see their pets as extensions of themselves and treat the animal in the way they themselves would like to be treated. The pet may also unconsciously symbolize a liked or disliked person and be treated accordingly. Other children look upon their pets as toys, so that as soon as the pet matures and loses its appeal, it is given away or destroyed. The pet may also be looked upon as a decoration and treated as such. Some children like or love pets because these are the only living beings they can relate to, having experienced so much hurt at the hands of people in their environment. Only after they have had a satisfactory relationship with animals can they make a start at developing human relationships.

The qualities of the pet itself may evoke certain reactions from its owner. In this connection, Foote (24) asks an interesting question: "Dogs are loved for being almost human, but children are rejected for being somewhat canine. What is it that we most value, human or canine characteristics?" (24, p. 217). The helpless quality of animals arouses a protective reaction in the average human being. Certain pets are bred to be helpless and infantile. "A helpless, rounded puppy crying for a missing bitch projects a powerful infantile image which few human females can resist" (51, p. 177).

Generally speaking, in our handling of the child and his pet we must remember that what is important to the child is also important to us. We must indicate to him that we take him and his wishes seriously and that we are understanding and not arbitrary in our decisions. The following case is illustrative:

> A fairly young couple had a set of twins and expected another child. They were concerned about the twins developing jealousy because an infant would require considerable attention. They acquired a young female terrier, hoping she would demand the attention of the twins through the period of anticipated crisis. (Had they normal communication with their twins the parents should have been able to explain the situation to them). The approach wasn't quite fair to the dog. She did gain the attention and the devotion of the twins — but terrier-like, she was boisterous and extremely energetic. She was too much dog, and the parents couldn't get rid of their mistake because she was already a favorite of the twins.
>
> In their anxiety to find a solution the parents were victimized by a self-proclaimed authority on dogs. They were told, and incorrectly, that spayed bitches become lethargic. The terrier puppy didn't survive what should have been a routine operation. The combination of circumstances was most unfortunate. The parents had told the twins when the dog was purchased that they would have their own pet to take care of while mommy was caring for the new baby. The fatal operation occurred the week before an infant girl joined the family. In the minds of the twins the death of their dog was somehow caused by their new sister. They hated her with an intensity that necessitated constant surveillance and the eventual intervention of professional help (46, pp. 15-16).

The Joys and Sorrows of Pet Ownership

I would like to lay certain misconceptions to rest. Some people who have never had pets visualize pet ownership unrealistically.

The pet runs to greet his master when he arrives home, bringing his slippers and the evening newspaper. The cat adds her welcome by licking her master's face. The pet, in other words, brings undiluted joy to the family.

This is quite erroneous. Pets need care. They need to be groomed, medicated, housebroken. They have to be walked even on the coldest nights in crime-infested streets. When traveling with pets, the owner is welcome only at certain hotels or motels. Pet owners in cities can live only in certain apartments. Low-cost housing is out of the question. Pets sometimes destroy shrubbery, chew on expensive furniture, claw exquisite draperies, and have accidents on rare Oriental rugs.

Living with a pet, adjusting to it, and making room in one's heart and apartment is sometimes trying. A pet, particularly a dog or a cat, must be planned for. Before the pet arrives, the family has to decide where the pet is to live and who shall assume major responsibility for its care; otherwise the family may discover that the pet's temperamental qualities are creating dissension among its members. If, through previous mishandling or lack of early affectionate care, the pet turns out to be a highly neurotic and agonistic animal, some of the family may consider the pet to be unsuitable and wish to send it away. By that time however, unsatisfactory as the animal may be, it has already established a firm niche in the hearts of one or two members of the family so that its tenure is secure, much to the discomfiture, annoyance, and even rage of the other members of the family. The following history of a family and its pet is illustrative:

> It was with considerable surprise that I discovered that a dog can become the dominant figure in a close family group, my own to be specific. Our dog forced himself into the core of our family life. In our relationships with each other and with him, during the time we had him, we each expressed our individual personality traits. It may be said that the dog created an encounter group within our family. When he was finally gone, it took the better part of a year to put the pieces together.
>
> Although our sons, aged ten, eight and four at the time, had been asking to have a dog for almost a year, we got Badger on an impulse. And yet, the decision was not really sudden, for my husband and I had been considering it for several months. When we passed Badger on a country road one summer day, we were hooked. We took the puppy into our life, and the remaining week of our summer vacation found me more tied to him than I had been to our own new born infants. They, at least, slept in between feedings at that age.

All my maternal instincts came to the fore. I literally carried Badger almost everywhere I went. In the beginning, all three boys were eager to feed him and take him out. But after three or four days, I began to wonder what I had gotten myself into. In spite of having help from the children when they were around, the puppy was obviously going to be mine.

By the time we got home to the city, we were beginning to realize some of the negative ways in which the dog would affect our lives. John, who was very much the center of attention in a household with two older brothers, suddenly felt that he had a rival for his mother's affection. He began to treat Badger much as he would a younger brother or sister. He became over-involved with the dog and expressed his aggression by being somewhat less than gentle.

Because of Badger, my schedule was limited and I was forced to come and go when I could get somebody to take care of his needs.

The novelty had worn off by now, and our boys were acting true to form. Dave, the oldest, the almost too responsible son, was fulfilling his obligations. He was also expressing resentment because Ben, our second child, was balking at taking the dog out. Ben's unwillingness to cooperate was making me angry. I had not prepared myself honestly for what it would mean to have a dog in the house.

Badger began to grow, literally by leaps and bounds. He was dirtying or destroying anything he could get his little teeth into. I felt angry with my husband because he did not exercise his mechanical skill to construct a dog-proof gate. Every time I left the house I went through a routine designed to confine the dog and yet allow him some freedom. Most of the time I came home to find at least part of the house in a state of siege.

With it all, I grew to love the dog more and more. And the more I loved him, the more I hated him. For with each joy came the hope that he would improve. And thus each setback was a greater disappointment.

For us, at least, Badger was not trainable. Except that we housebroke him, we could teach the dog nothing that he did not want to learn. He consumed everything in sight.

Ben began to use Badger as the object of his aggression toward his younger and older brothers, annoying the dog almost constantly. In fact both younger boys were creating nightmares for me because of their constant goading of the dog. Of course the children laughed delightedly at all the antics, but our oldest son was beginning to worry. Like me, he had formed a deep attachment to Badger and I was beginning to threaten to give the dog away.

Many times, as I threatened to get rid of him, I knew I was being dishonest as well as damaging. Dave really feared that I would carry out my threat. He is a highly sensitive boy, and Badger was a companion when he felt lonely. He tried harder than ever; by now he and I had assumed complete responsibility for the family pet. I could understand the responses of the younger children, but my husband's lack of involvement angered me. I began to prepare Dave for the inevitable, and yet I wanted to keep the dog as much as he did. The conflict was terrible.

Finally, I called the Pet Rescue Home and three weeks later they called to say they had an opening for Badger. I forced myself not to think as I put Badger into our station wagon and drove to Queens. All the while, I knew that no one who adopted him could keep him, at least not in the city. He was too wild. Still, I walked into the lobby, filled out the necessary forms, and took the dog upstairs to be examined by the doctor. As we sat there, the dog began to tremble, and I suddenly began to cry. I broke into such paroxysms of weeping that I could barely control myself. It was all I could do to get to a corridor and phone my husband for some comfort. I couldn't bear to give Badger to strangers, never knowing whether they'd love and care for him or turn him out into the street. And yet, as my husband told me to bring him home I cried that he was making a wreck of our family.

Well, Badger came home with me that day. Our children were confused, subdued, and happy to have him back. I was more tolerant of the commotion for a week or two. Dave was uneasy, and I felt he had lost all faith in me. The dog was soon being tormented again; things were the same as before. When we learned of a farmer in Maine who was willing to take another dog to chase the foxes from his chicken coops we agreed to let Badger go. Badger did not eat for a week after he got to Maine. But once we had ascertained that he had adjusted to his new home we were glad that he had missed us.

Dave never really expressed enough anger directly. He let us know how hurt he was by refusing to even discuss another pet when his brothers raised the subject. About a month afterwards, when John, then five, was being negative, I declared jokingly: "If you don't stop that, I don't know what I'll do." With an odd expression on his face he turned to me and said: "You'll give me away, like you did Badger." Then I realized that I would never really know the full effects of our mutual trauma.

My husband was happy to come home to a peaceful home again. I missed Badger for a long time, but felt relieved. We all feel, to one degree or another, that to have a dog is an immensely enriching experience.

I believe that Dave has resolved some of his feelings, because now when the children speak about another dog he joins in the discussion with interest. We all have that emotional pull to own another pet. At times I feel that a more realistic choice of breed, as well as the increased maturity of the children would make a difference. On the other hand, I think that their basic feelings about their respective positions in the family constellation are the same. It is therefore conceivable that we might use another dog in the same way they did Badger. I also wonder if having a pet to relate to would make it too easy for Dave to withdraw from difficult relationships, now that he is entering adolescence.

I am not willing to put any of us through such an experience again. Therefore, before we reach any decision to try again, we will have to be very certain that most of those negative events will not recur (4).

Another case in which the acquisition of a pet, improperly handled, created rather than solved problems:

> A neighbor's child, the brightest, nicest kid on the block — and an only child of working parents — enjoyed walking with my dog and myself. He kept asking his folks for a dog and they kept responding with vague promises. One day a playmate threw a dart which entered George's eye. He was rushed to a hospital where massive doses of antibiotics were given him because considerable dirt had been carried into the eyeball. George, it was belatedly learned, was allergic to the antibiotics. His body puffed up, and it was touch and go for him. Not knowing whether he would live or die, his parents promised George a dog if he would try hard to get well.
>
> After he came home George borrowed some books from me so he could pick out the kind of dog he wanted. His choice was one of the small terriers — but his folks presented him with a starved, scary, parasite-loaded Beagle pup. Promise number one broken. Soon the pup was very sick, and it didn't survive its first trip to the vet. George was told the pup had been placed with folks on the other side of town until it was well enough to come home. Promise number two broken and compounded with a lie. George was left to wonder if he was really important to his folks — and to wonder forever about the truth of every other statement they made (46).

By contrast, the following letter addressed to the writer movingly describes what a dog can come to mean to a family, especially to one of its members:

> Thank you for kinds words I read in the Anniston Star. A kind big hearted person to love God's world his own nature and the cripple. My baby boy has a dog 17 years old. Now almost blind can't hear good. And it is all he can do is walk. This dog has watched over us. Go to school with them. When school is out. He would go meet them. The dogs name is Bob. He has been shot 2 times hit by cars 3 times. My boy is cripple and draws $54.00 a month so I buy kerocene oil

and aspirins and put this in meat or bread so he can walk better. We have been giving him shots every year we can. But this year he is to sick. When he gets better we will take him. It cost so much to put him in the hospital 8 to 11 dollars a day. People told me to carry him and give him a shot get him out of the way. But this dog stood by me and pertected me bark at night and let us know when somebody is arround. So the children don't want me to carry him because they are afraid that Dr. will give him a shot. You know that would break their hearts and they would cry their eyes out. Bob has been sick with colds and I give him medicine so he would always get well. My cripple boy would pick up R.C. cola bottles sell them and buy potatoes chip. Tony my boy would eat and then give Bob part of what he ate.

I never throw my bread away. Or left overs because there are dogs and cats woundering arround hungrey. Birds can eat apple cores and bread crumbs. My baby girls has a poodle dog. My cripple boy has ducks chickens and 3 turtles he love everythings. I wish he had a zoo he loves talking to his pets. And I believe they understand him. Thannking you lots (68).

The question naturally arises as to what pet is most suitable for a child. Welch (71) discusses pets and their care in some detail (see Table I).

Pets and Human Development

TABLE I

Taken from M. Welch: Redbook's guide to
family pets. *Redbook, 127(5):* 88-96, 1966.

Type of Pet	Amphibians	Birds	Cats
Examples or varieties	Frogs and toads Salamanders Newts Alligators (not suitable — sluggish, grow too big) Turtles	Canaries Parakeets Parrots Myna birds Soft-billed birds Pigeons (outdoors)	Alley cats Domestic short-haired (20 breeds recognized by Cat Fanciers' Association) Persian (long-haired) Siamese Himalayan Abyssinian, Russian Blue, Burmese Manx (tailless)
Quarters needed	Terrarium: glass-sided box with movable lid of glass or screen. For one or two small amphibians, may be $1' \times 2' \times 1 1/2'$ (higher for jumpers). Use sand, gravel, moss or whatever is natural environment for particular species — half water, half land, usually (but for horned toad, all sand). Build-yourself directions in *Compton's Encyclopedia.*	Cage: oblong; roomy ($2' \times 2' \times 2'$ for one small parakeet); removable perches (for cleaning); no loose or bent wires; no chippable paint or rust.	Cats can have run of the house, or can be kept outdoors (garage, shed, under house) if food is protected from scavenging strays, etc.
Other equipment	Something for pet to hide in: artificial light and heater if room is not right temperature (usually 60-75° F.). Plants.	Food and water cups; bath dish; toys; mirror (if no mate); gravel or grit: treat cup; cover for cage (to simulate night and induce sleep).	Bed, unless you allow cat to sleep all over house and furniture. Sanitary tray, plus commercial litter, for indoor use.

Notes on Care	Keep water clean; siphon off sediment; supplement feed with live worms and insects.	Protect from drafts; be vigilant about parasites; watch feeding habits carefully (learn symptoms of boredom, disease, diet deficiency). Bathe — you may have to teach bird how. Give grit to all birds and learn the special food needs of your own. Parrot needs fresh fruit; canary eats "warble," not "roller," feed; most need extras during molting; soft-bills want live insects.	Inoculate against distemper. Ask vet's advice on feeding. Siamese need extra calcium, no fat. For indoor cat give grass (or vegetables mixed into food). No walking necessary for apartment cat; house cats will learn to indicate when they want to go out or door can be fitted with swinging in-out panel for free access.
Handleable?	Infrequently.	Not usually.	Yes.
Trainable?	Slightly.	Yes — to talk, mimic, sing, do tricks, perch on finger.	Somewhat.
Fun to watch?	Not too much. Amphibians are usually nocturnal.	Sometimes.	Yes — and to play with.
Hobby potential	"Raising" insects for food.	Breeding pigeons — racing or homing.	Showing, breeding.
Of further interest	The Japanese salamander may grow to 4 feet, but the common pet is only about 6 to 8 inches. Handle gently but keep hold; they dart away in seconds if let loose outside box. Chameleon short-lived; female apt to die eggbound.	Birds are not easy to raise, but canary is easiest. Bird talks better alone than when paired; best time to teach is usually when they are 8 weeks to 3 months old. Canary sings better if it can hear music. Parrots may scream. See *Cage-Bird Handbook*, Poe (Putnam's).	Siamese may yowl but others are quiet; least bothersome yet most responsive (on their own terms) of pets. Coax and reward — don't punish. Neuter at 5 or 6 months if breeding is undesirable.

TABLE I (continued)

Type of Pet	Dogs	Fish	Guinea Pigs (Cavies)
Examples or varieties	Working dogs: collie, St. Bernard, great Dane, mastiff, Doberman pinscher, German shepherd, Newfoundland, schnauzer, boxer, corgi Sporting dogs and hounds: Labrador, retriever, Weimaraner, pointer, setter, spaniel, greyhound, bloodhound, basset, beagle, foxhound, dachshund Smaller dogs: poodle, terrier (Boston, wire-haired, Bedlington, Scottish, Airedale, Welsh, etc.), bulldog Toy dogs: Miniatures or toys of above. Plus Chihuahua, Pekingese, Yorkshire and Manchester terriers, Brussels griffon	Over 500 kinds to choose from: live-bearers, mouthbreeders. Start with hardiest (goldfish) or starter-tropicals such as black mollies and guppies.	Short-haired, long-haired
Quarters needed	A.S.P.C.A. offers a pamphlet on how to build a doghouse outdoors. If the dog shares your quarters, he should be given a specified place to sleep with his own blanket or bed. Working and sporting dogs need more exercise than the others. If kept outside, be sure to give them free runs via wire-and-cable system; don't chain up. If kept in apartment, arrange runs in addition to daily walk schedule.	Straight-sided glass tank: allow 1 gallon water and 24 square inches of surface per inch of fish (not counting tail). Sand and gravel in bottom. Reserve tank for fry, or for cleaning out main tank.	Hutch: like rabbit's (below) but smaller (about 2' x 2' x 1' per pair). Hardware cloth or mesh floor with papers underneath is easiest to keep clean.
Other equipment	Collar; leash for walking (different leash needed for training): bed; grooming equipment (depends on dog): toys to chew that won't disintegrate into jagged pieces.	Plants as cover; light filter; food; rocks (careful: some may poison fish). Pure water kept at constant temperature (calls for heater). Correct amount of light (not direct sunlight); extra aeration (pump).	Manger for hay to eat; salt block; sleeping box; open-wire runway; gnawing board (for all rodents, lest teeth overgrow).

Notes on care	Only pet requiring license and vaccination against rabies. Inoculate also against distemper. Feed and groom as vet advises for particular age and breed. (Some dogs need regular ear-cleaning, toothbrushing, etc.)	Crowding, overfeeding and temperature changes are biggest hazards; feed dried foods daily but only as much as is eaten in 5 minutes. . . . Clean tank as needed, not necessary often.	Protect from cold (below 65° F.); otherwise they are hardy, easy to raise. Long-hairs need grooming (and they scratch); short-hairs are better. Feed like rabbits. They spend most of their time eating; food must be left in cage.
Handleable?	Extremely.	No.	Yes.
Trainable?	Very.	Slightly.	Somewhat. Can be taught to whistle on call.
Fun to watch?	Play with, rather than observe.	Yes.	Yes.
Hobby potential	Showing, training, breeding.	Collecting, breeding.	Breeding.
Of further interest	Make a dog part of your family, treat him as though he were almost human and you'll have something more than a pet. Write A.S.P.C.A. for information, or American Kennel Club, 51 Madison Avenue, New York, New York 10010, if dog is pedigreed.	Rule of thumb about mixing fish in tank; any fish whose mouth is big enough will eat a smaller fish. . . . Getting started with fish is bothersome, but afterward they are no trouble.	Keep in pairs of same sex or, to breed, 1 male with 2 or 3 females. Unlike hamsters, they get lonely if alone.

TABLE I (continued)

Type of Pet	White Mice	Rabbits	Snakes	Turtles
Examples or varieties	Not field or house mice, white mice are a special strain.	White, including chinchilla, Angora, Belgian hare. Don't keep wild rabbits.	Garter snake, grass snake, king, milk, black, green, hognose.	Water turtle commonest pet. Land turtle: wood tortoise, box, diamondback terrapin (may be against local laws to keep; check).
Quarters needed	Cage: metal (or wood frame protected by metal against gnawing), about 18" square per pair, second story to climb to. Metal tray bottom, newspapers under.	Hutch: 3' x 1 1/2' x 2' per adult, on posts and waterproofed against outdoors (dampness is a big hazard). As large a run as possible for exercise, of fine wire mesh, set 2' into ground to prevent burrowing.	Wooden box: hinged, wire-mesh top, glass front, padlock; 2' x 3' x 1' for several small snakes; big ones need a box as long as their own length.	Terrarium: easily cleanable glass, no top, allowing 1 square foot per 4-inch turtle. Enough water to submerge head entirely. Rock to climb on.
Other equipment	Ladder; exercise bar; trapeze; other toys; separate sleeping box attached; attached water bottle; cloth or paper they can shred: gnawing board.	Hay or shavings on floor, thick in cold weather; change daily. (Scrub and disinfect hutch weekly. Sanitation is vital.) Need untippable water bowl. Chinchillas need special "dust" for daily bath; protection from	Clean gravel and sand; shallow pan for water bath; hiding place such as flower pot; rock to rub against; tree branch.	Light: 60 watt bulb 8" to 10" above drying rock. Needs light 8 hours a day.

Notes on care	Feed no sugar, salt, cheese or meat. Feed twice a day – prepared food plus oats, bread, occasional vegetables, bread, milk, fruit. Protect from drafts (70° F is best). Keep clean.	Feed twice a day, pellets plus carrot; or dampened oats; clover, hay, green.	Needs sun 1 hour per day. Feed once a week. If preferred live food not available (frogs, mice, worms, bugs), train to eat meat.	Needs warm water (75-80 °F). Feed meat, fruit, vegetables 1 to 3 times a week. Clean water when meal is over (after about 2 hours). Supply extra calcium: Cuttlebone, bone meal, plaster of Paris. Fast of whole month won't hurt a healthy turtle. Don't overfeed.
Handleable?	Gently.	Yes.	Gently.	Yes.
Trainable?	Slightly.	A bit.	Slightly.	Slightly.
Fun to watch?	Yes.	Yes.	Yes. Especially when shedding. (Don't touch them then.)	Sometimes.
Hobby potential	Breeding.	Breeding, meat, pelt.	None.	Breeding.
Of further interest	Two females can be kept together, not two males. Main disadvantage is mousy odor.	Discourage screaming and thumping of hind legs from the first. Leave mother with babies alone for several days.	Until tamed and trusting, they may give off unpleasant odor when frightened.	

TABLE I (continued)

Type of Pet	Hamsters	Insects	Lizards	
Examples or varieties	All are basically the same, but sometimes distinguished as "Syrian" or "Golden."	Ants (best for child)	Chameleon Horned toad Iguana	
Quarters needed	Cage: metal and wire (will gnaw out of wood) about 1 square foot each, or 1 1/2 for nesting mother.	Glass box: 8″ x 11″ x 1/2″. Buy or make with ordinary glass and masking tape. (Easy directions in *Compton's Encyclopedia*.)	Terrarium (can be an old aquarium with hinged screen top added): add sand, gravel, water bath, plants (for water supply). Try to re-create natural environment, desert or bog accordingly.	
Other equipment	Shavings (change weekly; bathroom corner more often). Gravity-feed water bottle; exercise wheel; gnawing board.	Black cover (cardboard is fine) so ants have underneath darkness except when you watch them.	Light heater to keep temperature around 80° F. Plants, tree branch.	
Notes on care	Feed once a day — prepared mix or rabbit pellets, bread, nuts, fruits, vegetables, occasionally milk (only about 1 tablespoon). Avoid damp and draft; 50-80° F. best. Given food and water, can be left alone several days.	Keep soil moist but not muddy; feed about a drop of honey a week if you've started with real earth from an anthill.	Spray water on plants (lizards won't drink from dish). Catch soft insects (or buy live meal worms) for feed. Provide sun and warmth, also hiding place or shade. Feeding takes care of itself if live insects are put into box. Replenish as necessary.	
Handleable?	Gently.	No.	No.	
Trainable?	Somewhat.	No.	No.	
Fun to watch?	Yes.	Yes.	Sometimes.	
Hobby potential	Breeding (manage carefully).	None.	None.	
Of further interest	Good apartment pet (maximum weight, 5 oz. They like small space, have no odor). Start with 2-month-old; will live 3 or 4 years. See *Golden Hamsters*,	For "caught" bugs and how to keep them, see *Catch a Cricket*. Stevens (Young Scott Books); or *The First Book of Bugs*, Williamson (Watts).		

The Pet as an Aid to Learning

In the writer's opinion, young children learn best when they recognize that the subject matter to be studied is immediately useful. Further, the best way of learning how difficult a skill is and of remaining humble about possessing such a skill is to teach others. Pets, dogs in particular, are ideal tools for that purpose. The child learns that he must exercise patience if he wants the dog to learn, that outbursts of temper, though possibly effective with his parents, are only self-defeating when applied to the dog. He becomes aware of the fact that in training the animal he is teaching it to adjust to an environment which is basically alien to its nature. He further learns that he must repeat the same "lesson" over and over again before the dog can learn it, and that he will go through many unrewarding hours before achieving the satisfaction of seeing his dog master a new skill. The child unconsciously begins to apply these principles to himself, gradually realizing that learning is not always enjoyable and that it frequently involves much hard work. In this fashion the child increases his ability to master his environment and makes headway with the difficult learning and developmental tasks of adolescence and adulthood.

The child's interest in his pet will force him to seek information about the pet's food, care, and medication, which is most easily and quickly acquired through reading. From reading for information the child may gradually begin to read for pleasure. While learning to feed his pets the proper food for their needs, the child may come to recognize that he too has certain basic food requirements, so that he will develop a more wholesome attitude towards the eating of well-balanced meals. Furthermore, in his attempt to learn about his pet, the child begins "to learn how to learn," which in turn may help him to become more of a self-actualizing individual.

Children aged 4 to 10 are more interested in animals than in plants, and these interests may provide a broad approach to sex education and to realistic attitudes about life and death (43). It is much easier for children to understand animal life than plant life, their interest in animals being more intense and biologically based. Physiological processes are more easily observed in the animal than in the plant (43). It is thus easier to sustain children's interests in animals and to transfer this interest to other bodies of knowledge.

> For the child's interest in animals is far more lively and sustained, and needs less support and stimulus from us. It should, indeed, surprise us if this were not so. The movements and constantly changing behaviour, the warm touch, the voice, *the responses of the animal to the child's own behavior,* call out not only an interest in things happening, but a feeling of companionship, an immediate sympathy, which makes the relationship at once active and mutual. Plants and flowers are, as it were, mere instruments of passive pleasure; animals are active and adaptive creatures, which the child finds he can act upon or be moved by, much as in the case of human beings. Hence he shows a variety of attitudes toward them, according to the kind of animal, or his own changing moods and phases of development. The small animal, for instance, becomes to him a living toy, which he can tyrannize over or cherish (43, p. 169).

The larger animals require more understanding since they are so strange and inspire fear. Moreover, all of them become objects of fantasy.

Isaacs stresses that a child should be permitted and even encouraged to examine an animal so that he may learn something about physiological processes and the facts of death at first hand. "We have, then, to let our children face — when it comes their way — the fact of animal death, as a fact of nature as well as of the necessities of human sustenance" (43, p. 165). She found that children exposed to these experiences do not become cruel, nor are they shocked or frightened.

We should try to dispel the confusion which so many youngsters feel when, on the one hand we teach them to be kind and loving and not to kill, while on the other hand we eat dead animals and exhibit their bodies in butcher shops, dress in dead animal skins, and kill animals for sport, for protection, or because they are a nuisance (43). This confusion in children's minds can be cleared up if we are honest with ourselves and them. We can insist that neither we nor they should in any way unnecessarily expose animals to pain and that no one should tease or hurt animals.

When exposed to the above approach, children, instead of being cruel, exhibit kindness to animals. Their destructive drives are sublimated into a search for knowledge. "In other words, the impulse to master and destroy was taken up into the aim of understanding" (43, p. 166). "The living animal became much less an object of power and possession, and much more an independent creature to be learnt about, watched and known for its own sake" (43, p. 166). Thus children become sympathetic to living things and develop a deep interest in their lives and actions.

The Pet as an Aid to Successful Group Membership

The school-aged child has to sustain and deepen his contacts with the community and school. At this point, even more than in the previous stages, his attitudes are shaped by the people he meets. He must feel that he is accepted, that he is part of a family group, that he belongs. The child will find that his possession of a prized pet which can perform tricks has raised his status among his peers and has also given him positive group experiences and joy in living. Thus, through identifying with his peer group and finding that he has become an integral part of it, the child develops more respect for himself and for his abilities by introjecting the respect and admiration given him by his group. We find, for example, that when children who are submissive are taught a skill which is regarded very highly by their peers and in turn begin to teach this skill to others, such children become ascendant, achieve dominance in their group, and are sought out by their peers.

This acceptance by others on the basis of service performed is of particular importance in preadolescence, when the child has to start moving from concern about his own self to concern about others. He must now think of the needs of his friends and try to identify with their achievements. As a member of a "pet club" he might try to help his friends derive satisfaction from the training of their own pets. As an officer of such a club he would be concerned with the "pet" problems of his peers, thus earning their esteem.

Aggression and the Pet

A child needs both to love and to hate, and to express his aggression in acceptable ways.

Freud (26) considered aggression to be innate in animal and

man. Ardrey (7) came to the same conclusion, although he based his judgment on a different theoretical postulate. According to Lorenz (48), too, aggression in animals is innate, and a "fighting instinct" in man contributes to the development and differentiation of the self as well as to self-protection against hostile forces.

Our position is similar to that of Storr (67) who stressed that aggression "is a drive as innate, as natural, and as powerful as sex" (67, p. 109), and must therefore be satisfied in one way or another.

We also feel that aggression, unless perverted, plays a positive role in human development. It is through aggression that an infant differentiates himself from his all-encompassing environment, a child rescues himself from the smothering love of its mother, and a youth separates himself from the youth culture to become an individual. Modern life creates many tensions and anxieties. Insecurity of an economic, social, and political nature, violence in the streets, parental problems, conflicts with siblings and peers — all must be coped with. There are thus normal as well as abnormal family and social situations which call for aggressive responses.

I therefore do not wish to imply that through association with pets a child will become an entirely cooperative individual, rarely engaging in competitive activities. This in my opinion would be undesirable even if it were possible. Many youngsters seek out conflict either in actuality, in the form of competitive games, or vicariously through reading, radio, TV, movies, and the theatre. Conflict has a social and personal value (18). It provides a means for comparing oneself with peers and testing one's abilities. What we are concerned with here is how competitive striving in the raising and handling of pets can be used productively in the child's development.

Money Management and the Pet

Pets have to eat and food costs money. This is where the young child can get his first lesson in money management. The child should receive an allowance each week not only for his own but also for his pet's needs. It should be left to the child to budget this money. The amount can be worked out in cooperation with other parents whose children have similar pets. Of course, the needs and income of each family as a whole must be considered. The individual child's sense of responsibility and competence in managing money must also be taken into account. However, a pet allowance, if judiciously introduced, can teach a child a great deal. He should have some choice, within reason, as to the allocation of the pet money just as he should have some choice in the spending of his allowance.

Acceptance of One's Sex Role

We learn about sex throughout life. Likewise, our roles as males or females are learned in a gradual, almost imperceptible manner. With the ownership of pets the process of learning about male and female roles, about oestrus, pregnancy, and the rearing of the young becomes more vivid and natural. Children absorb this information very avidly and unconsciously apply it to themselves and to their future role in the procreation and rearing of families.

The Pet in Adolescence

With the beginning of adolescence the child begins to look increasingly to the outside world for love and companionship. However, afraid that he may not be able to meet the challenges and responsibilities of adulthood, the adolescent at the same time clings more tightly to the love and security provided by his parents. With the help of an animal companion, he may be better able to ride through the uncertainty of this period, which otherwise can be terribly threatening. This situation is illustrated in the following narrative:

> As a teenager, the writer had a dog named Pal. It is with nostalgia that she recalls the many long walks through the woods that were shared only with Pal. As the oldest of five children many responsibilities had to be assumed by her. Whenever the writer felt distressed she could always rely upon Pal for reassurance, love and security. The writer and Pal would retreat to their secret hideaway where the responsibilities would be put aside, play would ensue, and later they would return greatly refreshed (69).

As soon as a modicum of security is attained by the adolescent, however, he longs to abandon the support of the pet and come out into the world to face its adventures unencumbered. The pet at this point has already unconsciously become symbolic of the family and of dependence, particularly of the mother as a succorant figure. The need for the pet thus represents childish dependence. This factor, together with the redirection of the adolescent's interests to the opposite sex, leads to neglect of and eventual loss of interest in the previously prized pet. However, under the stress of loneliness or some other traumatic occurrence, the interest in pets may be reawakened and strengthened.

A study of the responses of 10- and 13-year old boys on the Rorschach has indicated that the 13-year olds saw a significantly larger number of timid animals than did the 10-year olds (3). This would seem to derive from the unsureness about themselves and their place in the world that young adolescents feel.

Animal Preferences of Children

Children have a tremendous interest in animals. When 137 nursery school and kindergarten children were asked to tell a story, 44.7 percent spoke about human beings, 34.30 percent about animals, and 20.93 percent about objects (computed by this writer from Pitcher and Prelinger, ref. 56, Table 2, p. 250).

A study was made in 1967 of the animal preferences and dislikes of 80,000 British children. These children, aged four to fourteen, were asked during a zoo TV program, "Which animal do you like most?" and "Which animal do you dislike most?" On the basis of 12,000 selected replies, the children ranked their preferences as follows: "1. Chimpanzee (13.5 per cent). 2. Monkey (13 per cent). 3. Horse (9 per cent). 4. Bushbaby (8 per cent). 5. Panda (7.5 per cent). 6. Bear (7 per cent). 7. Elephant (6 per cent). 8. Lion (5 per cent). 9. Dog (4 per cent). 10. Giraffe (2.5 per cent)" (50, p. 226). This confirms the results of a study done in the 1930's when child visitors to a zoo were asked about their preferences in animals. The order indicated was the following: (a) apes and monkeys, (b) lions and tigers, (c) elephants, (d) bears, and (e) sea lions (41). Several decades later, children in Montreal were asked the same questions. Again primates topped the list (41).

Morris (50) hypothesizes that small children see animals as parent substitutes and thus prefer larger animals which can afford them more protection. Later on when the child wishes to liberate himself from parental domination and assume the role of the parent, he prefers smaller animals, which he can see as his own children.

Morris concludes that we all have unconscious drives which make us "see other species as caricatures of ourselves" (50, p. 225). On the basis of his investigation of British children's preferences in zoo animals, he arrives at the following two principles: "The popularity of an animal is directly correlated with the number of anthropomorphic features it possesses," and "the age of a child is inversely correlated with the size of the animal it prefers" (50, p. 230).

Morris as well as other investigators found the horse to be three times as popular with girls as with boys, its popularity increasing until puberty and then declining. Morris ascribes this attitude to the fact that response to the horse has a "strong sexual element" (50, p. 231) and that the decline in its popularity coincides with the more covert sex play of the adolescent.

The following were the most disliked animals cited in the Morris study: "1. Snake (27 per cent). 2. Spider (9.5 per cent). 3. Crocodile (4.5 per cent). 4. Lion (4.5 per cent). 5. Rat (4 per cent). 6. Skunk (3 per cent). 7. Gorilla (3 per cent). 8. Rhinoceros (3 per cent). 9. Hippopotamus (2.5 per cent). 10. Tiger (2.5 per cent)" (50, p. 233). These animals were disliked because they were dangerous.

Animals Named by Children

Ilg, Ames, and Apell (42) studied the kinds of animals named by children on School Readiness Tests. A total of 301 children were examined, but since some children were tested at two or more ages, the total number of examinations was 700. Fifty boys and 50 girls were studied at ages 5, 5 1/2, 6, 7, 8, 9, and 10. The boys had a mean WISC IQ of 106 and the girls of 104.8.

The examiner asked each child to "name all the animals you can think of until I tell you to stop." The time limit was 60 seconds.

The investigators found a steady increase in the number of

animals named with age. The animals were classified into 5 different categories: domestic, zoo, intermediate (e.g. bear, fox, etc.), bird, and fish; on the whole, domestic and zoo animals were named most frequently, domestic animals leading at most ages with girls, and zoo animals at all ages with boys.

An examination of Table III indicates that the most common domestic animals named are dogs and cats. Interestingly enough, girls name dogs more frequently than boys. The most common zoo animals named are lions, tigers, and elephants.

Apparently the different results obtained by Morris (50) and Ilg, Ames and Apell (42) may be ascribed to the differences in the population sampled and the method of inquiry.

TABLE II

NAMING ANIMALS

Percentage of Responses in Each Class

	5 years		5½ years		6 years		7 years	
	G	B	G	B	G	B	G	B
Domestic	**39.0**	24.2	35.4	27.4	37.2	28.8	**35.5**	27.4
Zoo	35.5	**45.9**	**44.6**	**47.0**	**41.6**	**36.9**	34.4	**39.7**
Intermediate[a]	9.0	11.8	5.8	9.9	7.9	8.6	8.8	10.2
Bird	11.0	9.8	7.3	7.8	6.8	11.4	11.6	11.3
Fish	5.0	8.2	6.8	7.8	6.6	14.3	9.8	13.5

	8 years		9 years		10 years	
	G	B	G	B	G	B
Domestic	**40.3**	24.6	**35.6**	24.6	**34.2**	29.4
Zoo	26.7	**35.3**	26.5	**30.8**	29.2	**30.5**
Intermediate[a]	12.9	13.8	11.4	17.2	13.3	15.3
Bird	13.3	11.6	13.2	12.2	12.5	11.0
Fish	6.5	14.0	13.0	15.0	10.8	13.4

[a]Squirrel, bear, fox, etc.

Note: Boldface figures here are leading, not normative items.

Taken from Ilg, Ames, and Apell: *School Readiness as Evaluated by Gesell Developmental, Visual and Projective Tests* (42, p. 223).

NAMING ANIMALS

Number of Occurences

	5 years		5½ years		6 years		7 years		8 years		9 years		10 years		All	
	G	B	G	B	G	B	G	B	G	B	G	B	G	B	G	B
Dog	**28**	**14**	21	19	**34**	**23**	**42**	**34**	**49**	**38**	**48**	**34**	**46**	40	268	202
Cat	21	9	**22**	13	30	22	37	28	44	34	46	29	**46**	**45**	246	180
Horse	20	12	18	20	22	23	28	23	37	26	37	28	35	35	197	167
Cow	18	12	16	13	14	17	22	22	28	21	31	21	31	30	160	136
Rabbit	10	6	15	10	13	11	13	19	12	15	25	15	23	26	111	102
Lion	20	**30**	**26**	**36**	**27**	33	30	**38**	22	36	28	**30**	25	**35**	178	238
Elephant	17	20	19	17	24	22	**34**	28	**24**	27	25	25	**28**	26	171	165
Tiger	17	29	25	30	26	27	26	31	17	30	25	28	24	26	160	201
Giraffe	13	17	22	25	19	19	16	17	15	23	22	16	20	16	127	133
Bear	16	10	14	15	12	14	14	20	21	16	15	20	14	16	106	111
Zebra	9	8	13	12	15	10	19	12	9	14	12	8	20	18	97	82
Mouse	3	1	**5**	2	3	3	7	7	**12**	**12**	**12**	**15**	12	**21**	54	61
Deer	6	2	3	3	2	5	5	7	7	**12**	11	8	9	7	43	44
Fox	4	5	0	2	4	2	6	9	6	4	8	12	**15**	8	43	42
Squirrel	6	6	1	7	3	**10**	5	9	8	11	7	10	12	12	42	65
Some Bird	16	16	18	16	9	21	20	31	31	52	44	44	41	14	179	194
Chicken	5	3	4	5	7	13	17	12	18	11	20	13	16	16	87	73
Some Fish	2	4	7	2	8	12	9	15	7	24	21	13	20	14	74	84
Snake	5	6	4	9	6	14	13	23	8	20	16	24	18	16	70	112
Total	236	210	253	256	278	301	373	385	375	426	453	393	445	421	2413	2392

Note: Boldface figures here are the leading items at each age, rather than normative items, since no naming here reaches normative proportions.

Taken from Ilg, Ames, and Apell: *School Readiness as evaluated by Gesell Developmental, Visual and Projective Tests* (42, p. 225).

Animal Preferences of Adolescents and Adults

The reasons behind a person's choice of a particular pet have intrigued researchers for many years (45). Answers have been sought in such questions as: Do people have an ideal in mind for a pet as they do for a mate or child? Why does one person prefer a small dog, another a large dog? Why do some insist on a pedigreed animal? Is there a correlation between the personality traits of a pet and those of his master? Is there any verity to the claim of the well-known dog trainer, Blanche Saunders (60), that a dog should match its owner's personality?

Possibly both the symbolic meaning and a common sense evaluation of the traits of the animal determine its choice. Do one's feelings about one's inner self — for example, a fear of being intruded upon — determine the selection of a pet?

> This is my main point, the point of thought which is the centre of an intellectual world and of my paper. Although healthy persons communicate and enjoy communicating, the other fact is equally true, that *each individual is an isolate, permanently noncommunicating, permanently unknown, in fact unfound* (73, p. 187).

A dog intrudes; he demands love, he wants to be petted and taken care of. Some people admire these qualities; others do not. Some owners have a feeling of identification with their dog, liking him because he is sloppy or trips over his feet. Is it possible that authority figures who are terribly alone (e.g. Roosevelt, Johnson, Nixon) need a pet whom they can love and who asks little in return?

A cat, on the other hand, is not intrusive; it can fend for itself. Possibly such a pet is more desirable to people for whom preservation "of personal isolation is part of the search for identity" (73, p. 190). Note the facetious remark made by Camuti and Alexander, "Cat people are different to the extent that they generally are not conformists. How could they be with a cat running their lives?" (12, p. 41).

Pets and Psychological Regression

The reader should not be left with the impression that pets always exert a beneficial influence on children and adolescents. A great deal depends on the role which the pet plays in the life of the child or adolescent. Some children who fail to relate to their parents and peers may wish to escape into a world of make-believe. For the child who feels inferior and unhappy and finds it extremely difficult to get along with his peers, the pet may become a refuge, providing for the child's every emotional need so that he feels no necessity for rejoining the group. At times we find a disturbed home situation in which pets have come to play a crucial role in family pathology. Sometimes this manifests itself in school phobia, i.e. a refusal by a child to attend school out of fear that abandonment by mother or father will take place in his absence. In the two cases that follow, this fear of loss was symbolized by the children's pets.

Rhoda was a seriously disturbed 14-year-old school phobic adolescent whose attendance record in school had been very poor since the primary grades, although she had high average intelligence and superior reading ability. She had never been on a field trip with her class, and hesitated to leave the house even to go shopping with her mother.

When she was in fourth grade, Rhoda had an emotional breakdown, claiming she could no longer stand to live and begging God to let her die. Her parents placed her in therapy for two years, and then frequented a series of pediatricians, psychologists, neurologists, and psychiatrists.

For a long time Rhoda's mother concealed much of the problem from the school, but finally the school authorities intervened, undertaking a program of "desensitization" to ease her back into the school environment. She eventually attended class, but with many setbacks, managing nevertheless to be promoted to ninth grade. Attending high school meant riding on the school bus, and this Rhoda refused to do, so that she again had to leave school, spending her time at home watching television, sleeping, or playing with her dog, Casey, a very neurotic, oversexed male animal, very difficult for the mother to handle. Both parents loathed the dog, but were unwilling to get rid of it because of Rhoda's intense attachment to her pet. Rhoda also had a very large collection of stuffed animals which she had to keep by her in order to sleep.

Rhoda's family for a long time considered committing her to an institution, and the girl claimed she would rather go to one than attend school, except that she didn't want to leave Casey. When Rhoda was particularly nervous she would take Casey to bed with her. It was not known if there was any sex play or sodomy on these occasions, but there was at least the possibility of erotic and abnormal motivation on the part of the child. Rhoda had no friends and a very unhealthy relationship to the members of her family. Prognosis was guarded (53).

Fourteen-year old Mary, an 8th grader of slightly above average intelligence, was a passive, lonely, dependent adolescent whose school record was also marked by excessive absences for a variety of "illnesses." She, too, had a fanatic devotion to her numerous pets, her greatest love in life being her horse, Barney. Often Mary played truant in order to go to the stable where Barney was kept and ride him all day. All her creative writing in school involved a horse, and she once cried in class, to her great embarrassment, while reading a poem she had written about the death of one of her previous horses. She appeared unable realistically to differentiate the past experience from her present situation.

Despite her intense devotion to Barney, Mary gave the school bizarre excuses for her absences involving stomach and leg injuries inflicted by kicks from this supposedly beloved horse.

Other than Barney, Mary also tended numerous cats, hamsters, chickens and two dogs.

Her family was not receptive to therapy and the outlook for Mary's future development was not clear (53).

SUMMARY

The values of pet ownership in promoting normal child development may be summarized as follows: A child who is exposed to the emotional experiences inherent in playing with a pet is given many learning opportunities that are essential to wholesome personality development. His play with the pet will express his view of the world, its animals, and its human beings, including his parents and peers. Further, through play with the pet, the child may learn to resolve some of the problems of relating to his peers and of achieving a wholesome balance of dependence and independence with regard to his family. At the same time, the child can obtain some catharsis, as play with the pet permits him to release some of the accumulated tensions of school and home. In this play with a pet, the child frequently indicates his psychological and social needs, in a sense giving us a closer view of his developmental level.

Caring for a pet provides an opportunity for the child to toughen his ego. Of necessity, the child has to forego some of his pleasures and suffer inconveniences when he is taking care of the animal. This not only enhances the child's ability to handle unpleasant but necessary tasks, but also helps him learn to tolerate anxiety and to defer pleasure. Taking care of the pet may reinforce what has been called (22) the basic trust in one's ability to master one's urges and one's world. Acceptance of responsibility for the care of the pet will eventually lead to an acceptance of responsibility for establishing meaningful, satisfying human relationships. This will help give the child the security needed to lead an emotionally satisfying life.

REFERENCES

1. Ames, L. B., and Learned J.: Imaginary companions and related phenomena. J Gen Psychol, 69:147-167, 1946.
2. Ames, L. B., Learned J., Métraux, R. W., and Walker, R. N.: Child Rorschach Responses. New York, Hoeber, 1952.
3. Ames, L. B., Métraux, R. W. and Walker, R. N.: Adolescent Rorschach Responses, rev. ed. New York, Brunner/Mazel, 1971.
4. Anonymous: Badger and I. (An unpublished paper.)
5. Anthony, J. E., and Koupernik, C. (Eds.): The Child in His Family. In the International Yearbook for Child Psychiatry and Allied Disciplines. New York, Wiley Interscience, 1970, Vol. I.
6. Anthony, S.: The Child's Discovery of Death. New York, Harcourt Brace, 1940.
7. Ardrey, R.: African Genesis. New York, Atheneum, 1963.
8. Bender, L., and Vogel, B. F.: Imaginary companions of children. Am J Orthopsychiatry, 11:56-65, 1941.
9. Bowlby, J.: Child Care and the Growth of Love. Abridged and edited by Margery Fry. London, Penguin Books, 1953.
10. Bowlby, J.: The nature of the child's tie to his mother. Int J Psychoanal, 39:1-23, 1958.
11. Bowlby, J.: Attachment. New York, Basic Books, 1969.
12. Camuti, L. J., and Alexander, L.: A Park Avenue Vet. New York, Holt, Rinehart and Winston, 1962.
13. Cann, M. A.: An investigation of a component of parental behavior in humans. (Unpublished master's thesis.) University of Chicago, 1953. Cited by Hess, E. H.: Ethology and developmental psychology. In Mussen, P. H. (Ed.): Carmichael's Manual of Child Psychology. New York, Wiley, 1970, Vol. I, pp. 1-38.
14. Chukovskii, K.: Ot Dvukh do Piati (From two to five), 19th ed. Moscow, Prosveschenie, 1966.
15. Coleman, J. C.: Rorschach content as a means of studying child

development. J Pro Tech Pers Assess, 32:435-442, 1968.

16. Denenberg, V. H.: Education of the Infant and Young Child. New York, Academic Press, 1971.

17. Des Lauriers, A. M., and Carlson, C. E.: Your Child Is Asleep. Early Infantile Autism. Homewood, Ill., Dorsey, 1969.

18. Deutsch, M.: Conflict: Productive and destructive. J Soc Issues, 25:7-43, 1969.

19. Dice, R. L.: Man's Nature and Nature's Man. Ann Arbor, University of Michigan, 1955.

20. Draguns, J. G. J., Haley, E. M., and Phillips, L.: Studies of Rorschach content. A review of the research literature. Part I. J Proj Tech Pers Assess, 31:3-32, 1967.

21. Dubos, R. J.: Man Adapting. New Haven, Yale, 1965.

22. Erikson, E. H.: Childhood and Society, 2nd ed. New York, Norton, 1963.

23. Erikson, E. H.: Identity, Youth and Crisis. New York, Norton, 1968.

24. Foote, N. N.: A neglected member of the family. Marriage and Family Living, 18:213-218, 1956.

25. Freedman, D. G., Boverman, H., and Freedman N.: Effects of kinesthetic stimulation on weight gain and on smiling in premature infants. (Paper presented at the meeting of the American Orthopsychiatric Association.) San Francisco, April, 1966.

26. Freud, S.: Civilization and its Discontents. Garden City, N. Y., Doubleday, 1930.

27. Garai, J. E.: Formation of the concept of "self" and development of sex identification. In Kidd, A. H., and Rivoire, J. L. (Eds.): Perceptual Development in Children. New York, International Universities Press, 1966, pp. 344-388.

28. Geber, M.: The psychomotor development of African children in the first year and the influence of maternal behavior. J Soc Psychol, 47:185-195, 1958.

29. Gibran, K. V.: The Prophet. New York, Knopf, 1966.

29a. Hammer, E. F. (Ed.): The Clinical Application of Projective Drawings. Springfield, Thomas, 1967.

30. Harlow, H. F., and Suomi, S. J.: Nature of love simplified. Am Psychol, 25:161-168, 1970.

31. Hartup, W. W.: Peer interaction in social organization. In Mussen, P. H. (Ed.): Carmichael's Manual of Child Psychology, 3rd ed. New York, Wiley, 1970, Vol. II, pp. 361-456.

32. Hasselmeyer, E. G.: The premature neonate's response to handling. Am J Nursing, 11:15-24, 1964.

33. Havighurst, R. J.: Human Development and Education. New York, Longmans, Green, 1953.

34. Haworth, M. R.: The cat: Facts about Fantasy. New York, Grune & Stratton, 1966.

35. Hebb, D. O.: Organization of Behavior. New York, Wiley, 1949.
36. Hediger, H.: Wild Animals in Captivity. New York, Dover, 1964.
37. Helfer, R. E., and Kempe, H. C. (Eds.): The Battered Child. Chicago, University of Chicago, 1968.
38. Hess, E. H.: Ethology. In Friedman, A. M., and Kaplan, H. I. (Eds.): Comprehensive Textbook of Psychiatry. Baltimore, Williams and Wilkins, 1967, pp. 180-189.
39. Hess, E. H.: Ethology and developmental psychology. In Mussen, P. H. (Ed.): Carmichael's Manual of Child Psychology, 3rd ed. New York, Wiley, 1970, vol. I, pp. 1-38.
40. Hess, E. H., and Polt, J. M.: Pupil size as related to interest value of visual stimuli. Science, 132:349-350, 1960.
41. Iles, G.:My Home in the Zoo. Garden City, N. Y., Doubleday, 1961.
42. Ilg, F. L., Ames, L. B., and Apell, R. J.: School Readiness as Evaluated by Gesell Developmental, Visual and Projective Tests. New York, Harper & Row, 1965.
43. Isaacs, S.: Intellectual Growth in Young Children. New York, Schocken Books. (Reprinted 1966)
44. Ledwith, N. H.: Rorschach Responses of Elementary School Children. Pittsburgh, University of Pittsburgh, 1960.
45. Levinson, B. M.: Pet-Oriented Child Psychotherapy. Springfield, Thomas, 1969.
46. Levinson, B. M.: Kids are a responsibility. Dogs, 1(2):14-19, 1970.
47. Levinson, B. M.: Pets, child development and mental illness. J Am Vet Med Assoc, 157:1759-1766, 1970.
48. Lorenz, K.: On Aggression. New York, Harcourt Brace & World, 1966.
49. Miles, M. W., and Charters, W. W. (Eds.): Learning in Social Settings. Boston, Allyn & Bacon, 1970.
50. Morris, D.: The Naked Ape. New York, McGraw-Hill, 1967.
51. Morris, D.: The Human Zoo. New York, McGraw-Hill, 1970.
52. Perlman, E. A.: Pets and Children. (Unpublished manuscript.)
53. Piaget, A.: Two Case Histories. (Unpublished manuscript.)
54. Piaget, J., and Inhelder, B.: The Psychology of the Child. New York, Basic Books, 1969.
55. Piaget, J.: Piaget's theory. In Mussen, P. H. (Ed.): Carmichael's Manual of Child Psychology, 3rd ed. New York, Wiley, vol. I, 1970, pp. 703-732.
56. Pitcher, E., and Prelinger, E.: Children Tell Stories. New York, International Universities Press, 1963.
57. Report of the Joint Commission on Mental Health of Children; Crisis in Child Mental Health: Challenge for the 1970's. New York, Harper & Row, 1970.
58. Rheingold, H. R., and Samuels, H. R.: Maintaining the positive behavior of infants by increased stimulation. Dev Psychol, 1:520-527, 1969.
59. Ribble, M. A.: Infantile experience in relation to personality development. In Hunt, J. McV. (Ed.): Personality and the Behavior Disorders.

New York, Ronald Press, 1944, pp. 621-651.

60. Saunders, B.: How to pick a dog to match your personality. Am Magazine, 47:32-34, 1949.
61. Schaefer, C. E.: Imaginary companions and creative adolescents. Dev Psychol, 1:747-749, 1969.
62. Schaffer, H. R.: Objective observations of personality development in early infancy. Br J Med Psychol, 31:174-183, 1958.
63. Schaffer, H. R., and Callender, W. M.: Psychologic effects of hospitalization in infancy. Pediatrics, 24:528-539, 1959.
64. Searles, H. F.: The Nonhuman Environment. New York, International Universities Press, 1960.
65. Solkoff, N., Yaffe, S., Weintraub, D., and Blase, B.: Effects of handling on the subsequent development of premature infants. Dev Psychol, 1:765-768, 1969.
66. Sperling, O. E.: An imaginary companion, representing a prestage of the superego. Psychoanal Study Child, 9:252-258, 1954.
67. Storr, A.: Human Aggression. New York, Atheneum, 1968.
68. Stovall, A.: Personal communication. 7/5/70.
69. Sundaran, S.: An exploratory study of the feasibility of utilizing pets as a psychotherapeutic modality in the treatment of emotionally disturbed children. (Unpublished Master's paper.) Boston University, 1969.
70. Thomas, A., Chess, S., and Birch, H. G.: Temperament and Behavior Disorders in Children. New York, New York U. P., 1968.
71. Welch, M.: Redbook's guide to family pets. Redbook, 127(5):88-96, 1966.
72. Winnicott, D. W.: Transitional objects and transitional phenomena. Int J Psychoanal, 24:88-97, 1953.
73. Winnicott, D. W.: The Maturational Processes and the Facilitating Environment. New York, International Universities Press, 1965.

Chapter Three

THE PET AND THE ADULT

This stupid world where
Gadgets are gods and we go on talking,
Many about much, but remain alone,
Alive but alone, belonging-where?
Unattached as tumbleweed.*

W E all look for fulfillment, but our needs are different and our goals are pitched at different levels. The higher the spiritual, educational, and emotional development of a man, the greater are his needs. When his physical requirements are met, there are others which demand satisfaction. Man, however, can never attain this goal of complete self-fulfillment; he can only strive for and approximate it (8). As Browning (2, p. 630) said:

For thence, — a paradox
Which comforts while it mocks, —
Shall life succeed in that it seems to fail:
What I aspired to be,
And was not, comforts me:
A brute I might have been, but would
     not sink i' the scale.

However, in attempting to meet one's goals, the individual must take an affirmative attitude about his existence. Only through active participation in life can one learn to relate to others. Having a pet is one way to force oneself, if necessary, to take part actively in living. This participation, of course, may vary from person to person depending on the manner in which animal and master interact.

For self-fulfillment, man needs ever new experiences; he needs to explore. Rats, even though satiated, will explore a maze just for the fun of it. Man can find exciting activities at his elbow by observing the stars, though smog may sometimes obscure his view;

*W. H. Auden: *The Age of Anxiety*, 1946, p.44.

by hiking through the countryside; or just by playing with his pet and observing its development.

Preparation for Parenthood

We know that many couples either consciously or unconsciously prepare themselves for parenthood by taking care of a cat or dog, somewhat in the way girls play with dolls to prepare themselves for motherhood, and boys play with mechanical toys to prepare themselves for their life's work.

Searles quotes the ruminations of one of his patients who found that his pet dog had not only brought his wife and himself closer but had also in a sense prepared them for parenthood:

> Things are going along pretty smoothly (he began, in a tone of confidence which was unusual for him; he then said, of his wife:) She made the remark this morning that if the Boy Wizard (their name for me) made me more cocky than I am, something would have to be done — which was very pleasing to me, particularly in the light of so much in the past that was uncertain. . . .
>
> And the more I think about the child. . . the more I think it'd be sort of fun (slowly and thoughtfully) — uh — and I think I'd sort of be proud of being father to a cherub — I think it'd be sort of exciting — certainly a rather new experience — uh — and, uh — I certainly feel that if we're going to have children we certainly oughta have them now and not wait, because I think the older ya get, the less adaptable ya are, and the more trouble children are. I think the child — I *know* it'll be a good thing for my wife, who doesn't have enough to occupy herself. . . I think she'll be a good mother (tone of conviction). And I keep thinking about it's being a boy — and I keep wondering, "What the hell would you teach a boy about life and what life is about?" — I think I probably could do that. I suppose I'd have a tendency to overstress those things that were lacking in my own early life — uh — and I suppose I should be on guard not to overstress them — I feel that the set up we have out there (in a remodeled farmhouse) would be very conducive and very efficient for having a child, having children.
>
> *Certainly if the pleasure we've gotten out of this animal is any faint indication — it has been a pleasure,* much less of course (than that of having children), but *a mutual responsibility* (said in a tone of solid satisfaction) — *even when we we'd gotten pretty far apart in terms of our feelings toward each other, the dog always had a kind of bridging effect* — uh — I find that some of the things that used to irritate me about my wife, they don't seem to irritate me so much — . . . the

same things (i.e. things which they used to say to one another in contempt) are said, but they're said in a very different way — it's almost as if they're said on a basis of esteem rather than scorn. . . (10, pp. 86-87).

A woman who has successfully reared a pet will very likely have greater confidence in her ability to raise a child and be more ready to accept herself as a wife and mother. She will look forward to having a child as a positive and enjoyable experience, not considering its care a chore that she will be obligated to handle. Probably she will be more tolerant of the inevitable messes created by every infant and toddler, and will not feel disgusted when her child has had an "accident," thus helping him to develop a positive attitude toward himself. Such a maternal attitude will tend to minimize a child's developmental difficulties.

However, one must also consider the negative aspects of rearing a pet in preparation for parenthood. When a young animal is raised from puppyhood by a human being, not only does the animal develop an extreme attachment to its foster parent, but the human in turn develops an intense love for the pet. If, when a child arrives on the scene, it should become necessary to give up the pet, this situation may prove highly traumatic.

Prenatal Stress

It is well known that emotional stress in a gravid female can affect the foetus adversely (14). A mother's severe emotional stress during pregnancy may result in a hyperactive infant who "penalizes" his parents by staying actively awake all night and sleeping during the day! Thus anything that can lessen a woman's fear of giving birth and minimize tension during the prenatal period will benefit both mother and infant.

A woman who likes pets and takes care of them during her pregnancy may find this hobby both relaxing and comforting. First, caring for the pet may be symbolic for her of the care one gives to helpless infants. Second, observations of painless births by pets may lead the expectant mother to consider the possibility of undergoing natural childbirth, with its many satisfactions. If a woman is relaxed when giving birth the need for premature use of drugs or even the use of drugs at all may be lessened or eliminated.

Third, the regular airing of the pet, taking it for walks in the neighborhood, can help give the pregnant woman the physical exercise she needs.

Most mothers are very affectionate with their infants and feel amply rewarded by the baby's kiss or smile for all the sleepless nights, heartaches, and troubles they undergo. Yet some of these very same mothers become bitterly resentful when their children become toddlers and strive for autonomy by reaching out into the wider world. These mothers look upon such natural developments as desertion on the part of their progeny. It is advisable at that time for mothers with such an outlook to secure new pets for which they can care. Pets remain forever grateful and dependent on their owner. Moreover, this deflection of the mother's attention from her own child will permit the latter to grow up in a less harassed fashion.

Eventually our children outgrow us. We may still, however, have a need to nourish, protect, and love. Thus George Bernard Shaw, in discussing his mother and her disappointments, mentions that she had "three uninteresting children grown too old to be petted like the animals and birds she was fond of" (11, p. 146).

The Pet as a Child-substitute

Krutzmann, a well-known Canadian veterinarian, reports as follows:

> The love, care and attention these pets receive is often more intense than that given to a child. The case in mind is that of a first-aid man and his wife. Childless, but truly happy and in love with each other. Their main concern seems to be the health and wellbeing of their two German Shepherds. They live 400 miles North of Vancouver in a logging camp and are in constant touch by either mail or radio-telephone communication. They worry because there is medical help available in a nearby town for themselves, but no veterinarian closer than Vancouver. On two occasions they have phoned advising that the wife is flying down with a critically ill dog. Expense is of no importance and ever grateful are they for help received.
>
> Three o'clock in the morning, the telephone rings urgently. The night attendant wants to know what to do besides calling the police. A woman is inside with a severely sick cat. The husband still intoxicated is outside pounding on the door. Using abusive language,

he warns that if the cat stays his wife can stay as well. Just as he smashes down the front door, the police arrive and bring the situation under control. The woman insists on having her cat treated. She has paid her bill. He has failed to fulfill his responsibility and is now in the process of being summoned to appear in court, being sued for damages (7).

Occasionally when a couple divorces, a problem arises over custody of the family pet. This sometimes leads to acrimonious legal battles. There are cases where a couple divorces because one of the partners claims that his spouse pays too much attention to the family pet and too little to him.

Husband and wife, both actors, visit the hospital with their two German Shepherds. The husband's favorite is a big husky male dog. The man displays obvious pride and the dog seems to bolster his ego. The wife's favorite is a gentle female German Shepherd. A mother and "favorite daughter" combination. Husband and wife seem to suit each other and all four of them appear to be a good combination. Months later the wife registers as "Miss" using her maiden name. She is now divorced, but while love for husband has ceased, her motherly care and love for her pet still exists. Her former husband is more than ever depending upon his male German Shepherd to promote his own image of all male masculinity (7).

The Pet and the Isolate

Nowadays we find many alienated individuals living in apartments, hotels, rooming houses, or skid-row lodging houses, who lack, need, and fear human companionship. These men and women feel isolated and drift like flotsam on the eddies and whirlpools of life. They desperately need some being to love and care about them; they need to commune with nature if a fruitful relationship with human beings is ever to be reestablished. For such people, association with a pet may make the difference between maintaining contact with reality or almost totally withdrawing into fantasy. It may literally mean a choice between life and death.

These men and women have been so hurt by life and so disappointed by other people that they frequently echo the sentiment supposedly expressed by Horace Walpole: "I know that I have had friends who would never have vexed or betrayed me, if they had walked on all fours" (13, p. 161); or the one attributed to Frederick the Great, "The more I see of men, the better I like my dog" (13, p.99).

Some people in fact feel that an individual who does not enjoy animal companionship disqualifies himself from human companionship. Cowper found that an association with a hare which he looked upon as a friend was very helpful to him at a time when he was mentally depressed, anguished, and in emotional travail. He was heartbroken when his hare died after eight years.

> "Epitaph on a Hare" (1784)
> I kept him for his humour's sake,
> For he would oft beguile
> My heart of thoughts that made it ache,
> And force me to a smile (3, p. 414).

The meaning of an animal to an isolate on a personal, even intimate level, and the dependency of such a person upon pets for companionship may be seen from the following two vignettes:

"Self Understanding Through a Dog"

When I was twenty-one I left home to make my own way in the world, although the whole thing was very difficult for me. By the time I had reached thirty-seven I still lived alone and was rather lonely in a small New York apartment. I was teaching school during the day; by night I was swimming around in a lonely pool, only occasionally making contact with another who happened to be swimming my way.

Finally this loneliness drove me to overcome a fear called misocyny, commonly known as a fear of dogs. My family was one of a not small group of people who dislike many of the common little things that come together and form a style of living known as the all-American way. One little tradition that my family ignored was the one that says every child should have a dog. They disliked the animals themselves and I never felt any loss because I never harbored even the slightest sense of affection for them. My misocyny seemed to have come into existence when I did, for I can remember no instance where a dog frightened me in any way; my fear seems to have been neurotically based rather than of a rational, logical nature.

We did not ignore the animal kingdom altogether, however. My family always had at least one cat. There were alley cats to which I would throw scraps and would occasionally entice close enough to be stroked. I would gently stroke the length of its body and finish with a quick, almost vicious tug of its tail. In return for these scraps and for the sadistic affection it received, our basement would be prowled continuously by the cat so that rats and sundry vermin which it housed were at least thoroughly disturbed, if not disposed of.

Even these dear creatures never embedded themselves in my affection or were felt to be of a nature similar to my own; in other words, I stuck closely to people. Perhaps my supply of affection did not receive enough replenishment, or was not expansive enough in the first place to extend itself to things non-human.

In New York, however, my environment changed, and the loneliness which overcame me drove me to get a dog. A dog, out of all the possible types of pets from which I could have chosen (since I was not free to choose anything but pets) offered the most stable sort of affection I could hope to get. The one I acquired was small and of unknown origin but she had unquenchable wells of affection that could both be given to and received from.

I returned home for a week's visit during my vacation, and was forced, by my family's dislike of Poochie (that was her name) and my inability to either leave or say that Poochie was mine and meant something to me, to get rid of her in order to spend a week with my family.

Several years elapsed before loneliness snowballed with enough force to drive me to get another dog. I again named him Poochie. Although he was a French Poodle, he was poorly bred and not really worthy of a more impressive name. It was at this point that Poochie became an object on which to vent the emotions for which I could find no suitable outlet in day-to-day contact with my acquaintances.

My relationship with the dog swung between taking a motherly attitude toward it, behaving as if it represented my mother, or identifying with it. In my contacts with others, I described the dog as ugly. In reflecting upon people's reactions to my description I began to realize that I was describing myself rather than Poochie. Poochie assumed the role of representing aspects of both my mother and myself, which were so thoroughly mixed in my understanding that I could not separate my own attitudes and characteristics from those which I attributed to my mother. I often described the dog as stupid, inwardly comparing my own stupidity with my mother's seemingly endless stores of knowledge.

I bought Poochie a large toy bone that he gnawed on for hours. I was very jealous of the time and attention he spent on the bone. It recalled to my mind the time my mother gave to reading the newspapers when I was a child, instead of listening attentively to me.

I began to realize the extent to which I was letting selfishness rule my nature when people I spoke with said I was cruel and thoughtless because the dog was forced to spend long periods of time alone. Like my mother, I felt that because I had experienced pain and rejection in my life I had a right to inflict even more pain upon the world. Since there were no people close enough to me to be hurt, I let Poochie bear the brunt of my uncontrolled aggressiveness. I let the dog do without exercise for days unless I wanted some companionship on my walking excursions. I felt no concern for the dog's needs and instincts. These feelings, although they festered inside of me, I managed to accept, outwardly viewing the suffering of another creature as appropriate compensation for my own suffering.

There were many small ways in which my relationship with the dog was a direct reenaction of my relationship with my mother. I spoke to the dog in condescending babylike terms, often at those moments when the dog represented a loving mother-figure to me. My mother had often spoken to me in baby-talk long after such actions should have been dropped and our relationship achieved a higher level of understanding.

I blamed my own lethargy for the fact that Poochie very rarely got bathed, although living in the city really made frequent baths necessary for cleanliness and good hygiene. Rather than lethargy, this neglect represented my own personal rebellion against the constant harping and whining my mother subjected me to as a child because of my natural youthful exuberance, which often militated against immaculateness and overly tidy surroundings.

The dog seemed to follow me everywhere, as my mother seemed to do when I was younger, checking on my actions. I was under constant surveillance, first as a child and now as an adult. It upset me even to undress in front of the dog, because I was well past the time when I felt comfortable undressing in front of my mother. The dog even entered the realm of my sexual life (where, as in all my actions, my mother was never far from my consciousness either). Poochie tore up the blankets and bedspreads upon my bed. I didn't punish him of course, as it must have been a form of masturbation. He was trying to have sex with those blankets and I certainly can understand and empathize with his frustrations. Why should I have punished Poochie for something that was akin to my own personal frustration? I could never stand the dog even to be in the same room when I was making love with a man. Although he paid no attention at all to what we were doing, his presence was as emotionally upsetting as making love with my own mother standing there and watching every move I made, mentally criticizing my performance.

Fondling and cuddling Poochie, I would close my eyes and imagine he could return my attentions in a way my mother never did. In my fantasy-world Poochie received all the attention I never had, intensified because of the deep longing I still felt for this attention. Being affectionate to the dog was the love part of the ambivalence I really felt toward my mother. I punished him severely for misbehaving (as severely as my mother had punished me) sometimes by not feeding him for days at a time, and other times by telling him how bad he was. I would also tell my boy friend how bad the dog was, just as my mother used to talk about how bad I was to my father, Finally, matters reached the point where I didn't even take him on the street because I didn't want people judging me by this dirty, mangy animal. My mother used to say that people were always judging my actions.

I finally got rid of him. I had bought a new rug, on which Poochie continually made his business. When I yelled at him he would quiver or yelp and hide from me for several hours, eventually repeating his misdeed. This action of Poochie's reminded me of the times when my mother refused to speak to me for days on end because she was angry at me for some real or imagined misbehavior.

Eight months after I first got Poochie I finally got rid of him. He had come, a pedigreed stray, from the A.S.P.C.A. In the middle of the winter I returned him there, although not without trepidation and some regret. As I watched him resist being taken out of my sight, I tried to ignore the hollow feeling in the pit of my stomach as I imagined how I would have struggled to reunite myself with my mother if she had gotten rid of me before I had forced myself out of my home and her life. Even now, although I live alone, she is just as much with me as ever. I guess perhaps I'll get another dog soon (1).

"Me and My Shadows"

I have been a mistress of cats for three and one-half years, which in itself is no minor accomplishment. Up until that time I had spent all of my life frightened of them, for no apparent reason. Having been taught to be afraid of them by my parents, I had never been close enough to a cat to test my fear. A boy friend gave me a seven-week-old black kitten, and being ashamed to show him my fear I entered into a new world of delight by raising that kitten and seeing her grow into a robust black beauty. I subsequently took into my home and heart two more beauties — a Blue-Point Siamese and a cream colored Persian, lately acquired.

They have brought me great pleasure, and incidentally taught me many things about myself, about animals, and about other people. Not knowing about cats I had no way of foreseeing the rich education that they would bring to me. Each one came into a different home because I was a different person by the time I had learned, or rather been taught by each addition. Like many mothers with first-born children, I was thrown into a turmoil by the first cat. It took weeks to adjust to her, learn her ways, love her. I was not conscious of losing my fear, but after several weeks I could not recall ever having been afraid. Being sickly, she needed me, and would follow me, run to the door when she heard my footsteps and make me feel welcomed and less alone. My body became a climbing board, as did all the furniture. Scratched but loved, I learned not to care. She looked and played so beautifully that when talking to her I would say "What a pretty little girl!" in many variations, and after a few days she answered to "Little Girl" as she still does today, though she is no longer little by any standards. I was a most inept mother with her and consequently she is a nervous, aloof cat, who rarely goes to anyone else. She patrols the house and controls all the territory in it, sleeping nearest to me, and communicating with me on the very deepest level. She is my number one cat and I cannot conceive of being without her.

Being away so much, with full-time work and evening school, I decided she was lonely. I was wrong because the new kitten created a trauma in her life. She was enraged and pointedly ignored the new addition. She whined, prowled the house, had raging fits, hissed at me and the new cat, and took to the top of the tallest book case, not concerned with me. She was determined to get close to "Little Girl," and after one week they were inseparable.

The house is divided between them geographically. Both ignore my room-mate, who has lived with me for one year. After deliberately provoking her, the younger one occasionally strikes out at her (the only person she has ever done this to).

My room-mate does not like cats and, knowing this, they do not like her. "Chamois," the Siamese, loves to flirt with and entice into play those people who she senses as CAT people. She never makes a mistake, never picks a non-cat person. Like a child she is innately sensitive to people's feelings and is never fooled by their words. Because she was the second cat in the house and I had substantially grown in confidence as a cat person, "Chamois" is more playful, friendlier, less tense and less attached to me than "Little Girl." The household hierarchy breaks down in the following way: "Chamois" loves "Little Girl" best, and the latter loves me best. They fight several times a day and "Chamois" ritually loses, regardless of the fact that she initiates the fight and could easily win. She follows the black cat around, never letting her alone for too long a period of time. She abruptly awakens the older cat whenever she needs to be groomed, and often a fight will start because of her inconsiderate demands. Though she is a superb jumper, being a Siamese, the highest perches in the house belong to "Little Girl," and never has "Chamois" been observed to even attempt to jump on them. Two kitchen ledges have been relinquished by the black cat and "Chamois" lovingly prefers them to any of her own choosing. I am sure that their behavior has its counterpart in the behavior of human siblings, and I have become very aware of nuances of behavior. Hopefully this will furnish deeper insight into the problems of children, when I am a practicing clinician.

Watching them I am continuously reminded of children playing, fighting, copying and testing one another. Because I do not yell except to reprimand them, they immediately know by the pitch of my voice that they are doing something wrong, and they run and hide, waiting a respectable amount of time before reemerging.

I seem to see people differently now than I did prior to their acquisition. I always feel sorry for people who enter my house ignorant of the cats who live there, and who reveal fear upon seeing them. It was only a few short years ago that I was just like them, but the changes brought about in my life through the cats have made people like these seem unknowable to me. If, however, I see a glimmer of curiosity behind the fear, I quickly tell of my own fears, and how they were overcome by exposing myself to that which I feared. Most people I know who are frightened of cats have never been near them. They are stuck in someone else's fears and thereby deny themselves pleasure. Friends have come to this house and, like myself, been ashamed to show their fears, so that they spent an evening pretending interest. By the end of that evening they were well over their fears and on the way to becoming cat people. Perhaps the way to overcome is by overcoming.

The cats have helped me to grow and free myself of many middle-class mores. A house with cats is simply not as clean as a house without them. Most of my furniture is a shambles in spite of the expensive scratching post. Hair abounds in every room, on everything, and lies in layers on all my rugs. Dinner is a howling begging scene, guaranteed to break all hearts until these animals get some human food. Sheets retain their color and freshness approximately one night. All this no longer matters to me. The cats live for me, rush to greet and warm me. My possessions are things and give little pleasure. They and my pets are surely not equatable. Non-cat people find this difficult to understand (9).

The Mascot

A mascot has today become for certain individuals a substitute for animal worship. He is regarded as a totemic figure, a protector against evil. "According to all the most reliable mascot lore, if such a pet is treated well he is capable of carrying his lucky proprietor through no end of favorable circumstances" (4, p. 2).

For a mascot to be a token of good fortune for an army company, he must either be brought in by a friend, given to the company, or stroll in all ready for adoption. When an insecure draftee sees that a mascot has joined his company he feels relieved and more secure. He feels uneasy when the company is in the battle zone and the mascot is not around.

Frequently, when an army company is stationed in permanent quarters and there is no mascot available or the regulations do not permit one, the soldiers purchase parakeets, turtles, or other small animals. The presence of these pets makes the men feel more at home.

"Stuff," a canine mascot that was adopted by the Edgecombe Rehabilitation Center for drug addicts in upper Manhattan, is regarded by the director as "one of the best therapeutic tools" the Center possesses (15, p. 11). The patients have a chance to express love, affection, and care for someone outside of themselves, and they consider the dog one of their best friends.

The Adult and the Zoo Animal

Most people visit the zoo for relaxation and also partly to satisfy their hunger for nature, "a disease of civilization" (6, p. 67). They prefer young animals, and tend, when feeding is permitted, to offer food to the smaller species (even though these animals may actually be mature). They also prefer animals which remind them of humans, such as the primates and the bears, which can stand erect. Pandas and penguins, with their human-like walk, are also much enjoyed (6). The sea horse, because of its erect posture, is often selected as an ornament.

People for the most part like animals which respond to them, as this apparently makes them feel important. Many zoo visitors feel insulted when the animals ignore their overtures (6). Exotic animals such as tigers, lions, and giraffes are also of great interest to zoo visitors, particularly at feeding time. Shomer (12) has pointed out, in fact, that there is a universal "fascination (with) feeding zoo animals from the seal to the elephant, feeding fish, reptiles, etc., in aquaria, watching wild animals kill and devour prey." According to Shomer, the psychological meaning of this behavior has largely been neglected in the literature.

Some individuals who come to the zoo are voyeurs interested in observing the mating behavior of animals, whereas other visitors find this behavior offensive. Hediger reports that "in one of the largest zoos in the world a spacious open-air enclosure for baboons had to be pulled down because its inmates had behaved 'indecently' — as though there could be such a thing as an indecent animal!" (6, p. 116).

SUMMARY

Pets can help the adult cope with the tasks which maturity brings with it. Caring for and raising a pet can serve as a preparation for parenthood for both men and women, but it is particularly valuable to women who are tense and anxious during the prenatal period. Bestowing attention on a grateful pet can also ease the sense of abandonment which some mothers may feel when their erstwhile dependent infants become more autonomous and assertive toddlers.

For those adults who by necessity or choice remain childless, an animal can serve as a child substitute upon which to bestow tenderness and protection and toward which authority can be asserted.

For an isolated person without human ties, a pet can be a lifeline to reality and a chance to interact with another in a meaningful way.

Pet owners, if alert to the nature of their relationship with the animal which shares their household, can learn a good deal about themselves that is applicable to their relationships with humans.

Finally, the symbolic value of a pet as a totemic figure which protects against evil is embodied in the mascot, an important adjunct to groups facing dangerous or stressful situations.

REFERENCES

1. Anonymous, B.: Self-Understanding Through a Dog. (Unpublished paper.)
2. Browning, R.: Rabbi Ben Ezra. In Snyder, F. B., and Martin, R. G. (Eds.): A Book of English Literature. New York, Macmillan, 1928.
3. Cowper, W.: Poems of William Cowper. London, Johnson, 1800, Vol. II.
4. Dempewolff, R.: Animal Reveille. Garden City, N. Y., Doubleday, 1943.
5. Erikson, E. H.: Identity, Youth and Crisis. New York, Norton, 1968.

6. Hediger, H.: Man and Animal in the Zoo. New York, Seymour Lawrence/Delacorte, 1969.

7. Krutzmann, W. G. A.: Personal communication, 4/11/67.

8. Maslow, A. H.: Motivation and Personality. New York, Harper, 1954.

9. Schwalb, G.: Me and My Shadows. (Unpublished manuscript.)

10. Searles, H. F.: The Nonhuman Environment. New York, International Universities Press, 1960.

11. Shaw, G. B.: Selected Prose. New York, Dodd, 1952.

12. Shomer, R. R.: Personal communication, 6/4/71.

13. Sloan, A., and Farquhar, A.: Dog and Man. The Story of a Friendship. London, Hutchinson, 1925.

14. Thompson, W. R., and Grusec, J.: Studies of early experience. In Mussen, P. H. (Ed.): Carmichael's Manual of Child Psychology, 3rd ed. New York, Wiley, 1970, Vol. I., pp. 565-654.

15. Stuff: ASPCA Animal Protection. Spring, 1968, pp. 11, 16.

Chapter Four

PETS AND OLD AGE

Grow old along with me!
The best is yet to be,
The last of life, for which the first was made:
Our times are in his hand
Who saith, "A whole I planned.
Youth shows but half; trust God: see all,
    nor be afraid!" (2, p. 629)

OLD age brings with it a host of developmental problems and at the same time revives many problems which date from infancy and childhood. Just as any other developmental period creates new needs, so does old age (13, 14).

However, we must approach aging differently from the other developmental periods. There is no longer involved a question of growth and of looking forward. At best the aged person is engaged in a holding operation, i.e. standing still and defending already gained positions. On the other hand, we are dealing with individuals who have survived in a tough, competitive world, who are responsible citizens, who have been good workers or professionals, and have maintained themselves adequately. In old age there is a more or less deleterious change in body functioning. The physical powers are beginning to wane, the environment is becoming progressively less favorable to self-enhancement, thoughts of death recur more and more frequently, and all this in turn necessitates a change in one's self-concept. The person entering old age must find a new way of getting along with his own body and adjusting to a new style of life involving decreased physical effort and a lessening of demands on the self.

Many old people concentrate on the pleasures and achievements of the past because the present is dull and the future looks foreboding. With the loss of relatives, friends, and associates, the

97

aged gradually withdraw from active participation in human
affairs. The nonhuman environment tends to take over and play an
increasingly significant role in their lives. Objects and animals that
provided feelings of security in early life may again assume great
importance. This can very clearly be seen from the following case
history:

> Frau Schmidt came to the Shelter with her married daughter, who
> intended to adopt a kitten for her two small children. The old lady
> had no interest whatever in the matter and accompanied her daughter
> reluctantly to the room where the cats were to be seen. The daughter
> tried to interest her mother in the discussion of which kitten should
> be selected, but the only answer was, "Es ist mir Schnuppe," (I
> couldn't care less). The old lady was hardly looking at the cats, but all
> at once she came to life and pointed to a short-haired, two-year-old
> yellow cat who was in no way remarkable. "Sieh da! Sieh da! Das ist
> meine Katze." (Look! Look! That's my cat!) Then, in a flood of
> German came the story of how, when she had come to America at the
> age of seven, she had been obliged to leave her yellow cat behind her
> with a friend. She had never found another that appealed to her, but
> here was the well-loved, well-remembered cat of her childhood. She
> took the cat from its cage and stood there holding it against her as if
> she were challenging anyone to take it away from her. So Putzi found
> a fine home, an elderly woman found a companion, and a dream came
> true (15, p. 7).

The transition from interest in pets to interest in people may
reverse itself in old people with the narrowing of their social circle,
so that the pet regains a position of major importance.

Like children, the aged often display fragile defense structures.
It is not uncommon to find among senior citizens patterns of
regression to earlier, primitive defenses which include animals as
totems. Old people are in more frequent and open communication
with primary material than when they were young adults or
middle aged. Regression to the unconscious thinking of childhood
is also more frequent. Like a child, the oldster may consider an
animal so much a part of his world that he believes the pet feels
and thinks like a human being. Thus the pet that was an
unconscious totem in childhood may serve the same purpose again
in old age.

Subject to increasing debility, the aged become physically
dependent on the grudging care and affection of their children or

other people who have, willy-nilly, suddenly assumed an authority stance. This reversal of roles in turn rekindles the smoldering flames of unresolved childhood problems and ambivalent feelings about authority and dependency. Increasing dependence on other authority figures reawakens old conflicts of loyalty. Identification with a pet may at this point symbolize becoming a liked and accepted dependent. The aged person finds reassurance in the fact that the attitude of the domestic pet in his home has not changed; it apparently does not matter to the animal that his master feels old and unwanted or that his body has deteriorated.

It is important to note the kind of philosophy of life and frame of reference that develops in old age. Part of this frame of reference encompasses an attitude toward animals that in a way symbolizes an attitude toward the world. If during his earlier life the aged person managed to maintain a good relationship with the animate and inanimate world, if he acquired a liking for animals, this may in his declining years serve as an anchor for good mental health. As Joseph (10) has pointed out, "One of the big rewards of having loved dogs all your life is the fact that you will be spared a lonely old age as a result of your continuing affection." Also, through pets the aged may be helped to work through problems of aggression and despair and to develop some feelings of security.

There are varying ways in which one may seek and find security by being close to nature and to animals. Some people go on photography safaris, others engage in birdwatching, still others act as animal Samaritans and feed wild as well as domesticated animals. We thus find lonely old ladies, known as "night feeders," who, at considerable risk to themselves, go about feeding cats that live in abandoned buildings (18). Sometimes, when the aged translate their interest in pets into an interest in the preservation of wild animal life, they in a sense sublimate their fear of immediate death (20). It is also possible however that when an older person is interested in the preservation of the rare animal, it is because that animal symbolizes "his own impending doom" (16).

Retirement should be a reward for long years of labor and social responsibility, and should allow time for activities that disengage one from community efforts. A paradox develops, however, as a by-product of our "future-oriented society" (6). There is an intergenerational gulf, exaggerated by the great value placed on productivity — something the old person is either unable to achieve or not permitted to achieve because of circumstances beyond his control. The only "leveler" seems to be a financial one: "To be rich is to be recognized as a success; wisdom often is its own reward" (6). Obviously, this sort of recognition can be obtained by relatively few.

During the previous transitional periods, the individual was given great social and individual support, and the changes that occurred in his status were of a gradual nature (11). This is not the case for the individual preparing for retirement, for this transition is usually a sudden one, with little or no preretirement counseling taking place.

Before his retirement, the aging man, owing to internalized cultural pressures, was inhibited from showing concern over his diminishing physical and mental powers. He would unconsciously modify his tasks so that he need not face the fact that he could not compete as successfully as before with his fellow workers. His identification was with the young, productive, vigorous colleague.

With the retiree's change in role, there is an accompanying change in status. The aged person begins to resent bitterly the fact that he has lost status and can no longer compete on an equal footing with younger people. The gulf that he feels between himself and his former, still productively engaged, business associates tends to create a feeling of alienation (11). Furthermore, with the "withdrawal of normative control" (6), through loss by death of relatives, friends, and acquaintances who formerly exercised strong sanctions that the retiree misses, social sanctions that forced the now aged person to behave in certain socially prescribed ways are less operative (11).

Being lonely and isolated can, like sulphuric acid, corrode the personality and create a warped point of view on life.

Stekel (19) indicates that lonely individuals frequently will tend to transfer their unsatisfied love needs onto their pets, as can be seen from the following:

"My brother and I lived together here in our home on top of the Alleghenies since my mother died eight years ago. We both were retired. My brother died last June 23rd. And I am now alone in a big house and have only my little 'Pooky.' He stays constantly with me, and I take him every place I go in the car" (10, p. 134).

The acquisition of a docile, affectionate pet can, and often does, help the retiree through the somewhat painful process of accepting himself as an aged person relegated to a different role. Moreover, the retiree who feels that he has lost out in competition in the market place will never find in his pet a challenger or competitor who reinforces his feelings of uselessness. The pet plays an important role in the psychological economy of the retiree. How extensive are the ramifications of the pet's role? This is a subject which needs much more research and study.

It becomes imperative for the aged person to find a new role that he considers worthwhile and that is not in competition with the young. Adoption of a pet, which is immediately feasible, can lead to new interests, adventures, and untrodden paths. A pet can pave the way to new friendships; walking a dog can provide a ready introduction to people, and casual conversation about the dog may kindle new interests. Such new or, in some cases, renewed interests may give the aged person a reason for living.

Miss Halstead was a dried-up, fussy, precise, wealthy, autocratic old lady who lived in the Riverside Towers, a high-class and expensive residential hotel. She had lived most of her adult life with a sister, who had died the previous year. Since that time she had had three different paid companions, but none had been satisfactory. About two weeks after she had dismissed the third one, Miss Halstead was having a particularly desperate bout with loneliness and with a general feeling of being useless. In this mood she impulsively called the Shelter and asked that a cat be delivered to her — age, sex, color, breed, unspecified. The old aristocrat was accustomed to being waited on, and it evidently did not occur to her that she might better come and look for herself. I had been in the Riverside Towers and had a pretty good idea what kind of a cat I had better bring, so I took her a beautiful Siamese cat about two years old, a spayed female. To be sure, the management of the hotel did not allow cats, but to this restriction Miss Halstead has never paid the least attention. When I brought the cat to her she was reserved, but I could tell that she was favorably impressed. Morning and afternoon she takes the cat up on the roof garden, where she lets it run about and get as much exercise as it wants. Miss Halstead is stiff, formal, and remote in her dealings with people, but the maids say she talks baby-talk to her cat. She also prepares its meals, and while the food is of a more expensive variety than most people would feed to a cat, she does not overfeed it. Moreover, she has it under excellent control and refuses to spoil it. It is to be regretted that this woman could not find human companionship that was adequate to her needs, but she is now at least the recipient of the two things she needed most, two things that all her money could not buy: unquestioning devotion and unstinted affection (15, p. 7).

Similarly, the old man may identify with his pet, giving it all the love he himself may be desperately craving but is unable to receive (19). How satisfying to have a living creature reciprocate his affection and reward his care! This may help the aged person develop an idea of being wanted and loved and give him a different concept of self. The pet can even provide "someone" with whom he can share his loneliness and with whom he can communicate, at least on a nonverbal level.

There is a widespread mistaken impression that if an aged person engages in a long conversation with his pet or even merely speaks to it on occasion, he is hallucinating. On the contrary, when a person has a warm and close relationship with his pet, it is only natural for him to talk to the pet as one might speak to a human friend. When an aged person in particular communicates in this fashion with his pet, he may unconsciously see it not as a dog but as a representative of someone in the dim past, who died many years before but with whom he still yearns to communicate.

With a pet, the aged person finds that he has a creature with whom he can communicate, who is not bored by hearing the same story over and over again, who is very much interested in the reminiscences of his owner, and who arches his back, curls his tail, and licks the aged man's face to show appreciation for shared confidences. This exploration of the past usually helps the old person to abreact some of his emotions and arrive at a better understanding of the present, thus moving towards a more satisfactory adjustment to the present.

As a result of the interchange between the aged individual and his pet, a personality change may occur not only in the person but also in the pet. This may be seen from the following case history adapted from Berman (3):

Miss L., a well-educated, unmarried professional woman in her early sixties, lives alone in a well-appointed apartment with a large 11-year-old turtle named Napoleon, given to her by a friend when she was recuperating from a serious illness. At that time the turtle was tiny but lively, and seemingly quite intelligent. Since Miss L. could do little else during her convalescence, she gave the turtle a good deal of attention, talking to it, giving it the free run of the apartment on a string (so he wouldn't get lost), and responding to signals which it apparently developed to indicate its desires, e.g. for food, for exploration, and for tub swimming. By coming up to the instep of Miss L.'s foot, Napoleon indicated that he wanted to climb on the lap of his owner, and he did the same to visitors he liked. He showed such signs of jealously when another turtle was brought into the house that Miss L. gave the newcomer away for fear that Napoleon would starve himself to death.

Napoleon gave evidence of having a sense of time of day and of the season; he listened with apparent attention to classical music and submitted to being housebroken. Miss L. believes that there may be an element of extrasensory perception in her pet's responses to her, as Napoleon has performed several actions just when his owner was thinking about them.

In any event, this turtle received a rare chance for development under the care of an owner who was fascinated by his potential for learning, and he seems to have rewarded her efforts to teach him in a most satisfactory way.

Some old folks see themselves as cheated by life and unconsciously, like children, feel that the people they love have deserted them. They are afraid to love again because loving and losing at an advanced age can be very painful. They may become depressed and develop somatic complaints. The knowledge that there is still someone anxiously awaiting one's homecoming, even if this be just a pet, can frequently avert serious emotional and even physical problems. It is well known, for example, that the best way to cope with the depression caused by the loss of a love object is for the person to go through a period of mourning and then if possible find a substitute for the lost object. A pet can serve as a new love object, one to whom a person can unabashedly give all the love he wishes without fear that the pet will not reciprocate or will desert him. A pet can become a bosom companion and a "substitute" for relatives and friends who have passed on. This can be seen in the following case:

Mr. Foster was a man of seventy-two whose wife had recently died.

His son and daughter-in-law tried to spend every week-end with him, although they had to drive 100 miles each way to do so. The son wanted his father to live with him, but the old man refused. He still had friends in the small town where he had lived most of his life, he did not wish to invade his son's home, and he was sure that he would not be as happy elsewhere as he was in his own familiar surroundings. During the week he was alone, and it soon became evident that he was not eating enough to stay healthy. He and his wife had had a cat, but it had died about a month before his wife did, and he had not had the energy to replace it. The son came to the Shelter to get a cat for his father, in the hope that the animal might relieve the old man's loneliness. He selected a four-year-old, neutered male of placid disposition and quiet habits. A month later the son reported on the results.

His father had been delighted with his pet, who soon adapted himself to the old man's uneventful life. At mealtimes he occupied a chair at the table, although he was not fed there, and contributed purrs and a variety of remarks in answer to conversation, with the result that the man ate more than formerly. In the afternoon they sat together in the garden. By the end of the first week an elderly lady who lived next door had made friends with the cat and through it with the man. The lady had remained a spinster from choice, but she liked cats and she enjoyed talking with her neighbors. Gradually the two senior citizens fell into the habit of eating their noonday meal together, with the cat acting as chaperone. The son soon put matters upon a business basis by paying the woman a sum each month for feeding his father at noon, thus insuring one adequate meal each day. The old man and his cat are inseparable. Both are old, both want affection, and both enjoy the quiet life (15, pp. 6-7).

Many aged people are so used to their miseries — which they ascribe to illnesses of old age — that they are not aware of the fact that surcease through the possession of pets is possible, and they therefore do not seek to adopt one. The miracles that can be accomplished through the possession of a pet may be seen in the following true story:

Mrs. Mason was a recently bereaved widow. She was escorted to the Shelter by her sister and brother-in-law, both of whom were greatly worried — as was her doctor — by her loss of weight, her depression, her threats of suicide, her constant tears. Mrs. Mason had had a cat, but in the confusion during the last days of her husband's life it had run into the street and been killed, thus adding a bit more to Mrs. Mason's feelings of bereavement. She did not really want another cat, but her relatives thought she would make a faster recovery if she had something to love, to take care of, and to be responsible for. The widow looked apathetically at several and was not intrigued by any of them, but finally I persuaded her to select a spayed, year-old Manx cat, named Trixie. The cat had previously had an over-indulgent owner and was constantly demanding attention; she was also full of pussy-cat ways of getting what she wanted, but in return she was eager to deluge her owner with affection. I thought that Trixie's unending demands were just what was needed to bring Mrs. Mason our of her depression and loneliness. The woman needed affection and occupation; with Trixie in the house she was sure to get plenty of both. After the cat had been with Mrs. Mason for a week, her sister called me to say that the situation was greatly improved. At the end of six weeks Mrs. Mason came to the Shelter and made a substantial donation because she wanted to thank us for the help we had given her in her time of need. She credits Trixie with saving her sanity, and while this estimate is probably too high, the cat did serve to take her mind off her immediate troubles and to bring her back in touch with reality (15, p. 10).

Any observant person will have noticed old men and women sitting on park benches in the summer or at railroad stations or bus stops in the winter, doing nothing but staring into empty space. Even when at home, they seem to have nothing to occupy their time and continue gazing at nothing in particular. A pet would bring the breath of life to these escapees from life, as it would to those who live alone and have to fill the emptiness of their existence with the constant chattering of the TV or radio. The presence of a pet can make the difference between intolerable and tolerable misery, as happened in the following case:

Mrs. Golden was a vigorous woman of middle age who was married to a man much older than herself. He was at least seventy-five years old. Although his general health was good, he had become completely deaf with a type of deafness that is helped little by a hearing aid. For the last two or three years Mr. and Mrs. Golden had hardly spoken to each other, not because they had quarreled but because communication was so difficult. Most days Mr. Golden did a little gardening, and once in a while he did an errand for his wife at a nearby store. Some days he sat for hours in a rocking chair on the porch, doing nothing. Often he spent half a day in his small room, looking at faded snapshots and his collection of picture post-cards. He was not much of a reader; he glanced at the morning paper each day, but it had been years since he had read a book. Mrs. Golden alternated between impatience at her husband's deafness and a genuine desire to make his life more interesting. One day a neighbor's cat wandered into the yard and spent an hour sitting on the old man's lap. He was so delighted that Mrs. Golden decided to bring him a cat of his own. At the time we had in the Shelter a small-boned, delicate, black and white, spayed, angora female, who was small and light enough to sit on someone's lap without putting the person's legs to sleep, although she was full-grown and in blooming health. She was a friendly, affectionate, sociable little animal; moreover, she had grown up in a family of men and boys. Little Pearl seemed made to order for the situation. Mrs. Golden reported two weeks after the cat's arrival that her husband was far more alert than he had been for years and that he was taking an interest in people once again. He was by nature a shy man and had become even more reserved because of his deafness, but there was nothing shy about Pearl, who made friends right and left and carried him along with her. He had even been to a men's club and played chess with another oldster, something he had not done for the last three years. At home Pearl follows him about, accompanies him on a leash to the store, sits with him by the hour, and sleeps on his bed at night. In spite of his deafness he can "hear" the vibration of her purring, and he takes great delight in even this small contact with the world about him. Mr. Golden is still a deaf and isolated elderly man, but he is a good deal happier than he had been for a long time (15, p. 8).

Old people can adjust to new situations, learn to play new roles, and change their habits and be very useful, provided that we permit them to play roles which are within their physical limitations. One such role, which is sorely missed by grandchildren nowadays, is that of the frequently present grandfather. Parents today are too busy to spend much time with their children. A doting grandparent who has all the time in the world, who comes with his pet (usually a dog) to take his grandchildren for a walk in the park or playground, can be of inestimable value to these children. This new role enhances the grandfather's self-concept as he finds that he is needed, respected, and loved.

Contrary to societal preconceptions, many aged people continue to have an active interest in sex and sexual activities. However, in this as in many other situations faced by the aged, society looks askance, so that sexual interest or activity that is approved or looked upon with envy when engaged in by a younger individual is considered lecherous, indecent, and immoral in an aged person. This attitude is paralleled by the internalized belief of the aged person, both because of cultural expectations and the fact that his reproductive powers are waning, that he is no longer desirable sexually and thus, because of the high premium placed on youth and potency, is no longer wanted at all.

This attitude hits the older woman with particular force. She cannot be fruitful and bear children, and though children may no longer be desired per se, her inability to produce them makes the woman feel depleted.

As a result of the situation described above, we find among many old people that depression is a frequent companion of even a normal aging process, as are gastrointestinal difficulties which may represent a displacement upward of genital interest to culturally more acceptable areas of the body.

Pets can play a crucial role in alleviating this situation. An interest in pets, since they are small and dependent, can unconsciously give rise to a feeling of having children and continuing to be the head of the family. Concerning oneself with the sex habits and breeding of pets can vicariously satisfy an individual's sex drives. It may also reduce the aged person's ruminations about himself and his ailments. This is well-illustrated in the following case in which Dr. Axel Munthe (17, p. 58) prescribed a dog as a remedy for an ailing, deaf countess who for years had been complaining of colitis. The countess became so preoccupied with her pet, taking him for regular walks in her garden, watching very carefully over his diet, concerning herself about his digestion and elimination, that she forgot about her own "illness" and became well.

> "He is a horrible little brute," wrote the Abbé, "who sits in her lap and snarls and growls at everybody; he has even bitten the maid twice. Everybody hates him, but the Marquise adores him and fusses about him the whole day. Yesterday in the midst of the confession he was suddenly sick all over her beautiful teagown and his mistress was in such a state of alarm that I had to interrupt the function. Now the Marquise wants me to ask you if you think it might possibly develop into colitis and asks you to be so kind as to prescribe something for him. She says she feels sure you will understand his case better than anybody."

Mythology has it that an aged person can benefit from associating with someone younger than himself. Thus, in the Bible, when King David became old, he was advised by the elders of

Israel to take himself a young maiden.

> "The idea that strength and life are obtained by the old from the
> young by incorporation — sucking, eating, cannibalism — as well as by
> way of body contact and absorption, or by passage of spirit from a
> distance, appears to be ancient and universal. Medicine men and
> witches, sorcerers and magicians, even evil or good spirits who can
> heal or harm by taking out of a person into themselves what is bad or
> what is good, are commonly gray, wrinkled, bent and gnarled, or have
> a long white beard (9, p. 87).

By sleeping next to a young animal such as a cat, the aged
person may unconsciously feel that some of his vigor is returning
to him.

It is worth noting that showing affection for animals is not
considered demeaning by our society. In fact, such an emotion is
supposedly an indicator of one's nobility of character. The senior
citizen can therefore express his love for his pet and unashamedly
give vent to his sorrow on its death, while vicariously expressing
his sorrow for the death of his world and of himself.

Very frequently a pet is a living memorial to a deceased life
partner, and must be preserved by the surviving spouse. Occasionally however, a pet's presence may be a reminder of guilt-laden
memories, and so it must be destroyed. Dr. W. G. A. Krutzmann
(12), the Canadian veterinarian referred to earlier, has confirmed
this in a personal communication to the author:

> The most notable of my observations usually involve women more
> than men, as in the case of widows. The surviving pet must be kept
> alive at all cost since it seems to represent the only link with their
> deceased husbands. The opposite case, of husbands surviving the
> wives, more often than not results in euthanasia of the pet since the
> presence of the pet brings back memories of their lost one that they
> cannot bear.

The loss of a canine or feline companion can represent real
tragedy for an elderly person. When the aged observe their pets
dying, it brings forcefully to their consciousness the realization
that they too will die before long — this despite the fact that we
cannot really acclimatize ourselves to the thought of our own
death because we cannot accept the idea of our total annihilation
(8). The aged person who suffers the loss of a loved pet should be
encouraged to acquire another one as soon as possible.

It is deplorable that in our society so many old people have to give up their pets in order to qualify for public housing. In many cases they refuse to do so, and remain in substandard housing. This situation is described in the following letter:

> I'm a widow over sixty-nine years old. My husband was Veterinary here over thirty-five years. I applied for an apartment in a public housing and was refused, because I have a seven year old kitty — she goes out once a day, otherwise is with me. I love her and share everything with her. I took her when a neighbor died and they were to have her destroyed — she first was left a young kitten on my porch — but at that time I had a black persian and he was my kitty and if I go first I hope she will be cared for (7).

In order to maintain a pet in good health, its owner must feed it properly and exercise and groom it. To help a pet when it is sick or otherwise indisposed, the aged owner may have to engage in activities he did not think he was capable of handling. In taking care of his pet's needs, the old person may therefore be taking care of his own. Even when it is difficult for him to do so because of physical disability, the owner will carry on because he is attached to his pet. When he shops for the animal he will also shop for himself; when he selects food for it, he may also give some attention to selecting palatable food for his own fading appetite. Exercising his pet forces him to engage in physical activity beneficial to his own health. Finally, accepting signs of aging in himself may become easier when he observes them also in his beloved pet.

Dr. J. Antelyes (1), a well-known New York veterinarian, has provided the following illustration of what a pet can mean to an aging person:

> Mrs. G., a widow in her mid-sixties, whose children were all married, lived alone in a small apartment. She was obese, chronically bedridden, and always "doctoring." She could walk only a few steps without assistance, complained of continual pains in her chest, back, and legs, shortness of breath, asthmatic attacks, and cardiac weakness. She would frequently take twenty or more medicines daily for relief of her broad spectrum of symptoms. Three months after a married daughter had given her a puppy, she stopped telephoning and visiting her physician, reported that her symptoms had disappeared, and began to lose weight, decided not stay in bed any more, and took only an occasional tablet for dyspnea. At last report, both dog and

owner were quite healthy and appeared to be enjoying their relationship immensely (1).

As a person gets older, he increasingly restricts his activities to those that can be performed with comfort. The selection of a pet must be made with this in mind. Since the pet should, so far as possible, meet the physical, social, and emotional needs of its aged owner, an expert may need to be consulted concerning the choice. The pet chosen should be of intrinsic interest to the person and should not represent a financial burden. Lowie (15) suggests, as noted above, that a mature sterilized cat be provided for those aged people who like them. Such a cat does not require constant care and, as it is not very active, is usually quite content to remain at home near its master, rarely going outside.

For the aged person who has developed anxieties, feels beaten down by physical handicaps, and has a desire to escape from his infirmities, a bird may be helpful. Through identification with the bird he may have the illusion of being able to escape from difficulties through flight, thus alleviating his anxiety. Furthermore, the bird, which is generally recognized as a phallic symbol, may give vicarious sexual gratification.

An aquarium may offer the ideal form of pet life for the very old or nonambulant person. Fish require little care, and watching them in an aquarium can be very amusing and relaxing. It can also provide insight into problems of life and death as they unfold in the aquarium.

SUMMARY

With today's increase in life expectancy, we have an ever-growing number of lonely old people, particularly women (as women on the whole live longer than men). Yet old age is different from the other periods we have discussed. This should be a period of fulfillment, a time when men and women have arrived at their goals. They have at this point made their mark on the world, big or small. Old age should not be treated as a transitional period to death, and thus safely neglected, but as a period worthwhile in itself, with its own share of satisfactions as well as sorrows. In our youth-oriented culture, however, we add insult to injury by denigrating the aged and thus adding to their burdens.

The aged not only face the problem of a loss of status on retirement from work or from managing an active household, but begin to find that the greatest source of frustration is within themselves. They have absorbed into their self-concepts the idea that once a person has retired from previous occupations, whether voluntarily or not, he or she is no longer able to do many things which previously were very easily managed. Whether this loss of ability is true or not for the individual in question does not matter. Once one believes this to be so, one acts accordingly. The aged person looks at himself and discovers that his body no longer corresponds with the idealized self-image he has carried within himself for so many years. He becomes convinced that his body is damaged or diseased. Since he also equates being young with being desired, loved, and wanted, he feels like a superfluous commodity. Like any other human being, the older person wants to be needed, admired, and approved of. He wishes to transmit what he knows to others, to teach new things, even new tricks. He wishes to create and be challenged. A pet such as a dog, which acts like a perpetual juvenile, may be just what he needs.

A pet can provide a boundless measure of love, adoration, and unqualified approval. Many elderly and lonely individuals have discovered that pets satisfy their needs and enable them to hold on to the world of reality, of care, of human toil and sacrifice, and of intense emotional relationships. Their self-concept as worthwhile individuals is restored and even enhanced when they find that the pet they have been caring for loves them in return.

When an old person feels fulfilled, he will not have to follow Dylan Thomas' advice:

> Do not go gentle into that good night,
> Old men should burn and rave at close of day;
> Rage, rage against the dying of the light. (21, p. 1247)

REFERENCES

1. Antelyes, J.: Personal communications, 3/26/71, 8/24/71.
2. Browning, R.: Rabbi Ben Ezra. In Snyder, F. B., and Martin, R. G. (Eds.): A Book of English Literature. New York, Macmillan, 1928.
3. Berman, M.: The Turtle: A Responsive Pet. (Unpublished manuscript.)

4. Buhler, C.: Loneliness in maturity, J. Humanist Psychol, 9(2):167-181, 1969.
5. Busse, E. W., and Pfeiffer, E. (Eds.): Behavior and Adaptation in Later Life. Boston, Little, Brown, 1969.
6. Cumming, E.: New thoughts on the theory of disengagement. Int J Psychiatry, 6:53-67, 1968.
7. Duclos, M.: Personal communication, 6/7/71.
8. Freud, S.: Civilization, war and death. In Richman, J. (Ed.): Psychoanalytical Epitomes, London, Hogarth Press, 1952, No. 44.
9. Goldfarb, A. I.: A psychological and sociophysiological approach to aging. In Zinberg, N. E., and Kaufman, I. (Eds.): Normal Psychology of the Aging Process. New York, International Universities Press, 1963, pp. 72-92.
10. Joseph, R.: A Letter to the Man Who Killed My Dog. New York Frederick Fell, 1956.
11. Kent, D. P.: Social and cultural factors influencing the mental health of the aged. Am J Orthopsychiatry, 36:680-685, 1966.
12. Krutzmann, W. G. A.: Personal communication, 4/17/67.
13. Kutner, B., Fanshel, D., Togo, A. M., and Langer, T. S.: Factors relative to adjustment in old age. In Kuhlen, R. G., and Thompson, G. G. (Eds.): Psychological Studies of Human Development. New York, Appleton Century-Crofts, 1970, pp. 583-595.
14. Levinson, B. M.: Pets and old age. Ment Hyg, 53:364-368, 1969.
15. Lowie, M.: Cats and People. Berkeley, Berkeley Humane Society.
16. Morris, D.: The Naked Ape. New York, McGraw-Hill, 1967.
17. Munthe, A.: The Story of San Michele. New York, Dutton, 1965.
18. Rice, B.: The Other End of the Leash. Boston, Little, Brown, 1968.
19. Steckel, W.: Patterns of Psychosexual Infantilism. New York, Grove, 1959.
20. Szasz, K.: Petishism: Pets and Their People in the Western World. New York, Holt, Rinehart and Winston, 1969.
21. Thomas, D.: Do not go gentle into that good night. In Aldington, R. (Ed.): The Viking Book of Poetry of the English Speaking World, New York, Viking Press, 1958, vol 2.

Chapter Five

THE PET AND BEREAVEMENT

DEATH

Stop kidding
Take off your Sanchina mask!
I don't fear you;
You're wanted and expected.
Do stop your night prowling,
Come, in broad day light, proud,
A knight in shining armour.
You are welcome!
I am ready.
I shall not delay your errand
By mumbled prayer; intravenous, penicillin or sulfa
Take me up for new adventures!
I am interested in being
Not becoming.
But first, let's stop
At Sirius, the dog star.

THE BEREAVEMENT EXPERIENCE

EVERYONE faces the developmental task of accepting death and handling bereavement. Since bereavement is one of the most traumatic events in a person's life (2), he needs a good deal of help in coping with it. Developmentally speaking, the "closer and freer" the relationships between parent and child in the early years, the more chances a child has had of differentiating himself from his parents in a wholesome fashion, the greater will be his resilience as an adolescent and adult in integrating the trauma of bereavement (7). Resolution of the trauma would depend on, among other things, how important the deceased was in the psychological economy of the bereaved and what the past experiences of the bereaved person had been with the death of both humans and animals.

113

There is a general progression in the gamut of feelings about death, depending upon the age of the deceased. The younger the deceased, the greater the mourning for him, the culture having defined him as more valuable and hence more of a loss than an older person. This evaluation is unconsciously reflected in the bereaved individual's intensity of mourning.

Since the bereavement experience tends to remind each person of his own inevitable death, the handling of those experiences will also depend to a great extent on how satisfactorily one has resolved his life's problems. The more resolution there has been, the less fear and the greater acceptance of death is experienced. Generally speaking, unless a person has really lived, he cannot bear to die. However, as Tillich (39) has so aptly expressed it: "The anxiety of fate and death is most basic, most universal, and inescapable. All attempts to argue it away are futile" (39, pp. 49-50).

Moreover, to refuse to feel sorrow over the loss of our relatives and friends, because to do so would be so devastating and painful, is to refuse to live. Mourning is cleansing and healing. "In all mourning rituals, we try to cleanse ourselves of earlier hostile wishes. We move toward the deceased or toward those they may have represented" (27, p. 22).

The greatest regret of those who have lived through the horrors of concentration camps is the fact that they were not permitted to mourn the dead, and they thus reproach themselves because they are living while their loved ones are not.

If the relationship between the survivor and the deceased was open and unambiguous, the circumstances of the latter's death may not occasion any guilt feelings. On the other hand, if there had been no such communication, the circumstances of his death may bring about feelings of anxiety and guilt (7).

Animals are part of nature and remind us that we too are an inseparable part of nature and of the universe. Possibly this is one of the psychological (unconscious) reasons that a pet is so often helpful in coping with bereavement. Searles (37, p. 122), for example, remarks that when a person feels that he is related to nature, it tends to minimize "his fear of death. It helps him also to find a sense of peace, a sense of stability, of continuity and of certainty." Thus the pet can serve as a solace, a psychological shock absorber, which helps to soften the severe knocks one gets along the road of life.

Bereavement frequently results in insecurity, anxiety, fear, distrust of the world, and physical discomfort. It brings to a focus, sometimes with explosive force, the underlying tensions, strains, emotions, and inherent strengths of a family. The effects of bereavement vary depending upon the age, conceptual development, and emotional status of the bereaved.

As noted before, we tend to personify animals and to feel that they are members of the family. It was customary at the beginning of the twentieth century, for example, in some European countries, to notify the farm animals of the death of a member of the family (18).

Pets have played an important mental hygiene role in the history of the race. They may also be most important in helping an individual to face the meaning of life and death, and in helping him pass through the critical period of mourning more constructively.

The mature adult realizes that death is a normal phenomenon, that it is part of life and gives meaning to life. In many homes however, the emotionally immature adult, frozen in his grief, has not himself accepted the reality of death, and in his pathetic efforts to avoid facing the inevitable will even assure a child that death is in its essence a prolonged sleep. Thus in a sense he comforts himself.

Even professionals in mental hygiene shy away from the discussion of death. There is practically no advance preparation for the inevitability of death, and hardly any provisions exist for the therapeutic experiences that would minimize the effect of death and ameliorate its trauma (9).

The help which pets can give adults in coping with bereavement is illustrated in the following cases:

> The writer, for one, is acquainted with a woman whose husband was killed in an automobile accident. She was inconsolable until someone had given her a puppy. This puppy, through the care she bestowed on her and the puppy's affectionate barking and licking of her hands and face, enabled her to recover her equilibrium and go through the bereavement period unscathed.

Mr. and Mrs. Lincoln are grandparents. One of their grandchildren had been born with an inoperable heart defect, and no one expected him to live for more than a couple of years. The grandparents had a large, quiet house and adequate means for being comfortable so they had been caring for the child almost since its birth, in order to relieve the strain on their daughter, who had three other children. With them the child lived a very quiet life that was kept interesting by the ingenuity of his grandmother. One afternoon he was sitting at her feet in the garden, playing with some blocks; all was as usual until the little boy gave a sigh and died. Although Mrs. Lincoln had known that her grandson would not live much longer, she was unprepared for the suddenness of his passing. For days she and her husband were inconsolable. They could find almost nothing to say to each other, and the house seemed very empty, especially for Mrs. Lincoln who was there alone all day. In order to fill up a little of her spare time she accompanied a friend to the Shelter to help her select a kitten. Suddenly it occurred to Mrs. Lincoln that she would be less lonely if she had a cat in the house. Without giving herself time to think the matter over, she selected a large, long-haired, neutered black male, about two years old. She then departed wondering audibly what her husband, who was not overly fond of cats, would say when he got home. The very first evening, as soon as the two sat down to dinner, Ezra — the cat — jumped up into the chair where the child had once sat, settled himself on a corner of it, made it clear that he did not expect to be fed at the table, and launched into a loud purr of contentment. The orchestral effect was pleasant. As the meal progressed, Mr. and Mrs. Lincoln found that they could talk naturally to each other for the first time since the child's death. Within three days the cat had found out for himself at what time the man came home from work and was always waiting at the gate for his return. If he went out into the garden, Ezra accompanied him. In the course of the next two weeks the edge had been taken off their loss, and they could be themselves again. Some of this effect was, of course, due merely to the passage of time, but both Mr. and Mrs. Lincoln feel that the cat had contributed a good deal to their recovery (26, pp. 22-23).

Mr. Jamison was a young man, a teacher of English composition in a high school. He was engaged to be married. One day his mother and his fiancee drove to a nearby city to make some purchases, but on the way home in the five o'clock rush-hour, they were involved in an eight-car pile-up on a freeway, and both were instantly killed. Mr. Jamison's work and friends combined to pull him through the first month of grief and of isolation in the house, in which all three had planned to live. Since I was an old friend of his mother, he stopped in one evening to see me and to ask if I had any suggestions as to how he could get the reading of his pupils' themes up to date. They had been accumulating since the tragedy, but every time he sat down to read them, the silence of the house closed in upon him, and he had to rush out of it. He said he had no close friend who was in a position to move in with him, and asked if I thought a cat might help him at all. I said I would select the most suitable one I could find, and he could keep it for a week and find out if its presence helped him. The cat I chose was a charming, amiable three-year-old, spayed tiger, of no great distinction in appearance but of deep attachment to people – a gently-reared animal who had never apparently heard a harsh word. The young man took Susie home for a week and was delighted with the results. She met him at the door when he came home from school, sat on a corner of the desk while he read themes, curled up on the foot of his bed at night and purred him to sleep. The week's trial was so successful that he adopted little Susie permanently. As he says, "She's always there, she's always affectionate and gentle, and she can't talk" (26, p. 23).

DEATH AND THE CHILD

Let us consider the child – the meaning of death to him and the help which a pet can offer in coping with it. Death is an object of concern to children. It is notable in one study that 10 percent of the stories told by children aged 2 to 5 were concerned with death (computed by this writer from Table V, ref. 28, p. 252). Moreover, there is a progressively increasing interest in death during that age span. On a word association test given by one investigator, in response to the words *very sad* "forty-five children out of ninety-one referred to death. Mother's death was most frequent, followed by siblings and then pets" (28, p. 105).

To the very young child, nature is animate (8, 32). Plants are sentient beings and animals think and talk. Animals and human beings may easily be transformed into each other. Fairy tales, biblical stories, and religious myths that he has heard of this kind are meaningful and believeable.

Because of the subterfuges used by some adults, children may think that their deceased parents continue to live in faraway lands, possibly on a nearby bright star. Some of them feel that their parents in the sky constantly observe their behavior and either approve or disapprove of what they are doing.

Yet when we attempt to give a child realistic explanations of the mysteries of life and death, he may find these stories unacceptable and create his own myths to provide more acceptable explanations. This tendency has been commented upon by Chukovskii (8) and Mitchell (28).

Years ago when we had large families, and unmarried aunts, brothers, sisters, grandparents, and grandchildren living under the same roof, death was a common experience in children's lives. They could observe relatives die, learning at first-hand about courage and fortitude and gaining some understanding of the people with whom they lived. Today however, exposure to the death of family members occurs relatively infrequently for children, and it therefore hurts them with doubled force. They are unprepared; the deaths are unexplained and unexpected and the unknown is much worse than the most dreaded known reality. When a loved one dies, the child suffers a loss of affection and security. He hears vague and confusing explanations which he feels conceal some horrible truth. He becomes sensitized to the existence of a mysterious terror in whose presence his giant protectors tremble.

The very young child readily accepts the commonly offered explanation that death is similar to sleep. Like preliterate people (20), he too cannot conceive of death as total destruction. He visualizes death as a very prolonged sleep, as in the story "Snow White." The body does not decay. The person feels, thinks, experiences, senses, yet cannot cry out or move. The dead exist, silently sharing the child's meals, his joys, and his sorrows. Death has no more finality for him than it does in the game of "cops and robbers," where the participants are resurrected as the rules of the game require.

The child is aware, however, that the immobilization of death is much more complete than that of sleep and is not voluntary. He has already experienced such a state in his nightmares, when he was frozen with terror. He may develop insomnia and ask to have the light on when he goes to sleep, or have his parents sleep with him. To compound his difficulties, he is reluctant to discuss his fears because he considers them shameful. Since adults are ashamed to talk about such fears, how can he? What he wants most of all is to find something that will help him integrate his experiences. At this point, having a pet may be most important.

The young child thinks of the animal as similar to himself and sometimes even more important than himself. Young children very readily identify with animals (5). In children's eyes, the grown man, the father, belongs to the animal world (10), clinical observations in pet-oriented child psychotherapy indicate that some children unconsciously believe that they may be transformed into animals and that animals may become children. This is similar to the belief of hunting cultures that in "primal times all animals were people" (20).

Some children notice that their pets commit crimes — mate and defecate in public, kill mice, birds, and other inoffensive creatures — and still are not punished. They envy the animals their freedom to engage in such fascinating and (for them) forbidden activities, and wonder why their pets escape punishment. They feel, however, that when punishment does come, it will be very severe.

Many children cannot conceive of death as a natural, lawful event, occurring fortuitously. They feel that someone is responsible. Jersild (21, p. 357), for example, remarks that for children who have been frightened by the thought of an avenging God who punishes youngsters for their sins, death has not only the implication of "annihilation and nothingness" but is "the ultimate in loneliness and isolation."

In this connection, it may be noted that children tend to perceive anything unfavorable that happens to them as punishment. For example, as noted by Bergman and Freud (4, p. 138), when a child becomes ill, he may find this to be a "confirmation of the belief that wrongdoing, however secretly performed, is open to punishment, and that other, still undetected misdeeds, whether actually carried out or merely contemplated in fantasy, will likewise be followed by retribution of some kind."

Pitcher and Prelinger (33, p. 179) note that children at four see "death as aggression (and especially as punishment for the ill-doers)."

The critical illness of a parent usually brings about the mobilization of all of a family's resources. At this juncture, the very young child may feel neglected and consequently may harbor unconscious death wishes against his parents. The young child who has not yet learned the difference between angry wishes and angry deeds becomes most anxious when his father dies. He may become terror-stricken, expecting the same fate. Since at this period the child is egocentric (32), is unable to generalize, and tends to explain death on the basis of the fact that the deceased wished to desert him, he may direct his aggression inward and become depressed. He may also feel that it is not worth while to love, that adults betray the trust children place in them by deserting them and leaving them alone just when they are needed most.

Children, when they feel abandoned through death, may develop feelings of loneliness and hopelessness. They may develop very poor appetites and stop eating or even neglect their natural functions. They may wish to die so as to join their loved ones in heaven.

Whenever possible, the child should be prepared for a parent's death. Serious illness should not be considered a closely guarded family secret, but should be discussed in the child's presence in terms he can understand. The parent's death will not then appear to be a sudden desertion.

Some parents feel that if there is serious illness in the family which the child is aware of, especially if death is an imminent possibility, he should no longer be gay and continue with his usual childish pursuits. However, parents usually do not object if a child is happily occupied with his pet, which thus relieves him of the adult imperative to feel sad at a time when he sees no reason to do so.

When someone close to the child dies, some well-meaning parents, hoping to help the child to overcome his fears and anxieties attendant upon bereavement, allow him to share their bedroom. This tends only to increase the child's sense of guilt. It is by far preferable to have a pet share the child's room or even sleep with him until the acute phase of bereavement is over.

In fantasies of bereaved children, themes of rebirth and reunion with the loved one after death occasionally appear. Children may dream of space saucers picking them up and reuniting them with their parents, who have moved to a nearby star. The child fantasies that only through death can he achieve his ultimate desire — a loving reunion with his deceased parent — thus obtaining forgiveness for his evil thoughts and making atonement for his guilt. The love of a pet provides comfort on the plane of reality, thus minimizing the need to escape into fantasy.

Occasionally, a pet given to a child by a parent is identified with that parent. If the latter subsequently dies, the child may express his anger at the parent's desertion by attacking and even killing the pet. This is a frequent occurrence among emotionally disturbed children. By experimenting with death and inflicting it on an inoffensive creature, the child apparently imagines himself to be the master of life and the conqueror of death. At this critical juncture in the child's life, his need for affection, support, companionship, and ego gratification are no longer being adequately met. Many an adult depression may be traced to this feeling of desertion in the child's mind (17).

Perhaps the bereaved child will turn to the surviving parent, who may not be ready to offer any comfort. The parent may be so involved in his own grief that he pays scarcely more than fleeting attention to his child. The child is frequently told not to disturb his parent, the implication being that the child is a burden. He is saddled with the responsibility for being quiet. This serves to deepen the unconscious guilt of the child, who sees that he has been deserted not only by the deceased parent, but by the living one as well, a feeling that may be particularly traumatic at a time when the child is already anxious about his standing in his family.

We sometimes find that the surviving parent looks to his children for comfort, thus denying them the right to be with friends of their own age and choosing. A pet to which the parent can transfer some of this affection and need for support can be most useful.

At a time of fundamental change in family dynamics, a pet can be of great solace to a child whose entire world seems to have come crashing down around his ears. The child's grief, tears, fears, and terrors, as well as his feelings of guilt are entrusted to the pet, whose silent, undemanding acceptance of the child's emotions, along with his unfailing admiration and love for its young master, bring sorely needed comfort. In playing with his pet, the child may be better able to work out his feelings of guilt, fears of punishment, and attempts to make restitution for the wrongs he has committed (24). He is then better able to accept his loss and will not need to deny it by escaping into a make-believe world. The child may thus be able to emerge relatively unscathed from the traumatic experience, because the pet has served as a warm, stable, protective bridge between the never-forgotten past and the future.

Introducing a pet into families which face the loss of a parent can in many cases prove to be a valuable mental hygiene measure. The pet gives the child a living companion that will not usually be a competitor for the surviving parent's affection. Even more important, "the dog represents a protector, a talisman against the fear of death, which is first experienced as separation anxiety" (16).

DEATH OF A PET

A young child may first become aware of death through the death of an animal. He may observe or accidentally stumble upon a dead animal, bird, or insect (28). The effect of this discovery differs, depending on whether a group of children is present to help dilute the shock, or the child is alone. When in a group, the child tries to model his behavior to correspond to the behavior of the children who are with him. He can thus accept the death of an animal in an impersonal, matter-of-fact way, looking upon it as one more facet of nature, provided of course that he was not personally involved with the animal.

Thus Susan Isaacs (19, pp. 178-179) describes the reactions of some very young children toward animal death as follows:

24.11.24 In the garden the children found a dead rat, and spoke of it as a "mouse." They said, "It's dead," and ran about holding it. Mrs. I. took it away for fear of infection. Dan said, "You won't hurt it, will you?" Mrs. I. took it to the other end of the garden, and hid it. Dan asked her, "Where have you put it? You've not hurt it, have you?"

16.2.25 Another dead rat was found in the garden; the children looked at it, and talked about it very interestedly. They helped Mrs. I. to bury it.

If the child is alone when he finds the dead animal however, an

entirely different reaction may occur. Mitchell (28, p. 77) reports
that one child's interest in death began as follows:

> As a very young child — perhaps five or six years of age, I
> remember stumbling on a dead hedgehog in some rhododendron
> bushes. The little carcass was alive with maggots, and the stench was
> both new to me and quite appalling. I ran to my mother and cried for
> at least half an hour on her lap. . . . I felt the utmost horror at the
> physical aspect of death.

When a child's pet dies, there are times we can safely talk about
it freely and times we must overlook or underemphasize certain
aspects of the death, if possible. When a pet dies from natural
causes — disease, accident, old age — we can discuss the causes
with the child. However, the death of a gerbil baby resulting from
its mother having had it for breakfast is too threatening to be
revealed to the child. Such an event may, if known, precipitate
harmful unconscious fantasies. It is advisable therefore to inform
the child that the gerbil has died, without going into details as to
how the death occurred.

Pets do not have a very long life span, yet the death of a pet is
interpreted by the child as punishment for its misdeeds. Who
caused the pet's death? Why was he punished? Where does the
pet's body go? Does the pet have a soul? These are some of the
questions the child raises at that point. The child may also wonder
if he and his parents will die. If so, and if his parents die first, who
will take care of him? Expressing these concerns gives the child an
opportunity to discuss his real or fancied guilt over the death of
his pet, to appraise his own feelings about death, and to come to
terms with it.

Children may participate in mock funerals and reenact the
death of their pets in an attempt to master their fear and to
understand their emotions.

Hall and Browne (15, p. 25), in discussing the funerals of cats,
indicate that quite a few children bury their pets with some ritual.

> Numerous funeral ceremonies are described, and by far the larger
> number of the dead pets are buried with more or less ceremony,
> though a few express a desire to have them stuffed so that they could
> keep them. While it is evident that both imitation and play, with a
> large dramatic element, are to be found in the descriptions of cat
> funerals, there is also much genuine grief and tenderness, and a desire

that the dead pet shall be gently cared for and respect shown to her memory. Flowers are placed on the grave, not only at the time of the funeral but for successive seasons.

Mitchell (28, pp. 46-49) describes the funeral of a bird which was not a pet:

The incident took place when I was visiting a day "progressive" school in a morning in spring in the late fifties to talk about opportunities for scientific activities for young children. In this school the first half of each morning was free for the children to choose their own activities, and there was an open access to classrooms and gardens so that children between the ages of five and eleven could mingle with other than their own age group. There was no religious observance or instruction in this school. I walked into a classroom mainly occupied by sevens to eights and was having a look at the Nature display on tables and cupboards when a bird flew in through the open door. The following is a verbatim report on what happened:

ROSA: "Look, there's blood on the window."

JILL: "The poor bird's hurt himself."

A little knot of girls gathered round the bird where it had fallen on the classroom floor. Rosa rather gingerly picked it up. By now the class teacher was standing on the fringe of the group. Jill seized her hand and said: "Joan, can we have the little bird in the classroom and look after it? Can I get a box to make a bed?" The teacher showed Jill where she could find an appropriate box and pieces of material for bedclothes and then again retired to the fringes.

By now other children from inside and outside had joined the group, mostly the under-nines. There was some shouting and bossing until the original group with the bird had got outside and were proceeding to arrange the sick-bed. Suddenly a boy shouted, "Oh, look!" The bird's head had dropped. For a moment there was silence, and then the same boy said, "He's dead," and wandered off. The first reactions of the rest seemed to be disappointment that they could not look after the bird and have a hospital in class. It was difficult to hear this part, but after a few minutes the class teacher was again called in to the group — "Can we have a funeral?" Immediately permission was given the children cheered up and became busy. I could only record scraps of conversation.

ROSA: "We must bury it. Go and see if the nursery will let us use their garden."

Here the teacher intervened and said they must use their own garden. So the bird in its box was carried in slow procession of about ten boys and girls to the garden and laid on the ground while John dug a grave. It was now that the rituals started.

ANGELA: "We ought to put flowers in its coffin."

JOHN *(looking up from the digging):* "It's got blue in its wings. It had better have blue flowers." Two girls went off to search for blue flowers. Meanwhile a fierce argument started between Rosa and Jill.

ROSA: "That coffin has to have a lid. You have to nail a coffin down."

JILL: "No, it's awful for it to have a lid. It's awful to be shut up."

JOHN: "Don't be silly. It's dead, isn't it?"

ROSA *(to Jill):* "How would you like to be buried in a coffin without a lid with all that soil all over your face."

JILL: "I wouldn't care a damn, you silly clot."

PETER: "Anyhow, I think we ought to have a cross. You should have a cross on a grave."

ROSA: "O.K. Good idea. Ask Paul to make one. Go on. Shout through the woodwork window. He's doing woodwork."

Paul, shouted at through the window, agreed, but a minute later reappeared saying: "Robert doesn't think it ought to have a cross. It might be a Jewish bird." The rest agreed that it could be, with the exception of John, who said they were crazy, and he had finished digging. By now the girls with flowers had returned and were arranging them around the bird. They also had a lid and without further protests from Jill the coffin was placed in the earth and very rapidly, and with obvious relief, covered over by John.

An uneasy silence was followed by Rosa's saying, "You sing something at funerals." They decided on "Speed bonny boat", and in the middle of the first verse the bell went for music in the hall. The children scattered to get instruments, etc, and all but one rushed across the grass to the hall. This was Chris, aged seven. He came up to me while I was lingering by the grave.

"Mrs M, what has happened to that bird? Who is that bird?"

"Well, who are you, Christopher?"

After a moment's hesitation, "I am my name." Then he went on: "I wonder if there is a part of the bird that comes out invisible and flies away."

Knowing that this particular child had atheist parents I thought it better not to comment. As he finally picked up his recorder and prepared to follow the others he said: "Mrs M, if I came back from my recorder lesson and heard that bird chirping again I'd drop my recorder and jump for joy all over the field."

He was the only one who had taken no part in the rituals and the only one who had verbalized his sorrow. But one can draw no conclusions from this about the value of ritual in allaying disturbance.

A group of fifty eighteen-year-old students, asked to remember any rituals associated with death in their childhood, all reported on something, mostly in connection with dead animals — either pets or, more often, dead birds found in the garden. All the remembered rituals occurred at home and no one reported on any which had happened at school. The following are typical:

"I remember the death of my budgerigar. We made a special wooden coffin, placed him tenderly on cotton wool, and had a procession down the garden with a cross. This was very different from the death of my uncle when I was ten, which occurred a little while before. The house was in mourning, drawn curtains, black dress. I was frightened of the darkness and the silence in a house that was usually very bright and alive."

"I remember making a cross when my pet rabbit died, and the drawn blinds when my grandmother died when I was nine."

Since the young child thinks that death is reversible (3, 13, 31) and that he is omnipotent, it is very easy for him to wish his parents and particularly his pet dead and then in his mind to resurrect them. "Death and killing are popular notions with three-year-olds. Death is a form of aggression, in most cases, which at least temporarily puts people out of circulation. But death is by no means final — it is a stunning rather than a knock out blow. Half the time the dead character comes back into action again" (33, p. 179).

However, when the child learns that death is final, he develops extreme feelings of guilt and nightmares in which the deceased pet appears in the shape of a ferocious animal. The child bewails his loss, begins to act out his feelings, and tries to assay through play activities what the realities of life and death are. He tries to curb his own fantasies and master his own anxieties. Finally, in a further attempt to lay his fears to rest, the young child exhumes his buried bird or fish and examines the decomposed body.

A student who described the "big ceremonies" they had when they found any dead animal — hedgehogs, fledglings, pets of all kinds — and recalls lighted candles, gravestones, and long chants, also made the interesting observation: "I also spent at least two weeks trying to bring five dead (drowned) puppies back to life. I had been told that if you stroked them you could get them alive — I dressed them up and spent fourteen days in secret with them talking to them — keeping them warm" (28, p. 49).

Every child creates his own burial ritual. But a ritual it nevertheless remains. Unnecessary as these actions may seem to the uninformed adult, through the ritual of endlessly and obsessively (or so it may seem) burying and disinterring the decomposing body, the child unconsciously punishes himself for his imagined guilt in bringing about the pet's death, and, after solving this problem learns finally to accept the reality of his loss. There is no return of the dead. The dead pet will not come to haunt him in his dreams.

> There is the example of a small boy whose pet dog was killed by an automobile. His first reaction was one of shock and dismay. This mood was followed by outrage against his parents who he felt were guilty of the death because they did not take proper care of the pet. The boy behaved like the adult who rages against God for neglecting his charges. Yet, the anger against the parents was but a substitute for his own guilt, for the youngster had on occasion expressed the wish to be rid of "that awful pest." The child then insisted that as part of the burial service one of his favorite toys be buried with the dog. The toy served as a kind of peace offering to the offended pet. Now, the lad was freed of his own anxiety and could continue to function effectively in his everyday activities. Thus the ritual combined the dynamics of guilt, assuagement, and reparation which possess a similarity in the mourning behavior of adults (14, p. 14).

Isaacs (19, 182-183) describes the funeral of a rabbit as follows:

> 13.7.25. Some of the children called out that the rabbit was ill and dying. They found it in the summer-house, hardly able to move. They were very sorry, and talked much about it. They shut it up in the hutch and gave it warm milk. Throughout the morning, they kept looking at it; they thought it was getting better, and said it was "not dying to-day."
>
> 14.7.25. The rabbit had died in the night. Dan found it and said, "It's dead — its tummy does not move up and down now." Paul said, "My daddy says that if we put it into water, it will get alive again." Mrs. I. said, "Shall we do so and see?" They put it into a bath of water. Some of them said, "It *is* alive." Duncan said, "If it floats, it's dead, and if it sinks, it's alive." It floated on the surface. One of them said, "It's alive, because it's moving." This was a circular movement, due to the currents in the water. Mrs. I. therefore put in a small stick which also moved round and round, and they agreed that the stick was not alive. They then suggested that they should bury the rabbit, and all helped to dig a hole and bury it.
>
> Later on, seeing the puppy lying on the grass in the sun, Duncan called out for fun, "Oh, the puppy's dead!" All the children went to see it, and laughed heartily when the puppy got up and ran at them.
>
> 15.7.25. Frank and Duncan talked of digging the rabbit up — but Frank said, "It's not there — it's gone up to the sky." They began to dig, but tired of it, and ran off to something else. Later they came

back, and dug again. Duncan, however, said, "Don't bother — it's gone — it's up in the sky," and gave up digging. Mrs. I. therefore said, "Shall we see if it's there?" and also dug. They found the rabbit, and were very interested to see it still there. Duncan said, "Shall we cut its head off?" They reburied it.

The reaction of child patients to the death of their psycho-therapist's dog has been detailed by the therapist as follows:

1. Early latency age children were the ones who expressed the most concern over the death of my dog 16 months ago.
2. Boys were more affected than girls.
3. Some of them are still talking about his absence.
4. The fact that he was old and sick made his death less anxiety provoking than had he been killed accidentally. This was revealed by the questions they asked, often repetitively needing reassurance.
5. Those who had dogs of their own talked of them more often, with renewed interest and concern.
6. Most striking of all was the reaction to my refusal to get a replacement for my dog. Two neurotic boys, both of whom distrust their mother's love for them, continue to bring this subject up. One expresses anger with me through this material. In the beginning, this same 8 year old child wanted several times to search my house, disbelieving the finality of the event (36).

It is most important for the child to go through the mourning experience and carry it to completion. If a young child's first contact with death involves the death of a pet which can be easily replaced, and if through the pet's death he can acquire some understanding of the meaning of such an event, we may then through an exposure to this inevitable stress of life immunize the child and strengthen his psychological defenses against the shock of the loss of key individuals later in his life. It will then be much easier for him to successfully go through the mourning period.

By losing a beloved pet while at the same time receiving support from his parents, the child may best be able to master the bereavement experience.

As death becomes less mysterious, more understandable, and in a sense "palpable," the associated emotions of fear become more manageable. Fantasies are cut to size by intruding reality factors, and the child is able to cope with his grief more adequately.

Children have deep ties to the dead pet, so that some time must be allowed to elapse before a new pet is acquired. Otherwise the child may be conflicted over what he considers "treason" (28, p. 113). It is valuable for a child to learn that a dead pet, like a dead parent, cannot be completely replaced. Nonetheless, when we replace a dead pet we in a sense endow the new one with all the qualities and virtues of the deceased. We don't have to learn gradually to love him, but can feel deep affection for him as soon as we obtain him.

By coming to love the replacement, the child learns that life must go on. He will recognize that, just as someone took over the care of the kittens when the mother cat died, some person will provide necessary care and support for him in the event of a parent's death. The death of a pet therefore serves as a kind of emotional inoculation against fears of abandonment.

DEATH OF A PET AND THE ADULT

It is not only children who can derive strength from coping with the death of a pet; the adult too can learn to deal better with the reality of life when he is face to face with the death of a beloved pet. At such times he can cry, possibly more openly and unashamedly than with the loss of a human friend or relative.

The traumatic effects of the death of a pet even on adults may be seen from the following remarks: "I often pay a visit to the remains of my dog, even though this may displease reasonable people." Or, "Can one ever be consoled after the death of his best friend?" (12, p. 107).

When his dog was dying, Gautier wrote as follows:

> I shall shorten this recital of the abominable night, the memory of which still shakes me horribly afterward. Strong spirits or persons who have never loved animals, or who know them only through books will consider me an imbecile. I don't care. I accept the insult. Only those who have lived with so faithful a friend as a dog is to man will understand me (12, p. 106).

Wechsler writes:

> What is hard to say to those who have never known a dog well is that his death is a highly human matter, and there is a loneliness without him.
> Perhaps I ascribed too much wisdom to him. But he was wise enough to know when I did not feel well, or when something had

gone wrong, and to exhibit his sympathy. Nervous and high strung, he was uneasy with strangers; but he was affectionate and sensitive to those whom he recognized (40).

In *A Letter to the Man Who Killed My Dog,* Joseph expresses his grief over the death of his dog in the following words:

> I am not a man who cries easily, but picking up her bone and rubber ball, her tag toy and the rubber bone that squeaked when she bit it, her food and water dishes, I cried as I haven't cried since childhood. I sobbed all the way while I was unscrewing her gym gate from the kitchen wall and putting her things away in the cellar. I was glad my wife wasn't there to see me cry that way, because I would have had to stop then, and then the hurt would have been worse (22, p. 42).

Such mourning may lead to a more open acceptance of death, without denying its reality.

> There is no surer testimony to the deep bond of affection between people and their pets than the long memories that remain. . . . And that being the case, it robs death of its terrible finality. Something lives on, if only in memory (22, p. 142).

In order to overcome his fears and atone for his fancied guilt, the adult too may engage in a complicated burial ritual. Some pet owners, for example, give their animals regular funerals, sometimes even with full religious services. These pets are buried in a pet cemetery and the owner may come at regular intervals to care for the grave (34).

Occasionally our pets are so dear to us that we do not want to be separated from them even in death. Falla, President Roosevelt's dog, is buried near him.

In his will Byron directed that his body be buried near that of his dog, Boatswain, for whose tombstone he wrote the following inscription:

> Near this spot
> Are deposited the remains of one
> Who possessed Beauty without Vanity
> Strength without Insolence,
> Courage without Ferocity,
> And all the Virtues of Man without his Vices.
> This Praise, which would be unmeaning Flattery
> If inscribed over human ashes,
> Is but a just tribute to the Memory of

BOATSWAIN, a Dog
Who was born at Newfoundland, May, 1803,
And died at Newstead Abbey, Nov. 18, 1808 (6, 59-60).

Some people may even wish to die near their pet's tombstone. A newspaper item of October 9, 1969, reports: "A physician paid a visit to the place where his pets were buried and then shot himself to death."

The emotions and thoughts of the aged when they contemplate the death of a pet are usually quite different from those of other age groups. The aged person has already had many bouts with death in all its nuances. Its bitter taste is nothing new to him. He may also have more difficulty in going through a bereavement period because he has had so many bereavements, the cumulative effects of which are devastating (23). Furthermore, it may be very difficult at this period in his life to find new friends and associates. He may be afraid to establish new relationships, even assuming that these are available within his immediate circle, for fear of having to undergo new bereavements and never recouping his losses.

However, there is a great difference between the death of a pet and that of a friend. A human being cannot be replaced but a pet sometimes can. This possibility was very well expressed by Lorenz (25, p. 207):

> Certainly the death of a faithful dog that has accompanied its master for some fifteen years of his life's walks brings with it much suffering, nearly as much as the death of a much beloved person. But in one essential detail the former is easier to bear: the place the human friend filled in your life remains forever empty, that of your dog can be filled with a substitute.

This is illustrated in the following case reported by Lowie (26, p. 10-11):

> Mrs. Edmonton was a wealthy woman who lived alone in a large house with her fourteen-year old cat. One day the elderly pussy had a stroke and died within the hour. Mrs. Edmonton had known in a general way that the cat was not likely to live much longer, but she was considerably shocked by her sudden loss. After rattling around in an empty house for a week she became quite desperate from loneliness. Before coming to the shelter she had visited several pet shops, but all she could find in them was one kitten after another, so she came to the Shelter to ask if we had an older cat. We did indeed.

A few days earlier a large, eight-year-old, short-haired, black-and-white, spayed female had been turned over to us by the executor of an estate. The old puss had had the best of care and had a charming disposition, but we were not sure we could place so old a cat. However, I brought her out to Mrs. Edmonton. It was quite unexpected good luck that the cat was an exact match for the one she had lost, with the same distribution of black and white fur. The lady was delighted and went off happily with her replacement for Sugar Bun. This story is included for two reasons: To show that wealthy people also have their problems and that any gently-reared cat can be placed. In most cat shelters Sugar Bun the Second would have been put to sleep; instead, she is earning her two meals a day by being a loving companion to a lonely woman.

PETS' REACTIONS TO HUMAN DEATH

A note should be made of the behavior of pets when their masters are ill or die. We have many verified stories of pets' devotion to their masters which surpasses that of their human friends (11). This, perhaps, is one reason why pets are so treasured by the sick, bereaved, and dying. Munthe reports the following:

It is strange and very pathetic to watch the behavior of a dog when his master is ill. The dog warned by his infallible instinct is afraid of disease, afraid of death. A dog accustomed for years to sleep on his master's bed is reluctant to remain there when his master is ill. Even in the rare exceptions to this rule, he leaves his master at the approach of death, hiding in a corner of the room and whining pitifully. It has even happened to me to be warned by the behavior of a dog of the approach of death. What does he know about death? At least as much as we do, probably a good deal more. As I write this I am reminded of a poor woman in Anacapri, a stranger to the village, slowly dying of consumption, so slowly that one after another of the few "comari" who used to go and see her had got tired of her and left her to her fate. Her only friend was a mongrel dog, who, an exception to the rule I have just mentioned, never left his place at the foot of her bed. It was besides the only place to lie on, except on the damp earthen floor of the wretched hole the poor woman lived and died in. One day, as I happened to pass by, I found Don Salvatore there, the only one of the twelve priests of our little village who took the slightest interest in the poor and the sick. Don Salvatore asked me if I did not think the time had come to bring her the Last Sacraments. The woman looked about as usual, her pulse was not worse, she even told us she had felt a little better these last days — la miglioria della morte, said Don Salvatore. I had often marvelled at the amazing tenacity with which she clung to life and I told the priest she might quite well last for another week or two. So we agreed to wait with the Last Sacraments. Just as we were leaving the room the dog jumped down from the bed with a howl of distress and crouched in the corner of the room whining pitifully. I could see no change in the woman's looks, but noticed with surprise that her pulse was now almost imperceptible. She made a desperate effort to say something, but I could not understand at first what she meant. She looked at me with wide-open eyes and raised her emaciated arm several times pointing to the dog. This time I understood and I believe she also understood me when I bent over and said I would take care of the dog (30, pp. 60-61).

SUMMARY

The death of a pet may provide an emotional dress rehearsal and preparation for the greater losses yet to come. When a parent dies, the pet may also become a temporary crutch that helps the child to hold on to life until the void can be filled and his shattered world can become whole again.

The adult, too, can derive much solace in bereavement from the companionship of a pet. As for his reactions to the death of a beloved animal, they are no less deep than those of a child, although the loss plays a different role in his psychological economy.

The behavior of animals upon the impending or actual death of their masters indicates the depth of the bond which develops between humans and their subhuman kindred.

REFERENCES

1. Anthony, S.: The Child's Discovery of Death. New York, Harcourt, Brace, 1940.
2. Arthur, B., and Kemme, M. L.: Bereavement in childhood. J Child Psychol Psychiatry, 5:37-49, 1964.
3. Bender, L., and Schilder, P.: Suicidal preoccupations and attempts in children. Am J Orthopsychiatry, 7:225-234, 1937.
4. Bergmann, T., and Freud, A.: Children in the Hospital. New York, International Universities Press, 1965.
5. Brill, A. A.: The universality of symbols. Yearbook Psychoanal, 1:63-78, 1945.

6. Byron, G. G.: The Poems and Dramas of Lord Byron. New York, Crowell, 1890.
7. Cattell, J. P.: Psychiatric implications of bereavement. In Kutscher, A. H. (Ed.): Death and Bereavement. Springfield, Thomas, 1969, pp. 153-162.
8. Chukovskii, K.: Ot Dvukh fo Piati (From two to five), 19th ed. Moscow, Prosveschenie, 1966.
9. Feifel, H. (Ed.): The Meaning of Death. New York, McGraw-Hill, 1959.
10. Freud, S.: Analysis of a phobia in a five-year old boy. In Collected Works, standard ed. Edited and translated by James Strachey. London, Hogarth Press, 1955, Vol. 10.
11. Gaddis, V., and M.: The Strange World of Animals and Pets. New York, Cowles, 1970.
12. Gautier, J.: A Priest and His Dog. New York, Kenedy & Sons, 1957.
13. Gesell, A. L., Ilg F. L., Ames, L. M., Learned, J., and Bullis, G. E.: Child Development. New York, Harper & Brothers, 1949.
14. Grollman, E. A. (Ed.): Explaining Death to Children. Boston, Beacon Press, 1967.
15. Hall, G. S., and Browne, C. E.: The cat and the child. Pedagog Semin, 11:3-29, 1904.
16. Heiman, M.: The relationship between man and dog. Psychoanal Q, 25:568-585, 1956.
17. Hilgard, J. R., Newman, M. F., and Fisk, F.: Strength of adult ego following childhood bereavement. Am J Orthopsychiatry, 30:788-798, 1960.
18. Hyde, W. W.: The prosecution and punishment of animals and lifeless things in the middle ages and modern times. U of Pennsylvania Law Rev, 64:696-730, 1915-16.
19. Isaacs, S.: Intellectual Growth in Young Children. New York, Schocken, 1966.
20. Jensen, A. E.: Myth and Cult among Primitive Peoples. Chicago, University of Chicago, 1963.
21. Jersild, A. T.: Child Psychology, 4th ed. New York, Prentice-Hall, 1954.
22. Joseph, R.: A Letter to the Man Who Killed My Dog. New York, Frederick Fell, 1956.
23. Kastenbaum, R.: Death and bereavement in later life. In Kutscher, A. H. (Ed.): Death and Bereavement. Springfield, Thomas, 1969, pp. 28-54.
24. Levinson, B. M.: The dog as a "co-therapist". Men Hyg, 46:59-65, 1962.
25. Lorenz, K. Z.: Man Meets Dog. Baltimore, Penguin Books, 1965.
26. Lowie, L. C.: Cats and People. Berkeley, Berkeley Humane Society.
27. Meerloo, J. A. M.: Mental First Aid. New York, Hawthorne, 1966.
28. Mitchell, M.: The Child's Attitude to Death. New York, Schocken, 1967.
29. Morris, D.: The Naked Ape. New York, McGraw-Hill, 1970.
30. Munthe, A.: The Story of San Michele. New York, Dutton, 1965.
31. Nagy, M.: The child's theories concerning death. J Gen Psychol, 73:3-27, 1948.
32. Piaget, J., and Inhelder, B.: The Psychology of the Child. New York, Basic Books, 1969.

33. Pitcher, G. E., and Prelinger, E.: Children Tell Stories. New York, International Universities Press, 1963.
34. Rice, B.: The Other End of the Leash. Boston, Little Brown, 1968.
35. Schilder, P., and Wechsler, D.: The attitude of children toward death. J Gen Psychol, 45:406-451, 1934.
36. Schildkrout, M.: Personal communication, 3/8/71.
37. Searles, H. F.: The Nonhuman Environment. New York, International Universities Press, 1960.
38. Szasz, K.: Petishism. New York, Holt, Rinehart and Winston, 1969.
39. Tillich, P.: The Courage to Be. New Haven, Yale, 1952.
40. Wechsler, J. A.: A dog's life. New York Post, June 3, 1963.

Chapter Six

ANIMALS AND PSYCHOTHERAPY

How do I love thee? Let me count the ways (3).

SPORADIC attempts to use pets in the treatment of human beings have probably been made since prehistoric times. After all, it is man and not animals who has a universal, constant need to be wanted, cared for, and loved. However, just a few instances are a matter of historical record. In the middle of the eighteenth century, animals were used as therapeutic agents at the York Retreat, an institution for the mentally ill in England. Although the written record of this experiment indicates that the association between domestic animals and emotionally disturbed people was beneficial to the latter, nothing came of the approach (7).

In 1942, a planned program involving dogs was inaugurated at the American Air Force Convalescent Center. Again, although good results were reported, the program was abandoned.

My own interest in using pets in psychotherapy was aroused quite by accident. One day my dog, Jingles, followed me to the door and warmly greeted a distraught mother and her disturbed child who had arrived several hours ahead of their scheduled initial appointment with me. Their premature appearance, which brought the usually invisible Jingles to the scene, proved fortuitous. The child's response to the dog's friendly reception paved the way to establishing a rapport that eventually aided the healing process. The child asked to be permitted to return to play with Jingles. In early sessions I was a more or less silent observer of their play and "communication"; my comments and queries were received with seeming inattention on the part of the youngster. But gradually I came to be included in the affection that the child felt for Jingles, who was in effect a willing and able cotherapist.

Pets, particularly dogs and cats, are useful in psychological evaluation, in psychotherapy (child, group, and family), and in work with physically handicapped and other exceptional children, at home, in school, and in special residential settings. Because they are especially helpful in dealing with children, and because this is the area in which most of my own clinical observations have been made, I shall concentrate the bulk of my remarks on the use of pets in psychotherapy with children.

A pet can considerably facilitate psychological examination of a child. The presence of an animal makes for a more natural situation, one that enables the child to feel somewhat relaxed and to be less aware of the fact that he is under observation. The young patient's reactions to the pet and his conversation concerning it (and "with" it) can provide important diagnostic clues to his personality and problems. Obviously, it requires some time and practice for the therapist to learn to detect these clues and to evolve some norms by which he can evaluate various types of behavior of child patients vis-a-vis his animal cotherapist. But any therapist who has experienced the difficulties inherent in an initial interview with a "problem" child, to whom he is a strange adult with a somewhat mysterious function, can readily appreciate the advantages of having a furry friend help "break the ice" and establish the beginnings of a meaningful rapport.

I have found pets particularly valuable in dealing with culturally underprivileged children. To children from a poverty background, who may also come from a broken home, contact with the therapist is especially frightening: his world is so different from theirs that the experience is doubly strange. Friendly acceptance by a pet can do much to bridge the cultural gap, ease the tensions of the initial encounters, and make the child feel at home and cared for.

Having used the pet in the introductory and evaluation procedures, one can then naturally include him in the therapeutic sessions. Of course, if one regards childhood behavior disorders as specific disease entities, then the use of pets in their treatment can seem tantamount to resorting to witchcraft. But if one looks at such disorders as maladaptive response patterns, then the rationale for using pets to help modify such patterns and persuade child patients to acquire more adaptavie life styles becomes apparent. Pet co-therapists add new dimensions to the therapeutic encounter and help meet the needs of a variety of disturbed children.

For very young children, pets offer a natural prop for the acting-out that precedes verbalization of experience. In the same way, children fixed at early developmental levels can gratify their regressive needs through play with the pet, then gradually achieve a measure of maturity that will enable the therapist to reach them.

For the child who is disorganized and fears losing control of himself, working with a pet means a setting of limits (there is just so much that an animal will allow!) that protects him against his own possibly destructive impulses and aids in bringing some organization into his thought and behavior. In contrast, the submissive withdrawn child, through the pet's acceptance of him and what he does, finds that he is able to loosen up and even to venture forth into areas that previously seemed forbidding.

Acting-out children, too, can benefit from the steadying influence of a loved pet. The case of 11-year-old Donald illustrates this well.

> Donald, the younger of two children in an emotionally disturbed family, had multiple problems which had gotten him into trouble at home, at school, and in the neighborhood. Diagnosed as exhibiting a psychotic reaction, he was suspended from school at eight years of age after disrupting the class with his aggressive, bizarre behavior. Tests showed him to have mild organic brain damage, a moderate hearing loss in one ear, a severe loss in the other (he wears a hearing aid), and borderline intelligence, although the school's impression was that his intelligence was normal. Donald played the role of scapegoat in his family, being the target of both physical and verbal abuse.
>
> At the end of a successful season in summer camp, Donald was rewarded by his family with a dog, Brownie. The dog was also intended to teach Donald responsibility and provide him with some companionship, as he was unable to keep friends. Donald fed the dog when reminded and accompanied his father when the latter took Brownie outdoors. The dog helped to unify the family members by providing opportunities for them to work together in caring for it and teaching it tricks.
>
> For the most part, child and dog got along well together. When Donald was overaggressive with his pet, Brownie snapped at him and put an end to the behavior, thus providing more effective control than human beings had been able to achieve.

Brownie also provided his young master with physical contact and affection which the child craved but was afraid to accept from people, against whom he struck out when they attempted to come close. The dog's love was not threatening, and Donald could love his pet in return, thus learning that affection and companionship can be enjoyable and not destructive.

The animal served also as a nonreactive listener, and in Donald's opinion, a comprehending one. This role diminished in importance as Donald learned to make friends and communicate with his peers. The dog served as a link to other children by arousing their interest, which then came to encompass Donald. Donald still does not like adults as much as he does his pet, but Brownie and other children are now on a par in his affection.

Brownie helped Donald develop patience and self-control as he cared for and trained his pet and discovered the limits of permissible behavior with her. She was a valuable adjunct in bringing about improvement in this severely disturbed boy (2).

Pet therapy is specifically indicated in the treatment of the nonverbal, severely ego-disturbed child whose contact with reality is tenuous. Such children are internally disorganized, have a short attention span, and sometimes think in solipsistic terms. It is difficult for therapists to enter their fantasy world and gain their trust. The pet has no such problem: the child quickly accepts him as a real playmate and accompanies him into the real world, at least far enough for the therapist to make contact.

Disturbed children generally have a great need for physical contact yet fear human contact because people have hurt them so much and so often. The pet can approach the child and make the needed contact. The young patient, as he fondles the animal, may even tell him his troubles. The pet asks no questions and makes no demands. Teaching the pet helps the child to affirm his own entity, to discover himself, his own body as separate from other elements in his environment.

Some schizophrenic children, especially, fear physical closeness to the therapist. They may sense that the hostility that emanates from them can alienate even the accepting therapist, or they may be so unsure of their own ego strength that they fear being overwhelmed by the stronger ego of the therapist. In playing with the pet cotherapist, the child makes his own world, with boundaries largely set by himself. The therapist becomes a participant in a common adventure, intruding into a corner of the child's world in which he feels relatively secure. Gradually the fears diminish, rapport is established, and the doors to communication are opened.

The child may be told to imagine that he is just like the dog he is playing with, that he should act like the dog — walk on all fours, roll over, even bark. The bodily sensations such acts evoke can help the child orient himself in his surroundings and reach out into the real world. With the pet as guide and model, the child can be drawn into experiences that can lead him to mental health.

For the child who needs love and something to cuddle, the pet provides much solace. For the child who needs to dominate, to master the situation, the pet serves as an obedient slave. For all disturbed children, who fear being judged and criticized, the pet offers unfailing, nonthreatening acceptance.

A child's use of a pet may undergo a gradual transition, reflecting a maturation process or better adjustment. A pet that is adequate at one point in therapy may be outgrown by the time another stage is reached, and the therapist must be aware of this. The need for a pet as a third participant in the therapeutic sessions may diminish. This heralds improvement in the child's coping mechanisms; it may even mean that he is ready to play with other children and to trust most adults.

Frequently the sequence is the following: Initially the child talks to the animal and uses him as a nonparticipant in imaginative play; at this stage the therapist is disregarded completely. Then the child progresses to the point at which the pet becomes the center of fantasied activity and participates in a role that the child assigns him. Eventually the need for the pet disappears, and therapist and child-patient carry on together, the pet becoming a nonparticipating part of a now-familiar background.

We must not think of pet therapy in terms of a willing dog acting as cotherapist in his master's office, however. One of the natural developments is that the dog provides an excuse for venturing forth from the office. Getting the child into the street enables the therapist to size up his young patient's reactions to many aspects of the environment: to adults and children, to traffic, to things of beauty, to the physically handicapped, and to responsibility — specifically, the responsibility of taking a four-legged friend for a needed walk.

The child patient may profit greatly from accompanying the therapist as he walks his dog. Seeing the dog out in the open, freely making his toilet and otherwise caring for his physical needs without reproof from the master, may help the child overcome feelings of guilt about some of his own bodily functions. Frank discussions about the frailties of the flesh may naturally arise and bring hidden fears out into the open, ultimately helping the child to understand himself and the world of which he is a part. The pet thus serves indirectly as a catalyst for learning and for developing awareness.

It may sometimes be of value to introduce a pet into a patient's family setting, though this requires careful preparation. Family dynamics change when a pet becomes a member of the household as we saw in Chapter Two. The needs and possible reactions of child, parents, and pet must be anticipated. Parents must be made to understand that they should set no preconditions concerning care of the pet by the youngster who is to be its master. They should be advised that when the child is ready to assume responsibility for caring for his pet, he will probably do so voluntarily.

The case of David and his family illustrates several aspects of pet therapy.

> David, the seven-year-old only child of ambitious professional parents, was brought to see me because of his nightmares and refusal to go to school. David knew that he was an unwanted child; his parents gave him everything but love. He was beset by fear and insecurity. I treated David's parents as well as the child, but it was with David that Jingles came to play an important role.
>
> David and I would visit the neighborhood grocery and candy stores to buy goodies with which to "bribe" Jingles to become his friend. As David became attached to the dog and comfortable in his presence and mine as we walked outdoors, he began to be less fearful.
>
> Particularly significant was a lesson David learned from my acceptance of Jingles' "badness." David wanted me to punish the dog for misconduct — for scaring birds or chasing a chipmunk, for example. When I pointed out to him that Jingles naturally had certain hates and fears and acted instinctively in response to these feelings, and that his behavior should therefore be accepted, David dared to

express his own "unacceptable" feelings about his parents and his teacher. He said that he wished his parents were dead and that he could live alone on a desert island, like Robinson Crusoe; he confided that he dreamed of drenching his teacher in gasoline "like they do in Vietnam" and setting him on fire. When David learned that such feelings were not regarded as monstrous, that indeed they were accepted, he was on the road to recovery.

Although they initially rejected the idea of letting David have a dog of his own (because a dog would be messy and would complicate their busy lives), David's parents finally consented to get one for him. The dog did much to help David acquire a sense of security and mastery in his own home. Its presence as a warm greeter, bed companion, and ever-present playmate helped David overcome his fears. In becoming master of his pet, David gradually became master of himself.

Sometimes a pet serves a useful and unexpected purpose, not at the beginning of therapy but some time later. This was the case in the treatment of John.

John, an eight-year-old adopted child who was much disturbed by the fact that his real mother had deserted him, could not accept his foster mother's reassurance that he was indeed a "chosen" child, that he was really wanted and loved. He felt that he had been taken "on approval" and feared he would be returned if he misbehaved. He threatened to kill his sister (also an adopted child) and himself because he was convinced that they must be very bad to have been surrendered for adoption.

My cat had been sleeping in her basket in the office for a few sessions before John noticed her. He began to fondle her and wanted to feed her. He asked questions about her, wanting to know where she came from. I explained to him that we had acquired her at the ASPCA, where she had been left as one of a litter of abandoned kittens. I told him how much we loved her and how my two sons often fought for the privilege of having her in their room at night.

At first John found it difficult to accept the idea that an animal that had been abandoned by her mother and her owner could be loved and accepted by others. He kept returning to this subject; he obviously began to see an analogy between the kitten's situation and his own, and to consider the possibility that he actually was loved by his adoptive parents. His recovery seemed to begin with our discussions about my "adopted" cat (6).

Some years ago I became involved as the clinician in a case where the parents in an upper-middle class family had finally acquiesced and granted permission to their importuning 12-year-old daughter to obtain a dog.

Karen had few friends and preferred to spend many hours alone each day reading. She had arrived late in the life of her parents, and her sisters and brothers were already married. Consequently she had little companionship within the home, and the puppy she acquired became her inseparable "best friend." Karen demonstrated more affection toward the dog than she had ever shown toward any human being.

A few months later, at the family's summer home, Karen was walking across the lawn one dark summer evening and did not know that little "Dizzy" was trailing at her feet. She inadvertently stepped on the dog's paw. Dizzy howled with pain and could hardly place the injured paw on the ground. Karen picked up the dog and rushed in to the house to ask her mother for money to take the dog to a veterinarian. Her mother refused to give her the money and admonished her saying, "You don't have to get so excited. He'll be all right in the morning. And why waste all that money on a dog?"

Karen took Dizzy to her room, placed him on a pillow on her bed, and put cold compresses on his foot all night. She didn't sleep a wink. In the morning she put Dizzy on the floor, but he limped seriously. She was sure that her mother would now recognize the necessity for a visit to the veterinarian. But she was mistaken, and the shock of her false expectations led her to a radical act. Suddenly she saw her parents in a new light. They were "cruel" people. She did not want to be identified with such a feelingless family. Of course there had been very poor communication previously so that her anger and disgust could not be expressed.

With some trumped-up story, Karen was able to borrow enough money from a neighbor to pay for a visit to the veterinarian and train fare to New York. Fortunately, Karen was a careful, sober girl or things might have turned out differently. She went to a friend's house in New York and for a few days her parents had an upsetting time worrying over the whereabouts of their daughter.

When they discovered where she was staying, Karen refused to return to her parents' home. So violent were her reactions and so emotionally upset did she become that the parents had no recourse other than to seek professional help. Obviously, Dizzy was not the nexus of this situation but the instrument that triggered its intensification. In the months that followed, Dizzy always accompanied Karen to my office and frequently crystallized the therapeutic situation. It is good when one can report satisfactory solutions to troublesome human problems. In this case, the results were most favorable, and not only is Dizzy a very important member of the family, but Karen has through him found many new strengths in dealing with human beings (8).

At times, emotionally disturbed children present their therapists with reports about the behavior of their pets which indicate that animals can mimic the symptoms of their young masters. Dr. S. Rubin (10) has described the case of a 13-year-old school-phobic girl who had five cats, some of which were males. Despite the propensity of male cats to roam for long periods out of doors when given the opportunity to do so, the patient claimed that she had great difficulty getting these animals to leave the house. During a two-year period of therapy, the youngster gradually gave up her almost psychotic attachment to her mother and her home, and although she did not return to school, she began a rather active social life and became more assertive and independent. At about the same time, the patient reported that her cats had also changed their habits, and were beginning to leave the house and to "socialize" with other cats in the neighborhood. The patient herself made no connection between these two events, but their simultaneous occurrence was illuminating to the therapist.

Though dogs and, to a lesser degree, cats are especially effective aids in the psychotherapy of children, other pets can also be useful — fish and birds, for example. I have an aquarium in my waiting room, and have found it quite valuable. Fish are particularly good for inspiring fantasies in children — fantasies that sometimes are played out in subsequent therapy sessions.

> Richard, a nine-year-old who had a primitive fear of being devoured, was "reached" through my fish. As he sat in my waiting room, he alternately opened and closed his mouth in imitation of the fish. I took some fish food and urged Richard to help me feed them. He reluctantly did so, and seemed concerned and perplexed about the competition among the fish for food. I casually remarked that the big fish didn't devour the little ones, but that all lived together in the aquarium in friendly competition. The next few therapy sessions were devoted to observing fish and discussing them. Richard's fear was somewhat assuaged by what he learned about the fish, and he later wanted me to show him how to start an aquarium of his own. My treatment of Richard was greatly facilitated by his interest in the aquarium and the lessons it taught him (5).

Quaytman describes her experiences in pet-oriented child psychotherapy (9, pp. 30-34) as follows:

> In treating children, it seemed quite natural to include animals in songs, stories, puppets, and toys, since I have both a dog, and a prolific female cat who produced two litters of kittens annually. At

first, I found it a useful projective technique to tell stories about my own animals. The particular choice of material depended on its pertinence to the treatment situation — the child's main problems, his self-concept, and the stage in therapy at that point. During one session that I recall vividly, I mentioned our new dog, Sean, and how "bad" he had been. I elaborated on his mischievousness, his undisciplined and energetic activity — all typical of a healthy puppy — to Steve, an eight year old boy. Steve's eyes lit up with the joy of identification, and in anticipation of hearing more. Comfortably, and with utter abandon, Steve used to experience and "go through" — in fantasy — all the dog's "destructive" activities I described, always asking for more: "What else did he do?" I then recounted how Sean chewed up a pair of shoes, or dug a hole in a chair, or urinated on the rug — all relatively mild activities when compared with what Steve would have liked to do, at least in his frightening fantasies, namely, blow up the universe. My attitudes towards the dog's behavior varied in the telling, depending on what I wanted to evoke in the child, and how he experienced the "badness."

One child may need to accept the animal's "destructive" behavior as representing his own unacceptable drives, with reassurance and without any introduction of consequences. Another, however, may be introduced in this way to the concept of discipline or "punishment" (which looms as such a fearful thing to so many children), that it is tolerable, that it is transitory and not annihilating, that it is wholly consistent with being loved. My descriptions of the dog's reactions, therefore, ranged from outright aggressive rebelliousness to a gradual understanding between dog and human which slowly develops into mutual respect and love.

Michael, age 6, was so emotionally restricted that he was unable to fantasy either verbally or in play. He used to sit rigidly in a chair and timidly throw a small ball to me — his only means of contact. This continued for months, since Michael was too fearful to respond to any other activity. When my cat produced a new litter, I described the process to him — how the kittens cried and how they nursed, snuggling up to the mother. I imitated the mother's purring sound and made the situation as vivid for him as possible in an attempt to reach him at his painful, orally deprived self. His response was immediate, as if this was the first communication in all these months that he had heard or understood: "Tell it again," and "Tell it again." The following session, after the usual request to "Tell it again," he tentatively suggested that I "be the mother cat" and he, the kitten. Michael curled up and meowed, crying out his need for nurture while I pretended to lick him and nurse him as a good mother cat should. This activity, with some modifications, continued for several weeks, and gradually other fantasy kittens were introduced into this game to make a litter, so that he could also experience the feeling of "closeness" of animals in a litter. There were many variations in the technique of using animals in fantasy and in role-playing which were effective in making contact with disturbed children. In many instances, they constituted the first real break-through in the building of a positive therapeutic relationship.

The first introduction of the live animal into the therapeutic situation was unplanned, and occurred in response to David's repeated requests to see my dog, Sean. I decided the time had come for these two to meet. Sean is a high-spirited Irish Setter, who was a puppy in love with life, children, and other animals, at the time David met him. David, age seven, had been in therapy for three years when he first encountered Sean. He was a small, round, soft boy with blond hair and blue eyes, and a seraphic expression which belied his inner turmoil and rage. Primarily, he denied his maleness, to the point of insisting he possessed no penis. David strongly identified with his mother whom he perceived as all-powerful, and felt contempt for the father, who was seen as weak and inadequate. In play and fantasy, as well as in his excellent art work, David revealed his intense anger at the mother, whom he wanted to devour and incorporate so he would possess "the power." His overt behavior was that of the nice, prissy, polite boy, who disliked the "rough" activities of other boys, and preferred playing with girls, whom he liked to boss.

At their first meeting, David was uneasy at Sean's uninhibited expression of enthusiasm and joy. To Sean, a boy was like another dog, namely, someone with whom to play. I decided the playroom was too enclosed to contain all this energy, so I took boy and dog out to a nearby park. Here Sean could move to and from David, and David could feel less threatened by the closeness and overt energy. I encouraged him to romp with the dog, to call him and see how he would respond, and to stroke Sean when he came up to him. When David seemed more comfortable and reassured, we returned to the playroom, where he was now able to stroke the dog and feel "cocky" because he had experienced the thrill of controlling this "wild" animal. At the end of the session, he mentioned that his father, who had brought him to the play session, was afraid of dogs. The father denied this (actually, as I discovered later, it was the mother who was afraid, but David displaced the fear onto the father), but the boy insisted, and I sensed the underlying hostility between these two.

In the following sessions, David related almost totally to the dog, rolling on the ground with him, having Sean lick his hands and face, and tentatively exploring the area around the dog's genitals, later gingerly touching them and asking questions about their size, furriness, function. Then, we were able to discuss the animal's maleness without David denying its existence, as he had whenever his own masculinity came into question. Castration fears were projected onto the dog and discussed. Not only was he reassured about this fear, but he was gradually able to experience the dog's masculinity as an admirable trait. When Sean became too active and frisky, David took the role of the highly controlling and finicky mother, and berated him. When I suggested that he felt angry at the dog if he playfully jumped on him or knocked him down, David replied that he couldn't be angry with Sean because he loved him. This led us directly into the experience of the coexistence of love and anger between David and Sean, which was later generalized to include relationships outside the playroom. David spent many sessions subsequent to this in acting out hostility to the dog, although still interspersed with much affection, and verbalizing his fear of retaliation if he should hurt Sean. During this period he became much more physically active with more open expressions of hostility on a motor level.

Sean's usefulness to David was climaxed in a dramatic incident. Prior to a session, David's mother called me aside to inform me that she is terrified of dogs and doesn't want David to know it, so would I "please keep the dog from running out to the waiting room at the end of the session." I agreed, and kept the dog in the playroom, until one session it occurred to me it could be most therapeutic for David to see his "all-powerful" mother manifest fear of an animal he feels he can control. At the end of the hour, I "inadvertently" left the door open and Sean bounded out. David confronted the "source of power" and saw her blanch and become rigid with fear. He took hold of the dog by his collar and unconsciously assumed the stance of a self-confident male reassuring the frightened female in an almost patronizing way. It was the first opening on the road towards acceptance of himself as a male, and his separation from identification with his mother.

Annie was a pretty seven year old girl who was fearful, angry and withdrawn. It took many weeks before she could be induced to leave her mother and come into the playroom. When she started to express her feelings they were always of anger and rage — no other affective experience seemed available to her. In her sessions, paints were flung around the room or poured on the floor; clay was hurled at the ceiling or light fixtures; language, when used, usually consisted of obscene words. Annie's well of anger seemed inexhaustible. One day, I mentioned that my cat had a new litter of kittens. She seemed quiet, but interested, so I reported more and noticed that she sidled up close to me, tentatively, but quite definitely. When the kittens were old enough to run about, I brought two of them and the mother cat into the playroom. Annie ran toward the kittens but they scampered under the furniture to safety. I suggested that perhaps they were afraid of her, that they didn't know she was friendly, and she would have to win them over — show them they could trust her. Sometimes kittens, like children are afraid of people they don't know.

However, *Midnight,* the jet-black mother cat with golden eyes, was more trusting and jumped onto Annie's lap. Annie was overwhelmed when the cat curled up and purringly dozed off in her lap, her face quivering with the onrush of new and unfamiliar emotions. She looked up at me as if for reassurance that this was really happening. Gradually, she stroked the cat and started to speak haltingly, but with unmistakable tenderness. When the kittens tired of their romping, they discovered mama on Annie's lap and crawled up to join her. This was the ultimate joy. For many weeks thereafter, Annie played with the cat and kittens, at first repeating over and over again play situations in which she acted out her new-found feelings of tenderness, trust and love. Gradually, as the kittens grew larger and friskier, she allowed herself to express anger too, by taking the role of the scolding mother. We were able to move gradually towards more direct relatedness to me with verbalized communication becoming more and more possible. We finally reached each other by way of the cat and her kittens. Perceiving the smallness and vulnerability of the kittens, whom she saw as being afraid of her, was the first non-threatening experience for Annie. Since the kittens belonged to me and trusted me, Annie moved, through them — as an extension of me — to me. Later, she allowed herself to sit in my lap, sucking her thumb contentedly and acting out her infantile needs. Thus, began the important discovery that there were other feelings one can experience beside anger, rage, and fear.

Rob is a tall, gangling, 14 year old schizophrenic boy who had been in residential treatment for several years, with no sign of improvement. He was finally discharged with the recommendation that he be hospitalized. His parents, who were fearful that his hospital stay might be permanent, pleaded for "one more chance on the outside" before commitment. After several conferences with previous therapists, it was decided that I would work with Rob.

He was painfully shy, fearful and withdrawn. His speech came in staccato, jerky spurts, and he experienced occasional memory lapses. At the first encounter between Rob and Sean, the dog was unobstrusively sleeping on a couch in the treatment room (Sean is now five years old and more sedate), and Rob could ignore him or move toward him, as he wished. Rob sidled over to the dog and very gently stroked his head, almost casually. For the next few sessions, communication between Rob and me was sporadic. When he had a concrete event to report, it was terse and quickly disposed of. His reply, when I asked about feelings or thoughts, was usually a shrug and "I don't know" or "I don't remember." About the fifth or sixth session, Rob started talking about his own dog and relating it to mine, thereby establishing a tolerable means of communication which was not threatening to him. He used the dog, in a sense, as a ventriloquist uses his dummy, symbolically speaking through him. For example, Rob once stated: "My dog is smart. Yesterday my mother and father had a big fight and he did the smartest thing." When asked what the dog did, he laconically added: "ran under the bed." I wondered how Rob felt when his parents fought, and he replied with a trace of humor, that he too, runs under the bed, finally admitting openly that he becomes upset. This was the first time he had admitted having any feelings or mentioned his family.

Each session, Rob sat near the dog on the sofa, stroked him, talked to him, and through him to me. One day, he tried to draw a picture of Sean, but was dissatisfied with it. Then he drew a "Hot Dog," which he labeled and showed to the dog, telling him that's how he would end up. Again, he spoke of his own dog and how his father "tricked" him, following this with examples of how the dog, in turn, "tricked" the father. Rob was thus able to express (through the dog) how he felt about his father's teasing. Although Rob can now discuss productively the interaction between his dog and his father, he is still unable to directly express his own feelings toward his father.

Rob is slowly beginning to speak directly about himself. One session recently, he brought some candy for Sean. When he gave him the candy he asked Sean for a kiss, which he got from a very enthusiastically slurping tongue in his ear. Rob said: "My dog kissed me there this morning. Now, Sean kisses me there, and when I get home my dog will kiss me and smell Sean. And that's how they kiss each other." In some dim, unconscious sense, Rob is expressing what happens between us. He is able to see himself as the agent through which the two dogs communicate. This is, somehow, safer than the realization that he and I communicate through the dogs. Recently, as he has begun to feel freer, he has taken to teasing Sean (as his father teases him). His conversation has become more fluid and is ripe with fantasies of "mischievous" activities, which have shifted from the dogs to his friends, and are now beginning to include him. As he is more able to communicate directly with me, the need for the dog becomes diminished – we can dispense with his dummy.

An animal co-therapist can play an important role in the residential treatment of very disturbed children. Fifty inpatients aged 6 to 14, at the Children's Psychiatric Hospital in Ann Arbor, Michigan, enjoy the companionship and comfort provided by a "resident canine" named Skeezer, who seems to sense each child's needs and may spend the entire night at the bedside of a child who is extremely depressed or sick. Living in a doghouse built with the aid of the children in one of the nursing stations, Skeezer has free run of the hospital and travels from floor to floor via the elevators. The dog joins patients for camping trips, picnics, and other outings. She greets incoming patients and their families, providing a relaxed, homelike atmosphere otherwise difficult to achieve. When Skeezer gave birth to puppies, the pregnancy and delivery touched-off discussions among the children which helped to correct many distorted concepts about procreation. An 11-year-old patient gained a needed sense of competence by taking the dog through an obedience course and winning a blue ribbon. Watching the dog being treated by the hospital nursing staff for minor injuries, the children gained security in recognizing that they too would receive the care they needed. The children share their treats with the dog and bring it presents after their visits home. The Chief of the Children's Psychiatric Service, Dr. Stuart Finch, points out that "Many of [the] youngsters enter the hospital suffering from disturbed relationships with both people and animals. In some instances, the first sign of progress has been noted in their relationship with Skeezer" (4, p. 16).

Pets are also frequently useful in the treatment of adults, as can be seen in the following (1, pp. 76-78):

> Jackie is my miniature poodle, She has had considerable impact on many of my patients. . . .
>
> I discovered Jackie's therapeutic potential the summer of 1959 when she was a tiny, fuzzy ball, fitting neatly into the palm of my hand. I had to take her with me to work because of a paint job at home. At the time I was a social worker in a mental health clinic connected with a suburban college.
>
> A little schizophrenic boy, Johnnie, whom I had seen for a while had consistently avoided talking to me. Also, he had a way of sliding out of the window and running around the campus which often kept me at the distance he wanted. On this particular day, however, Johnnie not only sat on the floor to play with Jackie, but actually asked me to take her out when he was ready for out-of-door play. He began to throw a ball to the puppy and directly requested my help in wiping the ball clean afterwards. For the first time he seemed engaged with something living. I was intrigued and decided to repeat the experiment during our next session. Soon a rapport was established between the little boy and the little dog, and in subsequent interviews

Jackie was told of a great many problem situations within my earshot.

The appointment days with Johnnie coincided with those of a highly schizoid woman, severely depressed. She had progressed slowly and still seemed frightened to discuss her need for tenderness. While we talked about this subject she picked up Jackie and gently caressed her. Her own demonstration of affection enabled us to discuss the issue with greater freedom. It evolved in the course of therapy that Jackie stood symbolically for the right to give and long for tenderness. Consequently, at termination of treatment, she acquired a poodle of her own.

How caring for an animal can help to abandon the determination to kill one's self was brought out by a young schizophrenic artist. This woman falls into periodic depression with suicide a very realistic risk. She dreads her feeling of void and is determined to shoot herself. Whenever her depressive phase sets in, I bring Jackie to the office. The dog's presence, she claims, irresistibly draws her toward living. This young woman's life-possibility is so precarious that I feared her suicide during my vacation. I decided to entrust her with the care of my dog. Both survived! Now, she is in the process of acquiring a dog for herself, uncertain whether or not to buy a poodle, since "they are more human than other dogs, and I might not be ready for this much closeness as yet." The acquisition of a dog signifies a beginning wish for emotional responsiveness.

A paranoid schizophrenic woman recently consulted me "because you can talk to me." Though she has lived in the same apartment for fifty-one years, she claimed to have no friends. She told me over the telephone in no uncertain terms of her dislike for dogs. And, sure enough, beyond the remark that Jackie's presence confirmed her being unwelcome, she hardly said a word during the first session. She just sat in coat and gloves and stared at the animal. The patient returned for a second appointment, however, and expressed great sympathy for "the poor little animal." Invited to tell me more of her compassion, she elaborated on the "tragedy" of not being understood, of "being made to keep quiet," and said, "It must be miserable to be all alone all day long and not a soul to talk to."

One of Jackie's most important functions is being "touchable," especially when comfort is needed. Once a young matron called for an appointment and was asked the routine question as to whether or not she minded dogs. She said she did, especially poodles because of an allergy, but she wanted to come anyway. She was in despair. She came in, squatted in front of a fish tank and pulled a reluctant Jackie into her arms. The flood of tears, once loosened, didn't stop and Jackie attempted to pull the tear soaked Kleenex out of her hand. This particular patient, endowed with keen powers of observation and a charming sense of humor, burst into heart-warming laughter at the puppy's antics. From that time the patient resorted to the fish-tank-Jackie-position almost routinely. The rhythm of the quietly moving fish seemed to quiet her turbulent mind, and Jackie's affectionate gestures made her feel "warm" inside. Endlessly the patient would cradle the animal, mumbling tearfully: "I need you. I must feel you. I love you because you are so cuddly." She also adopted my affectionate habit of calling Jackie "little monster." This patient, too, owns a poodle today! I do not know what it symbolizes for her now, but I imagine it to be connected with her beginnings of therapy.

Many patients, unaware of what they are doing, will drop an arm over the chair's ledge to search for Jackie's head in order to stroke it at the very moment they acutely need comfort. Jackie is the recipient of much affectionate patting. It is as though she were a stress-disperser, both for patients and myself. After a stressful session my left hand is dry and dusty from scratching Jackie's fur — often without my taking notice of having touched her; other times I am quite aware of it.

One puzzling question is why this dog is not used as a ready-made outlet for rage. Some of my friends, who dislike dogs, do not hesitate to shake her off when she begs for caresses. Some of my patients ignore her. No one has ever been rough with her or hurt her. Not even in dreams, unless I am too biased to recognize her in disguise. It seems as if the animal's gentleness gives silent recognition to the needs of patients for affection, and as if Jackie's requests for tenderness affirm my patients' rights to give it. The dog's appeal is seemingly innocent enough to overcome the barriers of shyness, and of shame and of embarrassment.

The most dramatic situation I remember contained within all its terror an element of humor. A psychotic girl had spent two hours alternating between catatonic stages of mute immobility and drunken running around the office. Finally she fell into a Japanese screen which came crashing down on her. Jackie, no hero by nature, fled in fright; then seeing the girl sobbing on the floor and dabbing her eyes with wet Kleenex, Jackie cautiously came over, attempting to lick the tears away and to get hold of the Kleenex at the same time. I did not know whether to laugh or to cry. When my patient finally pulled Jackie into her arms, trying to use her as a pillow, I sighed with relief. Once she could cradle the dog, I knew she would soon be able to talk. The eternity of the last two hours was over.

Another young girl, who likes to lie on the couch and to have Jackie on her stomach, could use the animal to explore some of her deeper fears. She had been crying and reached for her handkerchief, thus disturbing Jackie, who jumped off. The patient sort of fumbled around, trying to grab the dog, to pull her up again, and she looked let-down. When I remarked that apparently she had minded Jackie's

jumping down, my patient confirmed it with a simple "yes" and
proceeded to say: "Yes, I like her ... There is something constant
about animals. I was trying to explain the other night ... Sure, they
are a lot of trouble, it's as if they don't care how a person acts, they'll
accept anyone ... you don't have to put on a show ..." (she patted
the couch), "Come on Jackie, come on up. They'll accept whoever it
is and love them just for being themselves, I mean, just for
being; ... there isn't any great responsibility to have an animal love
you ... the fact ... I mean the fact, that, that you won't lose them
by doing something ... they don't quite understand." I remarked
that this fitted in with something she had said previously about her
fears of being deserted by her family and she continued: "Hmm ... I
remember whenever I went somewhere by myself I always had to have
a dog with me, simply because he was there... and he ... I think I
told you last week about stealing and all those things and a couple of
times when I'd go by myself and I wanted to have the dog come with
me so badly ..." (crying softly and almost suffocating Jackie with
embraces) "... I had the feeling that whether I did anything bad or
not he wasn't going to judge me ...

It was the first time my patient could so clearly express her dread
of being judged and consequently abandoned. I distinctly felt that it
was easier to speak of this precisely because she could clutch the dog
in her arms.

At least one state hospital has made use of animals in treating
withdrawn, regressed adult patients who showed no improvement
with other forms of therapy. Jacksonville State Hospital in Illinois
has a racetrack and stalls for 30 horses on the hospital grounds.
Horse owners rent these stalls and enter their animals in a horse
show and race conducted by the hospital. Ten to twelve patients
are taught to groom the horses. The director of volunteer services
who heads the program reports that the patients at first will not
talk to anyone, then begin talking to the horses, and after a time
talk to the other patients and to the horses' owners (11, p. 2).

A survey was undertaken by this writer to learn the extent to
which pets are being used by psychotherapists and to elicit some
thoughts and feelings about their use from those therapists who
have tried what seems to many to be a somewhat esoteric practice.

Procedure

We selected a random sample of 435 psychotherapists (50% of
the total membership) from the Clinical Division of the New York

State Psychological Association. A questionnaire regarding the use of pets in psychotherapy was mailed to this group, with a followup questionnaire to nonrespondents. A total of 319 replies was received. Most of the questionnaires were not answered in full however, and our statistics are of necessity based on the number of responses given to particular queries.

Biographical information on the respondents was obtained from the 1970 APA Directory (9 men and 7 women in our sample were not listed however, and age was not available for 18 men and 29 women).

Results

Thirty-four respondents indicated that they were no longer child therapists or engaged in the practice of therapy. Two hundred and forty-two (76%) of the therapists who responded were men and 77 (24%) were women. The mean age of the therapists was 48 for the men and 52 for the women.

One hundred and twenty-five (93 men and 32 women) respondents were familiar with the use of pets in psychotherapy. There was no significant difference in age, sex, or time elapsed since obtaining their highest educational degree between those who were familiar with pet psychotherapy and those who were not.

Fifty of 152 therapists (33%) had used pets as therapeutic aids at one time or another; 25 of 148 were currently using pets in psychotherapy. Of those who used pets and were willing to answer the query, 30 of 33 (91%) found them useful.

A majority of the therapists, 162 out of 278 (57%), recommended pets for home use. As we have indicated elsewhere (6), this is useful if there is concurrent treatment of both the child and the parents.

As indicated in Table IV, almost any living creature — depending on the exigencies of the moment, the animals that are available, and the ingenuity of the clinician — may be used in pet psychotherapy. However, dogs are favored, and cats hold second place. Of course these are the animals most readily available and most responsive to human contact. (It is much more difficult for a child to relate to other animals — with the possible exception of a horse, which however presents problems too obvious to mention).

Table V summarizes the therapists' views on the optimal age for pet psychotherapy. Most therapists, it will be noted, felt that pets were most useful with children aged 5 to 15.

Table VI presents a rough consolidation of the problems mentioned by the psychotherapists as treatable with the aid of a pet. Though the answers vary from a completely negative view to wholehearted acceptance of pets in psychotherapy, the general impression is that therapists see a wide gamut of emotional problems as susceptible to treatment by pet therapy.

The Pros and Cons

Fifty-eight comments were volunteered by the therapists, offering a wide range of views and interesting insights into therapists' reactions to the use of pets as therapeutic aids.

On the negative side, a number of therapists mentioned actual physical hazards in using pets — allergies especially, and occasional biting or scratching of a patient by the animal. Others noted the

TABLE IV

PETS EMPLOYED

	Dogs	Cats	Fish	Hamsters	Birds	Turtles	Other*	Total
N	30	19	6	3	3	3	7	71
%	42.2	26.8	8.4	4.2	4.2	4.2	9.9	

Note: Some therapists used more than one animal.
*Other include guinea pigs, gerbils, rats, horses, snakes, weasels.

TABLE V

AGE MOST APPROPRIATE FOR PET THERAPY

Age	5-15	15-25	25-45	45-65	65	All Ages	None	Total
N	46	11	10	8	2	4	1	82
%	56.07	13.40	12.19	9.75	2.43	4.88	1.2	

TABLE VI

PROBLEMS SUITABLE FOR PET THERAPY

Problem	N	%
All	3	6.4
Adjustment problems of childhood and adolescence	4	8.5
Anxiety states	1	2.1
Behavior disorder	2	4.3
Depression	3	6.4
None	1	2.1
Problem of identity	1	2.1
Obsessions	2	4.3
Phobia	7	14.9
Physical handicap	1	2.1
Schizophrenia	9	19.1
Severe deprivation (maternal deprivation, need for mothering)	3	6.4
Uncommunicative, emotionally and socially isolated children and preadolescents	10	21.3
Total	47	100.0

lack of physical facilities for pets in their offices. Some therapists took a dim view of the idea for personal or other reasons: "I am not a pets person." "I don't care for pets myself. I prefer people." "How about studying the use of people as an aid to therapy?" "Unbelievable! ...." "I am sure you'll find a rationale for such use. I doubt I'd call it psychotherapy. Therapy, yes; therapeutic, probably."

Other very personal reactions were also expressed: "I use pets to help me." "I do not use pets as part of the therapy except as they help to establish a view of me which I think is helpful." "I use pets occasionally — as an adjunct — to encourage one expression of positive, tender feelings, to present myself as a woman who loves openly and freely."

Some definite limitations in the use of pets were suggested: "The significance of pets to children varies with each child. If a child uses a pet to express certain psychodynamics, I will try to understand the interaction. If not, I don't see the value of introducing another variable. It may not produce the desired results." "Displacement object would seem to have limited value." "I can see pets as serving a therapeutic means in providing help to the isolated or withdrawn or alienated person, but do not see the value of sufficient pertinence to become especially involved in this as a therapeutic mode."

One therapist indicated that the animal he had was "too variable in his performance." Another noted a special difficulty regarding pets in the home: "I frequently find it necessary to take a great amount of therapeutic time reorienting families about their distorted value of pets in the home. Parents often try to use pets' purchase as a bribe or cure, and end up giving the children a 'weapon' and/or creating a neurotic dog."

Some therapists commented favorably on the use of pets in the home.

"Sometimes I recommend use of pets to youngsters, to 'empty nest' wives; at times for companionship, at times for learning responsibility."

"Have on occasion recommended as a temporary aid for affection-expressing for young women whose husbands were in service and who were on the verge of sexual acting out which they did not want to experience."

"I recommend pets for physically handicapped patients. Otherwise, I don't recommend but try to get them to choose their life."

Among the favorable reactions, many referred to the value of pets in helping withdrawn, asocial, isolated, or lonely children and adults. In some instances a pet was mentioned as an "ice breaker" for both the child and the parent who had brought the child for treatment. Therapists noted the transference role a pet may play and the manner in which a pet can serve as an intermediary for communication. One therapist stated that he used pets along with orally gratifying techniques and touch therapy. Another wrote: "I am a psychoanalyst and the dog is a sympathetic adjunct therapist. I even had a patient with a disturbed dog. I put my dog with her dog during the hour. Simultaneous therapy." Akin to this was the view expressed that "Behavior of pets, disordered or otherwise, reflects neurosis of master (mistress)."

This survey sheds light not only on the use of pets in child psychotherapy, but also on the therapist's attitudes and personalities. In many instances, the therapists' responses were very revealing of their own weaknesses and strengths, attitudes and prejudices.

The survey reflects considerable confusion and lack of direction concerning pet-aided psychotherapy. Some therapists seemed to view the pet as a "gimmick" to be used indiscriminately with every patient. They fail to realize that with the introduction of a pet into the therapeutic relationship, a subtle change in the dynamics of therapy takes place which in turn necessitates a change in the philosophy of treatment.

We need highly imaginative and extremely rigorous research to establish principles and boundaries in the use of pets in psychotherapy. The outcome of such therapy must be evaluated in terms of the needs of each individual patient. Many variables need to be studied, so that a truly refined therapeutic technique can be developed. Both patient-subjects and pets have to be carefully chosen. We need guidelines concerning what types of children are most likely to profit from this adjunct to more orthodox forms of therapy; we need to develop techniques for making effective use of pets in working with different types of disturbed children. And we need specific information about the kinds of pets best suited for the co-therapist role. Much must be learned about how to train dogs for special psychotherapeutic work with both children and adults.

I should like to see a comprehensive, planned program for the introduction of pets into psychotherapy – in private practice, in homes, in schools, and in residential treatment centers. Such a program would require close cooperation and collaboration between those involved in the treatment of emotionally disturbed children and those concerned with the training of pets. Both groups of professionals would have to learn from each other – and from their four-legged colleagues. A program of this kind would call for careful staffing, extensive training programs, and the expenditure of large sums of money. But I think it would pay big dividends in helping millions of children grow into mentally healthy adults.

SUMMARY

The use of animals in psychotherapeutic work with children or as supportive aides at home may be indicated. A group dynamics encounter is established when the pet is part of the therapeutic constellation. With the pet as a focus, the locus of therapy can be transferred outdoors, providing a wider environment in which to observe and interact with the patient. A pet aide, particularly a dog, may satisfy the child's need for physical contact without arousing in him the fear of undesirable emotional entanglements that accompany contact with humans. It is easier for a child to project some of his unacceptable feelings on to a pet. The animal may also assume different roles to a child. At one time the pet is protective and benevolent, while at others aggressive and malevolent.

A very young animal such as a puppy will help children work through their feelings of helplessness, dependence, need for nurturance and support, as well as aid them in becoming aware of themselves as independent entities. In therapy with older children, the use of a full-grown dog may introduce for consideration problems of protection, domination, the meaning of friendship, love, and responsibility.

Animals, since they have universal appeal, may also be used as a motivating device to promote group cooperation and "esprit de corps" among children. The use of animals in group settings varies, however, from their incidental use to provide a more homelike atmosphere to their direct introduction into the therapy situation. The use of animals in group therapy will depend upon the age of the children involved and the types of animals available and suitable.

Animals can also be used successfully in psychotherapy with adults, as therapists other than this writer have pointed out.

REFERENCES

1. Aschaffenburg, H.: Jackie. Voices, 2(1):75-78, 1966.
2. Austin, A.: A Case Study of an Emotionally Disturbed Child and His

Dog. (An unpublished manuscript.)
3. Browning, E.: Sonnet XLIII. Sonnets from the Portuguese. Edited with notes by W. J. Rolfe. Boston, Lothrop, 1886.
4. Dishon, C. Skeezer.: The canine child therapist. Today's Health, Jan., 1970.
5. Levinson, B. M.: Pets: A special technique in child psychotherapy. Ment Hyg, 48:243-248, 1964.
6. Levinson, B. M.: Pet psychotherapy: The use of household pets in the treatment of behavior disorders of childhood. Psychol Rep, 17:695-698, 1965.
7. Levinson, B. M.: Pet-oriented Child Psychotherapy. Springfield, Thomas, 1969.
8. Levinson, B. M.: Kids are a responsibility: Ask any dog. Dogs, 1(2):14-19, 1970.
9. Quaytman, A.: Animals as aids in child therapy. J Long Island Consultation Ctr, 3:29-35, 1963.
10. Rubin, S.: Personal Communication, 10/12/70.
11. Smith, Kline, and French Psychiatric Reporter, Fall 1969.

Chapter Seven

THE VETERINARIAN AS "THERAPIST"

THE PRAYER OF THE DOG

Lord
I keep watch!
If I am not here
who will guard their house?
Watch over their sheep?
Be faithful?
No one but You and I
understands
what faithfulness is.
They call me "Good dog! Nice Dog!
Words . . .
I take their pats
and the old bones they throw me
and I seem pleased.
They really believe they make me happy.
I take kicks too
when they come my way.
None of that matters
I keep watch!
Lord,
do not let me die
until, for them
all danger is driven away.
                    Amen   (6, p. 17)

I N the course of centuries, a quiet revolution has
occurred in the relationship between man and his domestic
animals. Dogs, cats, and horses once served as man's slaves. They
provided a cheap form of labor that liberated man from certain
drudgery. These animals also acted as man's protectors. Now the
roles have been reversed. The domestic animal has become the pet
which is frequently the privileged, protected member of the
family. Man serves and protects his pets; he tries to prolong their

lives with special diets, vitamins, drug therapy, and even major surgery (12).

Since the relationship between man and his pets has changed, the function of the veterinarian must also be transformed. The veterinarian, for example, is very much interested in "the characteristics and motivations of pet owners who seek veterinary services compared with those that do not" (9, p. 321). He can no longer limit himself solely to safeguarding the physical health of the family pet (7), but must learn to "recognize conflicting emotional attitudes in families" toward pets (14). He must become involved in the mental health of the family whose pet he treats (13). This trend is so inexorable that eventually veterinarians will become members of mental hygiene teams. The problems of interprofessional functions will not be insurmountable. No one group should retain a monopoly on ameliorating the mental health of our population. By working hand in hand and by sharing interdisciplinary knowledge, all service professions can bring much light to rather murky and confused areas.

Since man has neurotic as well as healthy needs, his pets are used to serve both purposes. Highly charged emotional currents are characteristic of the relationship between the pet and his master.

The veterinarian is witness to the complex interplay of personality dynamics in a family which owns a pet. From the behavior of family pets, the veterinarian can sometimes make a diagnosis of the family situation. The pets in a sense mirror the tensions of their adopted families, as we saw in the previous chapter. When pets are subjected to an unusual amount of disappointment and frustration, they may develop the same difficulties as their masters. Modern life places restrictions on both humans and animals, and many animals suffer from psychophysiological ailments.

> A cat with a chronic skin condition. Chronic, I feel, because the nervousness of the owner must be awfully hard for the animal to take. The woman reports that Toby, her male cat, vomited at three o'clock this morning, drank some milk at four o'clock and attempted to sleep a little after that. Even after repeated pleading she insists on taking a watchdog attitude about every movement the animal makes. Anyone's skin would be itchy with such scrutiny (11).

Another veterinarian reports the following case of canine anxiety with somatic manifestations:

A shy, tense, highly nervous male German Shepherd dog was frequently brought to the clinic by a fearful owner for treatment of intractable anal pruritus. Although this patient was a veritable terror at home or in the car, after a few visits to the veterinarian he became quite easily manageable. As a matter of fact, he was soon considered to be *excessively* cooperative.

This huge animal would jump up onto the office table by himself, and, although wild-eyed with fear and rigid with tension, he would readily submit to anal examination, ear cleaning, necessary injections and other routine treatment.

All those procedures however, had to take place with the owner out of the room. This man would bring his dog into the examining room, caution the staff strongly every time about how vicious the animal was, and quickly retreat to the waiting room. He never failed to be astonished at how easily we handled his pet, without tranquilizers, force, muzzles, ropes or other restraining devices.

"Aren't you afraid of him?" he always queried. "I can't go near him." This comment was always made even though the man obviously had no trouble in putting his dog on the leash into his car and driving to the office.

As we grew to know our client better, certain elements of family relationships became clear. The wife and adult daughter of the owner never seemed to have trouble with the animal. Although he was an excellent watch-dog, and threatened and bullied many people, he never actually bit anyone. He was hostile only to the father of the family. Apparently the dog was playing the role of a son in this home — a formidable rival for the affections of two females. Is it too much to ask that we consider this situation a type of "Oedipal" relationship? No evidence to the contrary exists, and analysis of some of the events may serve to confirm the hypothesis.

After one particularly trying visit (for the owner) to the office, the man drew one of our attendants aside, pointed to the dog and said, "Some day when he's well I want to bring him here, have you tie him up for me, put a muzzle on him, and then I can really give him a good beating." Of course, this man never did act out his aggressive feelings, but the verbalized fantasy was so richly satisfying to him that every word was uttered with obvious relish.

The patient himself was affected by the family situation. No lesion or physiological cause could be demonstrated to account for his persistent anal pruritus. Anti-allergy and tranquilizer therapy of many varieties failed to cause alleviation of his symptoms. The possibility was explored that the itching might be psychogenic in origin. Tactful questioning of the owner indicated that the anal pruritus occurred most often during times of family tension or when the dog was not receiving the attention he thought he deserved.

Veterinarians should not, and really do not, often indulge themselves by anthropomorphic history-taking, but unusual cases sometimes require imaginative methods. We suggested that the owner discontinue all topical and systemic medications and concentrate on trying to disrupt the anal itching behavior pattern immediately every time it started. We explained that an annoying inflammatory lesion may have caused the pruritus originally, but that it was now completely healed. The habit pattern which remained, however, could be eradicated only in a non-medical way by conscientious owner cooperation.

At last report this line of treatment has brought some improvement. As soon as the undesirable symptoms appeared, the dog's attention has been diverted by being played with, fed, taken out, spoken to, threatened, cajoled, asked to perform his tricks — in short any type of more acceptable behavior has been enthusiastically encouraged.

Such success, some critics may argue, is too dearly bought. After all, the dog is clearly the victor in the struggle for family dominance.

Yet is this really too high a price for an owner to pay? By indulging the dog the family has acquired an additional member (a surrogate son) whom they jointly share, yet possess totally, whose biological functions they control completely, and who will never grow up, get married and leave home to start a family of his own. Almost certainly, in fact, the dog will predecease every other family member. In the light of such an analysis, is the price really too high? And shouldn't the owners themselves make the decisions to pay or not to pay?

The veterinary clinician who is willing to give some thought to the emotional interplay between the pet dog and the individual members of the family with whom it lives, does not often have to wonder, "Why do these people put up with such a monster?" The explanation is often painfully evident. So is the reason why ordinary training by negative conditioning would neither be attempted by this family, nor would be successful were it to be tried under external pressure.

The family and its pet are in a delicate balance, an emotional symbiosis, which seems to be salutary for all. To demand that the balance be changed so as to conform to norms satisfactory for others, may indeed be more damaging than to encourage its dynamic continuance (4).

In his treatment of the pet, the veterinarian must at all times be aware of the meaning of the pet to its owner, particularly if the latter is an aged person. The following case is illustrative of this point:

The most dramatic of all is the case of the widow aged approximately 60, who suspected that something was definitely wrong with her dog who had been limping for two months. She had not wanted to present the animal for fear my diagnosis and prognosis would be too severe. The Collie dog involved was 13 years old. For 12 years she had shared with her husband the joy of having the animal around. Now this dog was all she had left in the world. Before I had even made any diagnosis she was crying. Sadly she talked about her lost husband and how he had loved the dog. The diagnosis of an osteogenic sarcoma of the left frontal leg and its eventual fatal outcome was more than she could accept. When she finally calmed down, I explained about the futility of surgery. My honest opinion was that the animal was suffering, and that euthanasia would be the kindest gesture. She refused and kept the animal on sedatives for another six weeks. She finally, after many tear-filled conversations on the telephone, consented to have the animal put to sleep (11).

Another veterinarian (3) describes a case involving a cat owned by a mother and daughter who shared a household:

The perceptive clinician soon recognizes the cat as a living symbol of an ongoing struggle for dominance between mother and daughter. It is regrettable that both protagonists regard the cat as the same symbolic persons (at different times, of course) — husband, lover, protector, son, heir, companion, friend or whatever the case may be. If the animal could symbolize a different character to each of the ladies, their competitiveness might be diminished. But a mother and daughter, both widowed and living together, hold strange, unconscious rivalries toward each other. Direct verbal assault is unacceptable, so expression of these feelings is often focused on something or someone else, in this case the cat.

For instance, in bringing a not-too-sick Choo-choo to the veterinarian for an a.m. to p.m. inpatient examination and treatment, the daughter has succeeded in depriving her mother of the cat's company for that whole day (3, p. 46).

This veterinarian has also described the "Teddy Bear Syndrome," a situation in which the pet owner has high dependency needs which he or she is using the animal to satisfy.

In a typical case, a loving pair enters the animal clinic — a maiden lady or perhaps a widow with her Yorkshire Terrier or minipoodle — entwined together physically and emotionally in obvious mutual interdependency. The "body language" here is apparently love, but in truth it is really fear — fear of separation. Although the picture may look like love, and certainly a basic element of love is no doubt present, the predominant emotion nevertheless is fear. There may be, in fact, too much fear and not enough love, for the mental health of both pet and owner.

Veterinarians benefit from analyzing such a situation by recognizing and treating the relationship for what it really is, not for what it seems to be on the surface. An owner such as this, for instance, often requires high level persuasion before consenting to treatment of the animal for its own good, pleading she "loves my Skippy too much to put him through" a minor dental procedure or radiography. On the other hand, she will readily agree to treatment if her own fears are noted and understood by the clinician. Thus a veterinarian who sees only the superficial side of the relationship, i.e. the professed "love," might argue: "Mrs. Jones, if you really loved your dog, you'd be happy to let me extract those foul teeth of hers." He might ponder why such arguments fail so often. A more analytically oriented colleague might take a different approach and say: "I realize you're afraid for Skippy to have her teeth taken care of, but dentistry is quite safe these days and she'll only be away from you a few hours." In this way, he makes contact with the sensitive part of the conflict in the owner's mind, hopefully sets it to rest, and enjoys a much higher rate of consent (4).

"The veterinarian is often the first to notice symptoms of emotional disturbance, when observing the behavior of people toward pets" (1).

One such situation is that of a well-to-do society lady whose hobby is the rehabilitation of stray cats. She picks up a stray cat every week, lavishes the best of care on it, and then looks around for several days for someone to adopt her protege. When she fails to find a charitable soul, instead of bringing the cat to an adoption service, she takes it to a veterinarian to be destroyed, as she feels it is heartless to leave the cat to its former homeless and forlorn existence.

Camuti and Alexander (8, pp. 24-26) recount the following story of emotional disturbance in the owner of a "pet" brought to them for treatment:

I had come to the end of my office hours when George, my assistant and general handyman, stepped into the consultation room and told me a woman was outside. I asked him to show her in.

She was past middle age, well dressed, carrying a small cardboard box.

"It's about my dog," she said, sitting down nervously beside my desk. "I live alone," she went on, naming an excellent apartment house, "and he's my only companion."

I asked whether she had brought the dog with her.

"Oh yes," she said, "he's right here."

She unknotted the string around the box. I looked inside and saw a small dog, a Boston terrier. There wasn't anything wrong with him. There couldn't have been. The dog was made of papier-mâché.

"Well," I said, wondering what her answer would be, "what seems to be the trouble?"

"The trouble?" she said indignantly. "You're a veterinarian. Can't you see for yourself?"

"I don't want to jump to conclusions," I said.

"The trouble," she said, "is ticks."

"Ticks?"

"Of course! They're all over the little fellow!"

I took another look. "Now that you mention it," I told her, "I see them very clearly."

"He's very uncomfortable," she said.

"I can imagine," I agreed. I poured a little mineral oil into a bottle. "Here," I said, "put some of this on him every day."

She thanked me, put the bottle in her purse, tucked the box under her arm and left the office.

A few days later, George announced that she was back.

"That medicine didn't help," she said sadly. "There's only one thing to do. You'll have to put him to sleep."

"If you're sure that's what you want," I said.

I took the dog from her. After she left, I put the toy on my shelf and forgot about it.

About a week afterwards, George came into the office. "She's here again," he whispered. "In the waiting room."

"Tell her I'm busy," I said.

"I did. But she won't go away."

I left my patient and went to the waiting room.

"Ah, there you are, doctor," she said. "I came to see you about my dog. The one you put to sleep. How is he?"

Her question brought some puzzled looks to the faces of the people in the waiting room. One man put down his newspaper and stared at us.

"Why ..." I began. "He's fine ... He's sitting on my shelf right now."

"Wonderful," she said. "I've decided to take him back."

"I'll get him for you," I told her.

The man with the newspaper jumped from his chair and bolted from the office. The other clients looked as if they might do the same thing.

Later, after I had given back the toy dog, George shook his head in dismay. "It's bad enough taking care of the real animal," he said, "I don't want any more of the cardboard kind.

"It was my fault in the beginning," I said.

"Yeah," George agreed. "You shouldn't have given him that medicine."

"I guess not," I said, "Mineral oil isn't a damned bit of good for ticks."

While most people can enjoy the friendship of pets while maintaining very satisfying human relationships, there are some individuals who have lost contact with people and distrust them. Such people may adopt numerous dogs and cats because these animals can be trusted. Since these animals represent a lifeline for their owners, the latter engage the services of a veterinarian to protect the health of their pets. A veterinarian who is aware of the emotional implications of such behavior can tactfully suggest to these isolates that they join a club where they will find other people with a similar interest in pets. By exchanging information with other pet owners they can decrease their veterinary fees by taking over some of the animals' care themselves.

Occasionally, the veterinarian meets homosexuals who give their pets ambiguous names. The sexual perversions practiced with animals may also come to his attention. By using tact, the veterinarian may influence such people to seek therapeutic assistance.

Parents often turn to veterinarians for advice when the child doesn't live up to his promise to feed, walk, and brush a dog they have acquired on his insistence. Mothers and fathers who find themselves burdened with (and resentful of) these additional tasks frequently turn to the veterinarian with their complaints. One hears an irate mother say, "I don't know what to do. Johnny promised to take care of the dog but he doesn't. Shall I punish Johnny? Shall I get rid of the dog?" Losing a dog under such circumstances may represent one more failure to an already failure-ridden and frustrated youngster. It may also produce intense guilt and anxiety. It would be helpful for everyone concerned if the veterinarian were sufficiently trained in the behavioral sciences to recognize the complex factors operating in those situations. Or (and these two possibilities are not mutually exclusive) he could be a cooperating member of a mental hygiene team and in this capacity make the appropriate referral for therapeutic aid to the troubled family.

A pet enlarges the scope of a child's experiences in ways both happy and sad. Johnny may derive rich feelings of gratification and success when Fido has been a good student, when the boy's friends beg to play with Fido, when Fido wins a blue ribbon at a local pet show. A boy who finds it hard to compete socially, in school, or in sports, may acquire through his pet a first positive insight into the joys, rather than the pains, of competition. Often it is the veterinarian who has made the suggestion and given Johnny the advice on how to prepare his dog for the show. Experiences of success in early childhood are the foundation stones of our ability to resolve life's problems. The success Johnny experiences with his dog can provide enough real satisfaction to prevent the boy from seeking imaginary satisfactions in a fastasy world.

Even the crises and suffering that a boy who is very attached to his pet can experience provide important growth and learning experiences. When a pet is critically ill, Johnny knows severe distress and anxiety. The death of a pet, as we have seen, can be a rehearsal on an attenuated scale for the suffering we all must face at the death of someone near and dear. However, this brush with harsh reality may be an experience which a particular youngster cannot cope with alone. Should the dead pet have been the only source of security and love for the boy, the shock may be seriously upsetting. Like' the many clergymen who now receive training in psychology in order to be of greater service to their congregants, the veterinarian needs special training to provide the most skillful help in such situations.

Veterinarians are generally sensitive to distress signals emanating from a troubled child. Unfortunately, the veterinarian rarely acts on these hunches because he feels that they are not his professional responsibility. For example, the veterinarian may be aware that a dog is being dominated and very roughly handled by a child. The child may even administer improper medications to the dog, insisting that the dog is ill. This child may assume an air of great knowledge and authority, challenge the veterinarian, and argue with his parent. The veterinarian may be fully aware of the fact that this boy is merely acting out, through his dog, his need to convince himself and others of his own importance.

Occasionally the veterinarian may be called upon to treat a pet in a family where the mother lavishes all her attention on the pet but neglects her husband and the children, toward whom she is probably angry and bitter. The change in the mother's behavior since the acquisition of the pet may have been so gradual that the family has barely noticed it. They merely feel that she is "ornery." With the proper training, the veterinarian would be able to institute the first measures of help and might thus even abort an incipient mental illness.

Parents sometimes wish to get rid of a pet that is old and too much trouble to care for. Their child, however, is very much attached to this pet and does not want to lose it. In such cases, the parent frequently brings the pet to a veterinarian and asks him to tell the child that the pet is incurably ill and should therefore be put to sleep. The veterinarian, instead of accepting such a task, can discuss quite frankly with the parents the meaning of the pet to the child, stressing that by taking good care of the old pet the parents can teach the child respect for the infirmities of age. By their actions they can also reassure their child that when he is ill, he is not worthless and fit for destruction. Similarly, when the cost of curing a pet bird may be ten dollars and the cost of replacing him two dollars, the veterinarian should emphasize not the market value of a healthy new bird but the sentimental value of the old bird and its meaning in the child's fantasies and daydreams.

Occasionally, upon the recovery of a child from a physical illness or accident, the child is afraid to engage in normal activities although he is well enough to do so. This condition, unless treated early, can lead to invalidism. The veterinarian might well step in at this point, after consultation by the parents, to discuss with the child the possibility of acquiring a pet. Becoming the owner of an active and wished-for animal can provide the child with an incentive to stop playing the sick role and become active in caring for his pet.

From time to time, parents leaving for their summer vacation make no provision for their pet or bring him in to be destroyed. Here again, the veterinarian can explain to the parents the meaning to their children of such an action on their part, pointing out that feelings of anxiety may be aroused, while ubiquitous fears of abandonment and thoughts of being "foster children" are strengthened. In the child's mind, his real parents certainly would be kinder than to rid themselves of beloved pets because they were somewhat burdensome.

There is a need for the organization of experimental mental hygiene clinics connected with the practice of veterinary medicine. As pointed out above, a veterinarian treating a pet may become aware of a disturbed home situation or of a child's mistreatment of an animal which points to a possible incipient emotional disorder of a serious nature. Early treatment of such problems is imperative if the outcome is to be a favorable one. A suggestion to the family by the veterinarian that they discuss the problem with a member of the experimental unit attached to the veterinarian's office might be more readily accepted than a referral to a community mental hygiene clinic. There are still too many parents who distrust psychiatric clinics and who see treatment as stigmatizing.

In the experimental mental hygiene clinic, specially trained dogs could serve as "cotherapists" or "seeing-heart" dogs.

Veterinarians could also be responsible for selecting and supervising the training of dogs assigned to residential schools for emotionally disturbed or delinquent children.

Pets should also be selected by the veterinarian to serve as companions for the aged, infirm, and homebound.

In view of the ever-increasing alienation in our society, there will be a growing need for pet animals. However, a critical point may soon be reached where with growing population density, the current practice of permitting household pets to evacuate in the street or park will have to be prohibited. There is currently widespread demand for such legislation. If enacted, this will surely lead to a decrease in the number of pets kept by city dwellers. There will thus be lost a valuable mental hygiene resource along with no doubt considerable diminution in the income of veterinarians.

> Loss of urban space will require greater control of animals, with greater requirements placed on sanitation and regulations. Without proper training and control, they may have to be eliminated from certain parts of urban society (10, p. 1037).

It will thus be necessary for veterinarians to train paraprofessionals who will condition animals in their formative period to utilize specially constructed sanitary facilities in the home or neighborhood.

SUMMARY

Only a few general aspects of the role of the veterinarian as a mental hygienist have been touched upon. The many specific ways in which veterinarians can exercise their mental hygiene functions will have to be elaborated by members of the profession. The delineation of this role will undoubtedly take years of experimentation, observation, and formulation (5). The mental hygienist must work not only to prevent emotional disorders among the minority, but to maintain and reinforce the emotional health of the majority. As an important participating member of a mental hygiene team, the veterinarian will face an analogous situation. He is very often the first professional to observe the aberrant behavior of a pet owner which may provide a clue to the beginning of a mental disorder. He can surmise what pressures are being exerted on the pet and, from them, the emotional pressures under which its master is laboring. The veterinarian who is sensitive to the mental hygiene values of his profession may initiate a referral to a colleague which will help prevent the development of a major emotional problem.

The veterinarian can be of particular help in mitigating stress between parents and children over the treatment of a pet by family members.

Research and experimental approaches to the use of the veterinarian's services in a mental hygiene capacity are much needed.

REFERENCES

1. Antelyes, J.: The psychology of pet feeding. Vet Med Small Anim Clin, 62:249-251, 1967.
2. Antelyes, J.: The petside manner. Vet Med Small Anim Clin, 62:1155-1159, 1967.
3. Antelyes, J.: Animal hospital: group communication. Mod Vet Prac,

August, 1969, pp. 42-46.

4. Antelyes, J.: Personal communications, 3/26/71, 8/24/71.
5. Armstead, W. W.: Veterinary education; problems and prospects. J Am Vet Med Assoc, 149:1401-1405, 1966.
6. Bernos de Gasztold, C.: Prayers from the Ark. New York, Viking Press, 1962.
7. Blenden, D. C.: Personal Communications, 4/13/70, 12/10/70.
8. Camuti, L. J., and Alexander, L.: A Park Avenue Vet. New York, Holt, Rinehart and Winston, 1962.
9. Dorn, R. C.: Veterinary medical services: Utilization by dog and cat owners. J Am Vet Med Assoc, 156:321-327, 1970.
10. Gay, W. I.: Opportunities for the veterinary scientist in medical research. J Am Vet Med Assoc, 153:1033-1039, 1968.
11. Krutzmann, W. G. A.: Personal communication, 4/11/67.
12. Levinson, B. M.: The veterinarian and mental hygiene. Ment Hyg, 49:320-323, 1965.
13. Parrish, H. M., Blenden, D. C., and Clayton, F. W.: The veterinarian's role in community health activities. Sci Proc, 100 Annu Meeting, American Veterinary Medical Association.
14. Speck, R. V.: Mental health problems involving the family, the pet and the veterinarian. J Am Vet Med Assoc, 145:150-154, 1964.

Chapter Eight

THE PET IN CARETAKING INSTITUTIONS

> . . . the world, which seems
> To lie before us like a land of dreams,
> So various, so beautiful, so new,
> Hath really neither joy, nor love, nor light,
> Nor certitude, nor peace, nor help for pain;
> And we are here as on a darkling plain
> Swept with confused alarms of struggle and flight,
> Where ignorant armies clash by night.
>
> — Matthew Arnold. *Dover Beach*

CHILD CARE INSTITUTIONS

DUE to a lack of adequate financial support, most residential child care institutions such as foundling hospitals, orphanages, and well-baby wards in general hospitals have an underpaid and poorly trained staff which is unable to give the children in their charge good personal care. "The burden of managing the behavior of children in a residential setting remains to this day a nearly unattempted challenge of great complexity" (5). The attention these children receive is impersonal and is based on a schedule rather than on the individual needs of the child (27). This type of care not only restricts social stimulation, but may also affect the intellectual development of these children, with the result that they are frequently impaired in social responsiveness and language skills, are retarded in mental development, and generally exhibit the behavior of perceptually deprived children. We also know that maternal separation can produce perceptual deprivation and emotional trauma (30).

One study found, for example, that infants six months of age or younger upon entering an institution did not protest when a mother substitute ministered to their needs, whereas babies of seven months or older could already recognize the difference in caretakers in their new surroundings and protested at the change (31).

The importance of very early stimulation for normal child development is well established. Infants who are handled often and are exposed to a variety of sensory stimuli are not only more resistant to stress in adulthood, but are more precocious in their overall development (9) particularly in the psychomotor area (9, 32). Lack of appropriate stimulation during the first 2 years of life may therefore affect the child adversely.

As a result of poor psychological care, institutionalized children often grow up to be hostile and apathetic adults. In the absence of human caretakers who can stimulate these children while still in the crib, we suggest the employment of specially trained dogs who can respond affirmatively to an infant's or toddler's adient responses, thus reinforcing his attempts at social behavior. Play with such dogs would not only increase opportunities for social interaction, but would also provide the child with an opportunity to develop his motor skills.

If possible, the same dog should remain with a child or group of children for the entire period of institutionalization, in order to avoid traumatic feelings of loss. If the child is subsequently placed in a foster home, where he might have difficulty establishing his identity and relating to the foster family (2), having his old pet or a new one with him, to which he can easily and safely relate, is helpful in making the transition.

In certain residential settings, pets have come to be considered a necessity. "It sometimes almost seems as if they should be paid members of the treatment team because of all they add to the interest, life, warmth, and often humor of the group" (2, p. 106).

PETS IN RESIDENTIAL SCHOOLS FOR EXCEPTIONAL CHILDREN

In a preliminary survey of residential schools, we investigated (21): (a) whether children were permitted to own pets or had access to them; (b) what kind of pets these were, (c) who cared for them, and (d) what role the pets played in the residential setting.

We selected a sample of 160 residential and day schools from the Directory for Exceptional Children (6) and mailed questionnaires to 40 schools under each of four categories. After one followup letter, we had a total of 121 replies — a return of 75.6 percent. The returns according to different types of school may be seen in Table VII. Some of the returned questionnaires were incomplete; others contained most interesting comments regarding the role of pets.

Of the 118 schools responding to the item on pet ownership, 48 (40.7%) permitted the children to own pets. The percentage of pet ownership varied with the children's handicap. Whereas only 4 (14.8%) of the schools for the blind and partially sighted permitted children to have pets, 9 (28.1%) of those for the deaf and hard of hearing, 20 (55.5%) of those for the emotionally disturbed and socially maladjusted, and 15 (65.2%) of those for the mentally retarded permitted the children to have pets.

The schools for the mentally retarded that had a census of fewer than 500 children permitted children to own pets significantly more often than those with a census of over 500. This finding was also valid for the schools for the emotionally disturbed and socially maladjusted; in turn the schools that had a census of fewer than 100 children were significantly more tolerant of pets than those having more than 100. Such distinctions did not hold for either the schools for the deaf and hard of hearing or those for the blind and partially sighted.

We did find that in 62 schools of 113 responding to the

TABLE VII

QUESTIONNAIRE RETURNS

Type of School	Number	Percent of Questionnaires Mailed Out
For the mentally retarded	23	57.5
For the blind and partially sighted	30	75
For the deaf and hard of hearing	32	80
For the emotionally disturbed and socially maladjusted	36	90

Taken from B. M. Levinson: Household pets in residential schools (21, p. 411).

pertinent items children also had access to pets belonging either to staff members or to the school. Thus staff and school pets were available to children in 9 schools for the mentally retarded; in 15 schools for the blind and partially sighted; in 18 schools for the deaf and hard of hearing; and in 20 schools for the emotionally and socially maladjusted. In half of the schools the staff cared for the animals; in the other half the children took care of them.

We wanted to learn, more or less incidentally, whether parents were permitted to bring their pets with them when they visited the institutions. Of the 80 (66%) schools that replied to this question, 61 (76%) permitted the parents to bring pets with them when they visited their children.

Table VIII indicates the kinds of pets that are commonly permitted in residential schools. The category "other" includes turtles, baby chicks, ducks, horses, mice, snakes, hawks, game birds, skunk, ocelot, frogs, guinea pigs, insects, white mice, and rats.

Pets, when available, are utilized principally as an educational rather than as a psychotherapeutic tool. Comments from the various schools included the following:

> "Pets are used rather informally to give the child pleasure and satisfaction, something to provide give-and-take affection, learn

TABLE VIII

TYPES OF PETS AVAILABLE ACCORDING TO SCHOOL*

Schools for the

Pets Available	Blind	Deaf	Emotionally Disturbed	Mentally Retarded	Totals
Dog	11	13	14	11	49
Bird	10	6	16	9	41
Fish	8	16	18	7	49
Rabbit or hamster	6	10	10	1	27
Cat	4	5	8	10	27
Other	11	6	8	2	27

*Some schools had more than one type of pet.
Taken from B. M. Levinson (21, p. 412).

responsibility. Some children can learn to relate in time to people using the pet as a wedge or a training ground."

"To gain some understanding of what animals are like, dogs or gerbils in particular, by feeling them, helping to care for them (our children are blind)."

"Classroom work acquaintance with the animal kingdom."

"Pets are kept primarily because the children enjoy them."

"Language training."

"For science experience, sex education."

"Brought in puppies to overcome a child's terror of dogs."

"Companionship for child until he feels more secure and assisting in establishing home-like atmosphere."

One school's questionnaire contained this remark: "We do not believe in the fancy therapy angle." Yet this very school apparently has an excellent pet program. It has "a full-time kennel master and a large husbandry department." Another school, which has a rabbit, cat, and fish, stated, "We do not use pets. . . . We permit but do not encourage pets."

Other schools that either for "practical" reasons or because of state regulations do not keep pets made comments such as the following: "Danger of scratching or biting the children." "No facilities within the living area." "Afraid of rabies or other health problems associated with the use of pets." "Sadistic treatment by youngsters."

Our survey would seen to indicate that most of the sampled residential schools do not permit children to own pets. Even in the schools that favor pets, the animals are not utilized to the fullest possible extent.

There seems to be a sharp division of opinion among various schools concerning how best to meet a child's needs within the residential setting. Fundamental differences in the philosophy of treatment and in the approach to child care express themselves in the attitude toward pets.

It does not seem to be universally acknowledged that children need love objects. Yet many institution children may be depressed, have a poor self-concept, and distrust close relationships as anxiety-provoking and painful because they have no one to love, care for, be protective toward, and have confidence in. In many institutions there is a constant turnover of personnel; the staff may be inadequately trained, impersonal in its care, occasionally not devoted to its tasks, and sometimes brutal and punitive toward the children. On the other hand, too much closeness between a particular staff member and a child may not be wholesome either and may arouse the wrath of other children who resent the favored child. In both situations a pet can be most helpful; it can become the constant companion of a child, one in whom he can confide all his misgivings, heartaches, and pain.

Occasionally a member of the staff "sacrifices" his time off, identifies with the child he cares for, and develops a feeling of possessiveness. This frequently brings about open resentment on the part of the child's parent. A pet, on the contrary, is not seen as a competitor for the child's affection and thus cannot undermine a parent's confidence in herself.

A pet can serve as a source of constant stimulation. Among seriously disturbed children, possession of a pet tends to decrease the need for head-banging, excessive masturbation, rocking, and finger-sucking. When the child finds that he has adequate pleasurable tactile contact and activity, he no longer has to seek these through his own body. The introduction of well-trained pets can also help children to abort early deviations in ego development and can aid in the establishment of favorable relationships with peers and staff persons. Pets can aid children in developing a favorable attitude toward themselves and confidence in others.

Frequently in a residential setting, preparations for sleep are anxiety-provoking. A child who can take his pet to bed with him may be able to avoid this anxiety, for the pet may help ward off the fears and nightmares that disturb sleep.

When pets are permitted to become a part of the therapeutic milieu of a residential school, therapy becomes reality-oriented, with a consequent strengthening of the child's ego. A child should be permitted to select his pet, and the pet should be considered the child's own. The pet should be allowed to sleep in the same room with the child, to eat its meals with him, and even to attend school with him.

In order to clarify the role of the pet and to utilize more fully this new means of treatment, it is necessary to educate para-medical staff — attendants and others — concerning their role and what behavioral changes can be expected in the children. In this connection, it would be advisable for members of the staff who have no love objects of their own to also obtain pets; for as Freud and Burlingham have pointed out in another context, ". . . the children should on no account serve as an outlet for the uncontrolled, and therefore unrestrained, emotions of the adult" (8).

We must remember that the cardinal principle of residential treatment is that every experience of the child should be therapeutic and lead to a speedier return to the community. Residential treatment should be flexible, variable, and sometimes unpredictable, like life in a normal community. However, living in a residential school, with its usual emphasis on regularity, conformity, and undeviating routine, may mean that the child is deprived of the possibility of making small, everyday decisions. He may find it impossible to discover a meaningful activity within the confines of what he is permitted to do. He then finds that he is completely dependent on others and must do certain things in an undeviating manner, whether he likes them or not. Finding time hanging heavily on his hands, he becomes bored, and life as a whole loses its meaning. In the course of his stay in the institution the child may find himself drained of all energy he needs for rehabilitation. Under such circumstances, what could be better than a pet to help break the deadly routine and in the process become the child's best friend?

Careful observations should be made of how different children with varying emotional and/or physical disorders handle their pets. These questions may then be explored: What limits should be set in the use of pets? Should pets be denied to children who transgress the limits?

A variety of pets to meet the different psychological needs of children should be considered a requirement in any child-treatment facility if such a facility is to be concerned not just with the physical, but also with the emotional needs of the child.

1. They should relate equally well to all children and adults and not tend to become a one-master dog.

2. They should be sensitive and yet be able to take rough play in their stride, whether from children or adults, without resorting to biting or withdrawal.

3. They should be good looking, intelligent, alert, inquisitive, of

a happy disposition, affectionate, and willing to please and to serve.

4. They should know a few tricks such as fetching, "shaking hands," "dancing," and begging.

5. They should obey the therapist's orders implicitly and be able to remember these orders for quite a while.

The Pet and the Habilitation of the Retarded In a Nonresidential Setting

Gores (11, 12) reports an experiment using mentally retarded boys and girls to maintain a pet shop. These youngsters, whose IQs ranged from 48 to 85, did an excellent job in caring for the animals and running the store. The only functions they could not handle satisfactorily were making change and answering questions about raising and caring for pets. These retardates were happy in their work, were partially self-supporting, and felt that they were making a contribution to society. As such they began to regard themselves and each other as desirable individuals.

An Experimental Day Center and School For Mentally Retarded Children

Anyone who has worked with the mentally retarded is aware of how the latter evaluate themselves, particularly those whose intelligence is closer to the normal range. Young retardates feel inferior, unappreciated, unloved, and generally worthless (7, 19). We must offer these youngsters a realistic opportunity to develop feelings of self-worth, respect for themselves and for others like them.

Today, the achievement of self-support marks a person immediately as competent and self-sufficient. Our mentally retarded youths have absorbed this evaluation by society and have made it a part of their self-concept. Those who cannot become self-supporting live perpetually under a cloud of inferiority, poor self-regard, and hopelessness. The mentally retarded person begins to feel that he cannot do anything worthwhile, retreats into helplessness, and does not even participate in those activities he can do well (20).

To help mentally retarded children prepare for productive, independent lives, special schooling is required (17, 26). An experimental day center and school can give the child an opportunity to establish good work habits, become accustomed to the discipline of work, and learn to regard himself as a worthwhile human being. Pets would be the major means for providing training. The staff of such a center would have to be very carefully selected. Only those who liked pets and did not consider them an intolerable burden could be engaged. The staff would have to undergo an orientation and training period to learn how best to work with retarded children and to maximize the therapeutic value of pets.

Prior to enrollment in such a program, the child would undergo psychological assessment to determine his assets and liabilities. This would help the staff determine the child's needs, his attitudes toward the staff and toward animals, and how much responsibility the child could be expected to assume at the outset for the care of a pet. It is anticipated that in such a setting, the animal would become the child's friend and not a burden to be resented, hurt, or cast off as soon as possible.

The pet would be introduced gradually to a child who was willing to take care of him, the amount of responsibility assigned varying with the child's ability to shoulder it. Children and pets would be under close supervision at all times. Eventually, the children would learn how to feed, groom, and exercise their pets.

There is a need nowadays for competent assistants in pet shops, animal hospitals, and pet grooming salons. Training of the kind described above should help many retarded children eventually to become employable in such capacities. Skills of this nature will not be automated in the foreseeable future, and well-trained retardates can compete on an equal basis with other workers in this field.

Pets can also help the mentally retarded adolescent or adult make the transition from the protected environment of a rehabilitation center to that of an everyday work situation. This is illustrated in the following case:

L. is a 16-year-old retarded girl, classified as trainable (although the project teacher expressed some doubt as to the validity of this classification), who took part in our project to teach domestic tasks in the home of a suburban housewife. L. Was somewhat talkative on the trips to and from her training home, yet exhibited some initial shyness. In this particular home there was a pet Labrador retriever of good size that L. promptly fell in love with. She exhibited no fear of the dog, and enjoyed using her work break to play with it. The dog learned to recognize L., and also seemed to enjoy the play. It seemed that in this situation, the presence of the animal and the "bond" that was established almost immediately with it by L. eased her into a new situation that might have been more traumatic without the animal — although we cannot be certain of this latter assumption.

In any event, girl and dog immediately hit it off, and L. persisted in regarding her time with the animal as a high point of her work experience (24).

Pet Fairs and Dramatics with Mentally Retarded School Children

Pet fairs and pet dramatic shows in either residential or day schools help socialize the retarded child and capitalize on his strengths. The child can have a role in the preparation of the pet fair or the production of the play in accordance with his ability and physical stamina. A play written by the children and the teacher can maximize the participation of the pet and give each child a role which can help him make a better social and emotional adjustment. For example, if the child is aggressive, we may give him a part which permits him to drain off his aggressiveness into socially useful channels. If he tends to withdraw, the participation of the pet will give him an opportunity to be in the limelight without being too aware of it.

There are also other desirable by-products. The social cohesiveness of the parent group will be immeasurably increased when the parents come to see their children's productions. There may also be a greater acceptance of their children by the parents when the latter realize that in spite of handicaps the children are able to turn in a socially acceptable performance.

Even a cursory exposure to pets is quite helpful to retarded as well as to emotionally disturbed children, as can be seen from the following description of a school trip:

THE CHILDREN

David L.   CA 14.4; IQ 62

Disturbed, retarded and delinquent. Repeatedly suspended from previous schools for severely aggressive behavior, chronic lying, stealing etc.; many social skills, including speaking vocabulary, at approximately normal level; severely over-weight ($5'$ - 175lb.)

John K.   CA 13.3; IQ 50

Can speak, but very rarely does; good gestural language and comprehension; stubborn when crossed, at which time frequently resorts to throwing (inappropriate) things; a great tease with a good sense of humor.

Nelson R.   CA 12.4; IQ 64

Generally gentle, considerate and cooperative, reflecting the un-usual warmth and understanding he gets at home. Robert has a dog, which has given him an occasional nip when he played a bit roughly, but without any "hard feelings" being harbored on either side. Robert is somewhat more insecure and fearful than his development and home-life warrant.

Richard M.   CA 9.2; IQ 55

Childhood schizophrenia. Writing and speaking vocabulary are near grade level (with a few strange lapses): he taught himself by watching TV. Didn't speak until he was 5. When he joined our class, he had almost no other academic skills, i.e., numbers, colors, geometic shapes etc. It seemed apparent that he has used writing and drawing (which he does very well) to protect himself from failure in most other learning situations. Fearful of almost any new experience, he withdraws, giggles, runs about, or hides when writing and drawing are denied him. Rarely expresses his feelings, especially his fears.

Martin M.   CA 8.11; IQ 41

Childhood schizophrenia and autism. Home background extremely bad until the father remarried two years ago. Martin has begun saying a few isolated words (appropriately) within the last few months; has shown an almost driving desire to learn (numbers, colors, how to write etc.) within the last two months. In September he was considered "uncontainable" and his previous school had to keep a lock on the door. Fearful of many things, especially of the sight or even sound of a dog; extremely destructive; broke windows, light fixtures, etc., and threw these out of doors or windows. Especially prone to throwing things (bottles, cans, etc.) under wheels of moving cars when outside, or to crushing or stamping on things in class. By

June, he was trusted to go to the toilet alone, to use the phonograph and other valuable equipment, to work with tools (hammer, saw, etc). Almost all observable negative behaviors were minimal by June, and even the sight of a dog no longer sent him into blind panic.

Jerry S.   CA 7.9; IQ 44

Chronic brain syndrome. Generally highly distractible, and unfocused. Almost constant flow of "excess energy," as evidenced by small random shaking of the fingers and feet, and high-pitched chattering or emitting of sounds. However, with strong encouragement and direction Jerry has shown a capacity to concentrate for limited periods, and has a good deal more "academic" knowledge than we had suspected.

THE TRIP

We were allowed 2 "charter-bus" trips for the school year. I planned this Animal Nursery trip for my class, as well as one to the Staten Island Zoo, as a sort of culmination of my year-long effort to encourage gentleness and compassion, reduce anxieties and fears, and lessen aggressive and hurtful behavior. The Zoo trip was scheduled for the second-to-last Friday of the school year, and the Nursery for the last Friday (on Fridays the children are usually aware of the coming week-end, and are somewhat "wound-up"; a special "treat" often provides a constructive outlet for this extra energy). One other class decided to join us for the Zoo excursion, and the whole school came along to the Nursery.

The trip to the Zoo was a "first" for several of the children, and there were the expected reactions; some fearfulness, some hyperactivity, and a fairly short interest-span. Since the animals were all out of reach, the children were of course limited to primarily visual stimuli, and rather over-whelming stimuli at that. This was not the best learning situation for brain-injured and disturbed children, but they remained quite concentrated for about an hour, showing particular interest in the animals that moved rather slowly but rhythmically, such as the pacers (tigers, etc.) the swimmers (alligators, turtles and otters) and the large birds. The gorilla frightened almost all of them, no doubt by his abrupt movements and loud grunts, and also his size and possibly threatening appearance. The virtually non-moving snakes were generally ignored, as were most of the very small animals. We broke for a picnic lunch for an hour, and then went back for a second look at animals of the children's choosing. The alligators, birds and otters got the nod. After about 15-20 minutes most of the children were quite ready to leave. It was a hot day, there were quite a few other (normal) children there, and several remarked on the "smells" inside. On the whole, the trip seemed quite rewarding to them, and we did have several chances during the following week to verify that they remembered some of the animals.

The Good Mother Animal Nursery is a small, not-too-clean, over-crowded and rather unprepossessing commercial enterprise. The animals were in very small cages or in open pens. The space between cages is narrow, and quite a few children were already there when our 50 descended on the (fortunately prepared) proprietor. It was smelly, crowded, hot and humid, but none of this mattered. My assistant teacher took two children (Richard and Martin), while Mrs. M., a mother who had come along as a volunteer, took Jerry. A teacher from another school had also come along as a volunteer, and she took charge of David, while I had John. Since it was soon apparent that both David and John would require a minimum of supervision, I was fairly free to circulate and stay with each of the children for a bit.

The Nursery sells prepared nursing bottles of "formula" and paper cups of dry food which the children may feed to all the animals. There was one large, open pen with puppies of fair size and stamina, about 3-5 months old, all quite eager to be played with and fed. The pen was of chicken-wire, and only about 2 feet high, so that the children could easily reach in or over to pet and feed the animals. There were perhaps 15 pups in this pen, and it was the prime attraction for David and Nelson in particular. There were also rows and rows of individual wire cages about the size and type of dairy bottle holders, each containing one quite young puppy. Several other pens held young pigs, calves, goats, and sheep. There were also a llama in an enclosed cage, some coyotes and other more "exotic" animals in very fine · mesh cages (which meant that the bottles couldn't be pushed through so the animals were largely ignored), and a slew of kittens and cats, also (sensibly) in fine wire mesh cages. Since these had pans of milk continually available there wasn't much chance that they would be attracted by the children's bottles, though several attempts were made to entice them. Monkeys were kept in individual cages bearing a sign, obviously largely ignored, requesting, "Please do not bottle feed." The monkeys apparently reach out and snatch the bottles from the childrens' hands, tear up the nipples and drink the milk in a few quick gulps. They are also rather rambunctious, and can be mean. There were also some bunnies in a small pen on the floor (the only animals that the children were allowed to pick up, although none of our children did), a few cages with assorted birds, and a few glass-enclosed terrariums with Tarantula spiders and other "exotica," also largely ignored.

The place was soon cleared of almost all the other children, probably more by accident than design. They had served a good purpose for us, however, since their example was an encouragement to our more fearful children. Within a relatively short time all the other classes from our school also left for the other pleasures of the area, and for the last hour or so of our stay we had the place virtually to ourselves (6 children and 4 adults). All the adults were highly enthusiastic about the Nursery, which was, I think, very instrumental in encouraging the children to stay for so long without losing interest. In discussing the trip afterwards with several teachers of the other classes, I found that most of them had been put off by the crowds, smells, heat, etc., and had consequently encouraged their classes to leave rather quickly. Also, few of their children were prepared to pay for the bottles and feed, preferring to spend any money they had on the rides etc. that they went on to. Our class, on the other hand, spent almost two hours at the Nursery, not one child asking to leave or showing any lessening of interest during that time. There were almost no "management" problems of any kind (with the exceptions noted below). This length of attention-span was remarkable evidence in itself of the success of the trip.

Individual Responses

David

For almost the first time in the month I had worked with him, David showed a gentleness and consideration that was quite touching. When the "mother" dog (in a separate pen) snapped at Jerry, who was rather determined that she take a drink, David was upset, and warned the others, "Shouldn't feed him (sic) because he's bad . . . just feed the good ones." Again, when he saw a monkey with a bobby pin in his mouth, he ran to the proprietor (without result, unfortunately) to warn him, "The monkey's going to choke to death. Take it away from him." David did not act completely out of character, however. Although he was very gentle and considerate with all the animals, he also managed to snitch some of the dry feed while he had the owner otherwise diverted. He also went up to other children (the "normal" ones who were there for the first half-hour or so) with offers to help feed the animals. He did this so nicely and with such apparent good-will, that it took several repetitions before we recognized his ulterior motive. He left each child he had so "helped" with his almost empty bottle, and went on to feed other animals with his newly-acquired full one. He never tried to palm off an empty bottle, however; until we stopped his enterprise he would seek out another victim when his bottle still had an inch or two left in it. The only animal he showed any fear of was the llama, and after I fed that animal a few times he did make a rather gingerly attempt to do the same. David talked about the trip during the remaining few days of school and cried when I put him on the bus the last day. This really upset me; apparently we had finally gotten through to this child . . . and too late.

John

John was enchanted from the start, and wanted to feed every animal, even trying to get the birds to drink from the bottle. He was quite vexed that the kittens had their own supply, and kept dragging me back for another try at enticing them to try his bottle, finally succeeding with a couple. He also bottle-fed the monkeys until the owner pointed out the somewhat inconspicuous sign. After that, although he was tempted, he would look at me and then point to the sign, shaking his head and saying "noo." He had been given my class keys (on a thong, the "symbol of office" that all of the children loved to wear). At one point one of the more adventurous monkeys reached out and grabbed them so hard that the hook broke, and the monkey managed to get most of the keys into his mouth. We called the owner to our aid, but since this monkey was rather "mean," we couldn't retrieve them (the owner subsequently mailed them to me when the monkey tired of them and dropped them). Each time we went by the monkey's cage after that, John held his bottle firmly out of reach and stuck his tongue out at the offender. He quickly found out how to open the small cages so that he could feed the pups more easily, but he made no effort to pick them up, although he did like petting them while they fed. He reluctantly stopped opening the cages when I told him that the pups might fall to the floor and get hurt or lost. He was also delighted to discover that the bottle would remain balanced when pushed through the mesh on the top of the cage. With the bottle in that position the pups had to stand on their hind legs to reach it, keeping their balance by holding on to the nipple with their front paws as they drank. John watched this performance with all the smug satisfaction of a successful circus trainer. He was rather more verbal than usual all day, and was particularly pleased with a song we made up to the tune of the Farmer in the Dell: "The monkey ate the keys, the monkey ate the keys, etc." The last two days of school he mentioned several animals by name when we talked about the trip.

Nelson

Since he has a dog, Nelson was quite free with the pups and very delighted right from the start. He was particularly happy with the larger pups in the front pen, as he could pet them while they fed. He was concerned that some were getting more than others, and made a special point of trying to feed those which seemed to be getting less, pushing the others away (quite gently), saying, "No, you've had some" etc . . . He says "I'm afraid" to most things, as he did here with all the larger animals, although I finally got him to pet the calves and feel their budding horns. He carefully avoided going down the aisle that led him near the llama's cage, but did so toward the end of the stay, when he wanted to get to some other animal. He also finally fed the pigs and sheep and goats and calves, remaining apprehensive of the big dog. His attitude seemed almost "maternal," and I think he would have gone right into the pen with the pups if allowed to do so. He kept saying, "Aren't they cute?" and "Not the big ones" (referring to other animals, not the pups). Both Nelson and David tried to guess what "breed" the pups were (they were mostly "X"), and when Nelson asked "is it a he or a she?" David said, "It's a *dog.*"

Richard and Martin

Both Richard and Martin were afraid at the beginning, Richard perhaps more so than Martin. Both held on to Leon's hands very tightly, but neither made any attempt to bolt or showed that they wanted to leave. They just didn't want to be left on their own for the first hour or so. At first, both of them stood as well back from any cage as the very limited space allowed. Very gradually, following Leon's example as well as that of the other children, both boys began to act less fearful, and finally, with strong encouragement, they fed the smallest pups which were entirely enclosed. They kept a tight hold on Leon none the less until about the last half-hour, when they finally dropped his hands. Leon observed that they both seemed very proud of being able to do this, and went about on their own after that with "Look at me . . . I can do it by myself" expressions. Neither child was afraid of the llama or the other completely caged animals; both seemed to like the calves best, perhaps because they were relatively slow-moving compared to most of the other penned animals and their pens were high enough to fence them in almost completely. Moreover, Leon admitted that they were his favorites. Martin was finally encouraged to pet a calf, but avoided the mouth area, giving the rear end a pat "to prove he could." Then he and Richard fed the pigs, who were lower than the top of their pens, and also slow-moving and quiet. Neither boy liked the monkeys, with their fingers reaching outside the cages, who jumped about so actively and made such noise. They did not seem afraid of the kittens or the birds (all completely enclosed) and Martin even tried to reach into the bird cage. After each of these children had become secure enough to let go of the teacher's hand, they gradually edged in closer to the various cages; Martin finally stood very close to the cows, fascinated (it was then that he was finally persuaded to pet one) and Richard tried to reach into the cage of a small, golden-colored puppy. Both boys then began to move about quite freely, feeding the puppies in the enclosed cages (never the ones in open pens), the pigs and the calves. Martin even managed the courage to pet a puppy! Though Richard didn't say much about the trip, either at school during the last three days or at home, his mother reported that several days afterward he drew pictures of a cow, a monkey and the "dog-house" for his brothers and sister. A day or two after the trip Martin added "monkey" to his vocabulary.

Jerry

Jerry was excited from the moment we entered the Nursery until we left. He named almost all of the animals correctly for Mrs. M. (as he had at the Zoo). He ran about fairly freely from the start and never showed fear of any of the animals. When he saw John open a cage he wanted to do the same, but he and Nelson both easily accepted the idea that the pups might be hurt or lost, and stopped. Jerry also wanted to get into the open pens with the animals; he rubbed the faces of the calves, pigs, sheep, goats, and puppies, and fed all of them that would accept the food. His infantilism revealed itself only in that he frequently took "nips" from the bottle himself (apparently without ill effects, though Mrs. M. was somewhat worried about this). He did not throw himself to the floor at any time, or indulge in any of his other "baby tricks," and although he kept up a fairly steady flow of chatter, it was meaningful; I don't recall hearing at any time the high-pitched sound he habitually makes, and when I had a chance to be with him as we left, I noticed that his fingers were still. This was an incredibly long period of concentrated attention for Jerry and he did have one long moment of crying and throwing himself on the ground shortly after we left. He was talked out of this fairly easily, however, and stayed calm the rest of the day.

Except for Bruce's minimal reaction to the monkey's taking the keys, none of the children showed any hurtful behavior toward any of the animals. The enthusiasm of the four adults contributed, no doubt, to the pleasure and "staying-power" of the children. After two hours indoors they might well have "acted up" a bit when we went out onto the sand for our lunch, but they waited patiently while Mrs. M. went for hot-dogs, and then sat down quietly to eat them. Martin just had to let off a bit of steam by throwing one bottle (there were dozens lying about everywhere); happily it caused no harm. When we headed back toward the bus, he carried the picnic hamper, walking by himself several yards ahead of us, stopping and waiting for us to catch up at corners etc . . . He was obviously terribly proud of being allowed this freedom and responsibility. On the way we passed a carousel, and decided to give the children one last treat. John was afraid to get on a horse, and sat in one of the stationary carriages, but the others climbed up on horses. We were surprised at Martin and Richard especially, and waited carefully to hold them or help them off when the horses started to move up and down. Although both were apparently surprised, neither was afraid, and Leon dropped their hands and got up on the horse beside them. All except John (who was more interested in the little ferris wheel) were giggling, and reluctant to leave when the ride was over (18).

Not all retarded children receive care of the quality revealed in the above narrative. Sometimes the only friend and protector such a child has is his dog.

Arthur was a sad sight; academically retarded (he couldn't read, barely wrote, poor attention span, etc.), he had bags under his eyes, wore the same clothes every day, was thrown out of the apartment by his mother, had no close friends either in or out of school, and spent much of the time stabbing pencils through rubber animals and growling while doing this. He was reported being seen wandering around the neighborhood (junkie and wino infested) at four in the morning. What he did have was a dog. He shared whatever food he had with this fairly large, mangy-looking dog. The dog licked him. The class would meet Arthur's dog. They would stand around the car saying to me, "Better watch out, he don't like strangers. We could sic him on you — but we won't." With the dog they were his friends. When the others ran to wherever they were going, Arthur would be still, stroking his dog, feeding him his cookies or whatever he and the boys had saved from their lunch (25).

Pets in Day Care Centers

Day care centers, in which very young children spend many hours away from their mothers at a time when both warm personal care and intellectual stimulation are crucial to their emotional and cognitive development, can benefit greatly from the use of animals in their programs. One agency which has found pets useful in a variety of ways has described the role of its animals as follows:

Our Centers are extended day programs for young children, and having animals is one of the strongest features of our program. . . . Many little people who have come in with varying emotional problems (and there are a great many in day care) were able to relate first to the animals before they could begin interacting with other children and other adults.

The commonest problem we encounter, of course, is separation anxiety. This is usually overcome quickly by diversion to the animals.

We have about 125 children in our extended day centers. Very often a child comes in, maybe a first venture from home. He clings to his mother — is perhaps overwhelmed by all the children and activities. An immediate diversion to the animals fixes attention away from himself and his apprehensions. Birds, turtles, rabbits — anything that *moves* captures his attention. To make his entry into the school easier it is helpful to "tie in" with the home by suggesting that he bring a carrot from home for the rabbit on his return. He is so preoccupied with this assignment he forgets his anxiety. . . .

An observation about my staff. Those teachers who truly care for the animals seem to possess the most skill and understanding of the children. One teacher in particular has an almost uncanny way with the animals (our vet says she has the tamest squirrel in captivity).

Over and beyond the usual care and responsibility for the animals, the use of animals in the actual classroom activities provides the teacher with opportunities for dealing with such things as shyness or aloofness. One 19-month-old just watched everything and never uttered a sound for two weeks. Then one morning our Siamese cat, who joins the children at story time and "gets in line" to go outside or to another building, teased the little boy. He squealed with delight and chased the cat around the room. He just seemed to "open up" and has been more responsive and assertive ever since. . . .

We're certainly finding our animals at the Learning Lab useful and enjoyable by children, teachers, and parents. Right now we have a mother duck who is hatching seventeen eggs. Such excitement (1)!

Pets in Nursing Homes for the Aged

It is not only the very young who can benefit in a variety of ways from contact with animals. The old and infirm, especially those who have been institutionalized, need pets perhaps most of all.

Admission into a nursing home for the aged, because it symbolizes desertion to many patients, can accelerate the withdrawal syndrome of old age (15). When a patient is separated from family and friends, removed from the home where he has spent many years as a self-sustaining individual, and placed in a facility where he may have to stay for months, years, or the rest of his life, his interpretation of the situation is of prime importance. Depending on the personality make-up of the patient, fantasies may or may not arise. The patient may feel that it was not his weakened physical state or his chronic illness or his inability to get along on his own which were the reasons for his transfer to a nursing home, but merely that his relatives and friends wanted to get rid of him (13). Handling these difficulties successfully demands of the nursing home staff much more than sympathy, kindness, and good will. It requires know-how, training, and skill (22, 23).

No doubt there are burdensome personnel and administrative problems involved in the management of the small as well as the large nursing home. Add to these the diversified activities and services required to satisfactorily maintain the mental and physical health of nursing home patients, and the problems become geometrically more complex. Of necessity, much more attention has been paid to the physical care of the patients than to their emotional well-being. They have been provided with rehabilitative activities such as finger painting, clay and plastic moulding, etc., rather than with psychological help. This is quite understandable in view of the cost of psychological services and the difficulty of obtaining them even if they could be afforded.

Most good nursing homes provide occupational therapy and put much effort into exercising to the full the remaining capabilities of their charges in order to defer deterioration. Attempts are made to rescue patients from idleness through such leisure time activities as games, amusements, movies, music, drama, story-telling, and on occasion even dancing.

It is not easy to get older people to participate in these activities. To begin with, the elderly are apprehensive about their ability to learn new things and fear the failures the new activities often represent. In addition, and more importantly, these various recreational and occupational activities, while extremely worthwhile and beneficial to the patients, do not resolve the basic dilemma of the nursing home population, namely the tremendous psychological need for unlimited affection, constant companionship, and opportunities to do for others (10, 33). Unfortunately, for most patients the loss of relatives, friends, and associates, and the decline of their own strength and capability have made the satisfaction of these needs practically impossible. As a result, the patients develop a tendency to regress to childhood, when the satisfaction of many of these needs was more easily obtainable.

It is well-known that removing a patient from his own home and placing him in a nursing home may threaten his sense of identity. This is why the patient frequently makes unnecessary requests for service from the overburdened staff. He behaves in this trying way in order to affirm to himself and others that he is still alive and still counts. Such actions can also stem from the change of role brought about by placement in an institution where the patient must take orders rather than give them. Let us remember that it is not only the Oriental who finds "loss of face" intolerable. Simple, perceptive people in our American culture have described the pain and ignominy of being treated "like a nobody."

Henry (14) stresses the great tragedy of preserving the human body while mauling and destroying the human spirit.

> In many primitive societies the soul is imagined to leave the body at death or just prior to it; here, on the other hand, society drives out the remnants of the soul of the institutionalized old person while it struggles to keep his body alive. Routinization, inattention, careless- ness, and the deprivation of communication — the chance to talk, to respond, to see pictures on the wall, to be called by one's name rather than "you" or no name at all — are ways in which millions of once useful but now obsolete human beings are detached from their selves long before they are lowered into the grave (14, p. 393).

If the nursing home were to provide for even one of the patient's many emotional needs — for example, constant com- panionship — it would require staffing on a one-to-one basis, which is obviously not feasible financially even if it were possible to find the necessary number of employees.

Nursing home patients, like any other adults, need someone to love and "lord it over." Canine and feline friends can serve this purpose better than humans. An obedient cat or dog can do wonders to help restore the patient's sense of identity and self-respect and to provide the nursing home resident with a feeling of ego mastery.

There is a great deal of security in holding on to familiar objects, familiar surroundings and old friends. For the person who has been cut off from all this by being moved into a nursing home and who therefore feels his identity threatened, the pet can provide an anchor to the internalized past as well as a refuge from the threatening new interpersonal relationships in the institutional setting. Moreover, nursing home patients, as they complete the cycle of life, begin to resemble children in many ways — except in the child's open solicitation and acceptance of love and affection. Elderly patients may feel that it is inappropriate for them to receive or to dispense kisses or hugs and may be too embarrassed to bestow such emotional behavior upon another human being. They find it acceptable however to demonstrate love unashamedly for a pet. Even younger adults are uninhibited in bestowing caresses on their pets. A pet can thus serve as a new love object to whom one can give affection unstintingly without fearing desertion or lack of reciprocation. A pet can become a "bosom" companion and a substitute for relatives and friends who have died.

Later on as the patient develops new, emotionally satisfying relationships, as so often happens in a well-run and psycho-therapeutically oriented nursing home, he may no longer need to cling for dear life to his pet as his only anchor. However, during the period of adjustment to the new setting, when the aged person feels that he has been rejected by family and friends and is likely to project his feelings upon his new associates, a pet can serve as a counterforce, and effect, even if only in appearance, a balance of power in favor of the old person. The patient does not worry so much about the way the staff and other residents may receive him, because of the reassurance provided by the loyal pet whose attitude toward its master is constant, regardless of the change in milieu. The love offered by a pet is unqualified and nonjudgmental. The pet will probably set his master a good example by adjusting to his new environment quickly, even if this requires an acceptance of some changes and minor discomforts.

The solace that pets can offer even dying nursing home patients may be seen from the following:

> When Cindy arrived at the Nursing Home, a tiny puppy six weeks of age, I took her around to the rooms of those patients who could not come to see her. Mrs. B. was in her final illness. She was within five months of her 100th birthday, which she did not live to see. Mrs. B. was totally deaf but had good vision and was mentally very clear for her age. When I came to her bedside with the puppy, she put out her arms

to take her and said, "Oh, I am so sick! *I just need something like that!*"

Cindy visited this patient frequently until Mrs. B.'s death on 12-10-68. Her family was very appreciative that she could have this joy (16).

For some of the aged residents of nursing homes, a pet may very well be the only remaining link with reality, tentative and tenuous at times perhaps, but a great improvement over the absence of any such links.

With the blurring of identity and the diminishing sense of self that are noticeable with advancing age, there is frequently an accompanying loss of interest in life. The somatic as well as psychological consequences of such an attitude are manifold and serious. The person will become increasingly apathetic, more and more inner-directed, and eventually will lose contact completely with his surroundings and with reality. Sometimes a pet can provide just the right antidote for such "death wishes," as can be seen from the following case record recently brought to my attention:

Mr. Keane, the subject of this study, had been an alert, fairly active seventy-year-old when he went into a rapid decline. At the age of sixty-five Mr. Keane had retired after thirty-five years of service as a teller in a local bank. He and his wife had looked forward to and planned for a time when they could enjoy their modest savings, move to a warmer climate and indulge some of their hobbies. Mr. Keane was an avid stamp collector and his wife had a green thumb which produced miracles with the rarest and most delicate plants. They had a simple, attractive and comfortable house in a small town in New Jersey.

As they were preparing to sell their house, less than two months after his retirement, Mrs. Keane suffered a severe heart attack, was an invalid for three years and died. The pain of the bereavement and the loneliness that followed seemed to immobilize Mr. Keane to the point where he left home only occasionally to market. Many of his friends had died and others had retired and moved away. Mr. Keane's one married son lived in California and urged his father to live with him but Mr. Keane remembered the resolution he and his wife had made "never to depend on children." Following the death of his wife, Mr. Keane suffered severe loss of hearing. A shy man by nature, deafness seemed to make him even more reserved. The music which had always been a dependable source of pleasure became more irritating than

enjoyable. Another condition which had been only a moderate inconvenience became acute during this period. He underwent two unsuc-
cessful cataract operations which left him with impaired vision. To the
few remaining friends it appeared as if he had aged fifteen years.

Mr. Keane became despondent, could not be left alone, and was
eventually placed in a nursing home by his son. There he ate very
little, remained inactive, and became very bitter and morose. His son
and daughter-in-law came to visit him frequently. One day they
brought with them their pet Persian cat. Mr. and Mrs. Keane had
owned a cat, but it had died about a month before his wife did, and
Mr. Keane did not have the energy to replace it, although he had been
particularly fond of the cat.

The son and daughter-in-law placed their cat on Mr. Keane's lap.
The cat promptly fanned the father's face with his tail. Then he licked
both sides of Mr. Keane's face. For the first time in several weeks Mr.
Keane appeared alert. He put his hand on the cat. Every day
thereafter the friendly Persian was brought to visit and daily the old
man's responses became more immediate. He finally asked, "Are you
hungry, Pinky?" Pinky was the name of the cat that had died.

The staff of the nursing home became very involved in the
remarkable "cat" remedy for their patient, and after several consulta-
tions with the medical staff and the social worker attached to this
institution, it was decided that the cat would be permitted to stay
with Mr. Keane, especially since there seemed to have been such
immediate rapport.

The father made remarkable progress and seemed to be very
pleased with the pet. At mealtimes, the cat sat on the chair next to
Mr. Keane and made purring conversational noises which the old man
interpreted through his fingers as he occasionally stroked the animal.
After several months, the cat and Mr. Keane became inseparable.
They now take brief walks together, which have been very beneficial
to Mr. Keane's health and appetite. "Pinky" (still called that) sits with
him by the hour and sleeps on his bed at night. Recently, Mr. Keane
entered a checkers contest. Pinky sat on his foot purring his
encouragement. The only important change in Mr. Keane's life has
been the development of the relationship with "Pinky"! Other than
that, the circumstances which obtained before he entered the nursing
home remain the same, but they certainly seem different to Mr.
Keane, who can now share whatever he does with an admiring,
obedient, and loving cat that is his constant companion (23).

Despite the problems and hazards of introducing pets into
residential settings, the advantages by far outweigh the disadvantages. For example, patients who suffer severe physical pain or

who have been immobilized for a long time tend to engage in autistic fantasies. They are also prone to develop distrust for the people who minister to them because these people often have to force patients to go through painful procedures. Such patients may internalize their feeling of hurt, pain, and despair with the rationalization that they are being rejected. Restraints imposed by the staff during convalescence because of medical routines which have to be maintained become an overwhelming threat. Forced to realize that he is not what he was before, a patient of this kind begins to worry about whether he will ever again be well. The conflict between his need to deny his continuing illness and the recognition of reality becomes unbearable. The patient may panic. His unverbalized fear may express itself in depression, refusal to eat, or constipation. A reaction formation may also occur, with the patient becoming apathetic. The presence of a pet who stays with the nursing home patient throughout this period of depression, and is in a sense a participant in the patient's autistic fantasies, may be the greatest remedy for apathy. At this time the fear of death is very great. The pet can serve well as a talisman against such fear. The following case history illustrates the effectiveness of attention from an affectionate animal in overcoming the depression of an elderly patient.

> Joe, a 77-year-old bachelor of low mentality, was admitted to a nursing home after spending his entire life on a farm. His retarded and emotionally disturbed sister had already been a resident of the home for some years, while a married brother lived in a neighboring state. Joe was a skillful sharpener of saws, knives and scissors, and once installed in the nursing home was given a number of such jobs to do by the local townspeople.
>
> Before Joe's arrival, a little terrier named Cindy had been brought into the nursing home, and the two made friends immediately, spending many happy hours playing together in the lobby. The old man would take the dog out for a walk, see that she had food and water, and return her to her doghouse at the proper time.
>
> When some legal matters arose concerning his sister, some of Joe's relatives, overestimating his strength and abilities, tried to involve him in handling the situation. As a result, Joe became "nervous and jumpy," complained of not feeling well, and was unable to sleep. He gradually became more and more lethargic and depressed, eating poorly and looking so sick that he was taken to a clinic several times and given medication.

During this period of depression, Joe neglected his sharpening business and seemed to have forgotten about Cindy, despite the nursing home director's attempts to interest him in playing with his erstwhile companion. The dog would be brought to his room and excitedly jump on his bed, kissing him and rolling over in an invitation to play. At first Joe just lay motionless and did not respond to the pet's overtures, then smiled or laughed quietly, and gradually began to respond more. After several weeks, he took to visiting the lobby once again, although he did not ask for the dog. Cindy, however, would fly out of the next room and jump into Joe's lap, making a great fuss over him. He would pet her for a while, return her to the director of the Home, and then leave. At first he came to the lobby for these little "sessions" once a day; later two or three times a day. Then he began to ask for Cindy, and finally resumed taking her out on walks and feeding her. The nurses' note at this point read: "Patient much improved the past week. More like his usual self after three months of depression." Joe went back to sharpening saws and appeared to be well and happy (16).

The frightened adult, to whom every movement at one point signifies pain or the threat of another critical medical procedure, finds it difficult once convalescent to follow instructions and engage in activities which were formerly medically contra-indicated. Having a pet around often provides just the needed incentive for attempting the resisted activities. The need for independence overcomes the regressive dependency needs. The patient has to get out of bed to feed and care for the animal, thus exercising his larger muscles. Minimal movements necessitated by picking up, petting, or playing in bed with the pet help to restore and maintain muscular strength.

Pets offer a pleasant, natural way of stimulating the curiosity of an otherwise apathetic patient. One way of making the environment more interesting is to provide ever-changing displays of fish, small animals, and birds. For the patient who has developed anxieties, feels beaten down by physical handicaps, and has a desire to escape from his infirmities, a bird may be especially helpful. Identification with the bird may lead the patient to alleviate his anxiety by imagining that he can escape from difficulties through flight. Furthermore, (as we pointed out in Chapter 1) the bird, which is generally recognized as a phallic symbol, may give vicarious sexual gratification.

Birds as pets in institutions probably offer the fewest problems of care, maintenance, and cost of any animal. In addition to these advantages, they contribute beauty and cheer, giving a warm, home-like feeling which helps counteract some of the unavoidable hospital look of a setting where patients need medical attention of all kinds. We can visualize an experimental ward where the free feeling of the outdoors is created with trees (natural or artificial) — surrounded by colorful and graceful canaries, parakeets and other birds in cages. If the patients chosen for this ward were carefully screened for their enjoyment of birds, it would be a pleasant experience for them to let these birds fly freely around the room several times a day. In the course of time, patients and birds would inevitably pair up, and there would be an opportunity to study the choices of the patients and the therapeutic effects of the birds on individuals as well as on the group as a whole.

An aquarium, on the other hand, may offer to the very old or nonambulant person the ideal form of pet life. Fish need little care. Watching them can be amusing and relaxing, and any patient can experience the pleasure of caring for fish in a well-balanced aquarium. Even from a fishtank one can sometimes develop insight into problems of life and death.

An additional benefit of introducing pets into the program of a nursing home is the fact that patients who have a fear of animals and who manage to conquer their fears by working with animals often develop a sense of security that helps them overcome not only this problem but also the fear of interpersonal relationships. Thus those who previously had been unable to join in any communal efforts might find themselves motivated by animals to participate in work committees assigned to pet care. Making decisions about pets might strengthen weak egos and foster cooperation among the patients. Arrangements for participation of patients in the care and maintenance of pets in an institutional setting must be made after serious consideration has been given to the emotional status and physical condition of the patients, with great flexibility of scheduling as well as provision for "backstops."

In a discussion of ways to remotivate patients in the back wards of a hospital, Dr. Herbert S. Caron, Research Psychologist at the Cleveland, Ohio, Veterans Administration Hospital, has written the following about the use of pets:

In implementing the program, kittens or puppies might be used as a display in a corner of a recreation room. This might provide a more meaningful, awakening, and conversation-provoking stimulus than the usual TV set. Discussions on the subject of obtaining their own dogs could be initiated with those who showed interest. In a suitably prepared experimental ward, the patient could be introduced to and trained with his dog who would be housed nearby.

Patients would then be able to spend a certain number of hours daily with their dogs and if transferred to a nursing home, would keep the dog, thus easing what is often a difficult transition. The graded responsibilities that patients would take on in connection with the care of their dogs (brushing, feeding, walking) would likely contribute to a sense of purpose, of "being needed," and might encourage physical exercise and general progress in rehabilitation. Dogs could be trained to respond to various commands and in some cases to pull a wheelchair. The dogs would receive a special program of training for obedience, relative quiescence and devotion to a somewhat immobile master. Training techniques and problems may be similar in many ways to those encountered in training lead dogs for the blind. However, the problem of housing dogs in modern hospitals or nursing homes poses additional obstacles (4, p. 36).

A necessary prerequisite for the introduction of pets into a therapeutic institutional setting is the reorientation of the staff to its main role. When the staff is able to maintain a focus upon the primary purpose of the organization — which is to help the patients — it is possible to present them with several plans for the introduction of pets. Many problems incident upon the introduction of pets into any setting must be considered. Routine, which is so precious to most administrators and staff, will probably be disrupted at times. There is also a need for insurance against damage done by pets — scratches, bites, and damage to furniture. Provision must be made for the medical and physical care of the animals. A budgetary provision is necessary for one or more attendants whose sole function would be to care for the animals. Consequently, the introduction of pets demands a considerable reorganization of routines and a somewhat different philosophy of patient treatment.

Whenever decisions have to be made regarding the patient and his pet, one must be certain that the staff will cooperate and that the pet will not be considered an oppressive and undue burden. Otherwise, the staff is likely to transfer its dislike of the pet to the patient. A careful, realistic estimate must be made of how much responsibility the patient is able to accept or can exercise in caring for the pet. Conferences may be needed to reconcile the conflicting interests of the patients and the personnel in the problems of the pet-patient and pet-staff relationships.

Generally speaking, the introduction of pets into any treatment setting will change the dynamics of the interpersonal relationships between staff members and patients. For instance, pets provide that continuity of contact for which there is such a need, particularly when one is dealing with the chronically ill or infirm. Substitutions for trained pet aides are likely to be considerably fewer than the turnover in human aides. Frequently the only recognition the institutionalized patient can get as a person comes from his pet. Through the pet, opportunities are provided to the patient to make certain choices which in turn promote a strengthening of the ego and the development of inner controls. There is a hazard however, which can be anticipated and watched for, that aggressive reactions will develop in adults who have spent a considerable time in a confined setting, whether this be a hospital, nursing home, or veterans' domiciliary. Unless properly handled, such aggressions may be directed against pets as well as against people. Precautions should thus be taken by introducing pets gradually into a new setting. Patients who have never had pets need a considerable period of learning how to handle them so as not to hurt them. Unless such precautions are taken, the introduction of pets may boomerang.

In institutions where provision has been made for introducing pets into the therapeutic setting, it should be the responsibility of some staff member to explore systematically with each patient his interest in animals, if any. It would be advisable to discuss his past activities with particular emphasis on feelings and attitudes toward nature and animals. It should be established whether or not the patient has or ever had a pet, and the kind of animal he prefers. One might ask the patient which animal he would choose to be if he were to become an animal, and into which animal he would least like to be transformed.

Several alternatives are available for handling the patient's need for a pet, when this is indicated. If the patient already owns a pet, he may be permitted to have the pet brought to the nursing home. If the patient does not have his own pet, he may be allowed to select one, if he so desires. If neither of these alternatives is possible, a third solution is to allow relatives to bring the patient's pet with them when they visit.

The question of how one designs and implements a pet aide program was carefully considered by Mr. Dov Rappaport, the former director of the Orchard Gables Sanitarium in Hollywood, California (28).

> I have discussed the research proposal with the health department here and while they have no objections in principle, they raised a great many practical questions, most of them reflecting their obsessive concern with sanitation. They suggest that we can simplify these problems by segregating the animals in a separate space, where they can be visited; or we can limit ourselves to caged animals or else select animals that are easy to keep clean. It is true that the greater the animal's freedom of movement, the heavier the burden of labor for the staff.
>
> The problems of keeping pets in an institutional setting grow with the decreasing independence of the residents. Congregate living in a home for the aged, where the residents are healthy, mobile and able to exercise many options in their daily life, is far more open to innovation. . . .
>
> The psychic needs of the population at Orchard Gables are greater than those of well aged. . . . And yet, among the ill, even more than among the well, association with animals can probably provide patients with very real opportunities for ego affirmation and reassurance of personal effectiveness and power.

Mrs. Eva Rappaport, the wife of Dov Rappaport, has offered several practical solutions to the problems of utilizing pets in an institutional setting (29):

> I would like to mention briefly and in a preliminary fashion some of the possibilities of animal housing that we feel would be both feasible and conducive to participation.
>
> In a pavilion-like structure erected in a central area of the sanitarium's garden, where it would be visible from most of the patients' rooms; made mainly of modular sections of framed, welded wire mesh with provision for wind control; roofed to admit filtered light and to keep rain out. Entry wide enough to admit wheelchair with double doors to prevent animals from escaping.
>
> With a staff member in attendance during the day, nurses would be in a position to bring patients to the animal pavilion and leave them

there to visit with the pets. For patients who develop personal relationships with individual animals, visiting hours might be scheduled during which they would be permitted to take favorite pets to their rooms or for a stroll on leash or harness.

Research Queries

The use of pets in therapeutic and custodial settings has been the subject of very little research. A number of questions require further study. For example, how does one select pets for patients? Which patients can profit from working with pets? What effect will the attitude of staff members have upon the success of such a plan, and what can be done to develop positive attitudes? Can patient attitudes toward pets become a diagnostic tool in differentiating those who will adjust to congregate living from those who are unlikely to do so?

SUMMARY

The introduction of pets into caretaking institutions for both children and older adults can serve multiple purposes. In residential schools for emotionally disturbed, retarded, and delinquent children, animals can provide the affectionate attention and warm contact which a usually understaffed institution cannot offer, and which is so essential for healthy emotional development. Animals can help to socialize these children and develop in them an ego-strengthening sense of competence and importance by furnishing opportunities for making decisions and carrying out responsibilities connected with the care of the animals. The animals can also serve as educational tools in classroom situations, providing a focus for observation and discussion about various aspects of animal and human life.

Day schools and day care centers dealing with both normal and exceptional children can make equally good use of animals as part of their programs.

For aged nursing home patients, pets can satisfy vital emotional needs by helping these patients to hold on to the world of reality, of productive activity, and of intense emotional relationships. Through the assurance that the pets they care for love them in return, an image of themselves as worthwhile persons can be restored to nursing home patients. Through the activity involved in caring for pets, the physical health of aged people can also be improved and deterioration retarded.

REFERENCES

1. Bennett, N.: Personal communications, 8/19/70, 9/6/70, 2/3/71.
2. Burmeister, E.: The Professional Houseparent. New York, Columbia, 1960.
3. Butler, R. N.: Directions in the psychiatric treatment of the elderly. Role of perspective of the life cycle. Gerontologist, 9(2, Pt. 1):134-138, 1969.
4. Caron, H. S.: A proposal for re-activating the patient who has "given-up": The use of dogs as companions. Newsletter for Research in Psychology (mimeo), 9:35-36, 1967.
5. D'Amato, G.: Residential Treatment for Child Mental Health: Towards Ego-Social Development and a Community-Child Model, Springfield, Thomas, 1969.
6. Directory for Exceptional Children, 5th ed. Boston, Porter and Sargent, 1965.
7. Finney, J. C. (Ed.): Culture Change, Mental Health, and Poverty. Lexington, University of Kentucky, 1969.
8. Freud, A., and Burlingham, D. T.: War and Children. New York, International Universities Press, 1944.
9. Geber, M.: The psychomotor development of African children in the first year and the influence of maternal behavior. J Soc Psychol, 47:185-195, 1958.
10. Giffin, K.: Personal trust and the interpersonal problems of the aged person. Gerontologist, 9(4, Pt 1):286-292, 1969.
11. Gores, S.: The pet field and mental retardation. Pet Shop Management, 19(1):38-41, 1965.
12. Gores, S.: New horizons for the Lambs. Pet Shop Management, 19(2):30-34, 1965.
13. Hacker, S. L., and Gaitz, C. M.: The moral career of the elderly mental patient. Gerontologist, 9(2, Pt. 1):120-127, 1969.
14. Henry, J.: Culture against Man. New York, Random House, 1963.
15. Killian, E. C.: Effect of geriatric transfers on mortality rates. Social Work, 15(1):19-26, 1970.
16. Kilmer, M. M.: Personal communications, 7/16/70, 8/20/71.
17. Kirk, S. A.: Early Education of the Mentally Retarded: An Experimental Study. Urbana, University of Illinois, 1958.
18. Lawrence, E.: Learning Experiences of a Group of Emotionally Disturbed and Retarded Children at an Animal Nursery. (Unpublished manuscript.)

19. Levinson, B. M.: Culture and mental retardation. Psychol Rec, 8:27-38, 1958.
20. Levinson, B. M.: The mentally defective child. Yeshiva Ed, 3(1):3-15, 1959.
21. Levinson, B. M.: Household pets in residential schools. Their therapeutic potential. Ment Hyg 52:411-414, 1968.
22. Levinson, B. M.: Nursing home pets. A psychological adventure for the patients (Part I). Nat Humane Rev, 58(4):14-16, 1970.
23. Levinson, B. M.: Nursing home pets. A psychological adventure for the patients (Part II). Nat Humane Rev, 58(5):6-8, 1970.
24. Overs, R. P.: Personal communication, 1969.
25. Perlman, E. H.: Pets and Children. (An unpublished manuscript.)
26. President's Committee on Mental Retardation. MR 67: A first report to the President on the nation's progress and remaining great needs in the campaign to combat mental retardation. Washington, D. C., U. S. Government Printing Office, 1967.
27. Provence, S., and Lipton, R. C.: Infants in Institutions. New York, International Universities Press, 1962.
28. Rappaport, D.: Personal communication, 10/2/69.
29. Rappaport, E.: Personal communication, 10/2/69.
30. Schaffer, H. R.: Objective observations of personality development in early infancy. Br J Med Psychol, 31:174-183, 1958.
31. Schaffer, H. R., and Callender, W. M.: Psychologic effects of hospitalization in infancy. Pediatrics, 24:528-539, 1959.
32. Whiting, J. W. M., and Landauer, T. K.: Some effects of infant stress in humans. In Beach, F. A. (Ed.): Sex and Behavior. New York, Wiley, 1965.
33. Wolff, K.: Rehabilitating geriatric patients. Hosp Community Psychiatry, 22 (1):8-11, 1971.

Chapter Nine

THE PET IN CORRECTIONAL INSTITUTIONS

With spiders I had friendship made,
And watched them in their sullen trade,
Had seen the mice by moonlight play,
And why should I feel less than they?
We were all inmates of one place,
And I, the monarch of each race,
Had power to kill — yet, strange to tell!
In quiet we had learned to dwell (1).

PETS IN PRISONS

"THE love of pets is so generally characteristic of prisoners that Lombroso concluded that it was indicative of inherent criminality" (4, p. 23).

The above quotation raises the question of why prisoners love pets and what mental hygiene needs these animals satisfy.

When a person is sentenced to prison, he is no longer known by his name but by a number. This loss of his name robs the incarcerated individual of the magic powers that most of us unconsciously ascribe to our names and leaves him, psychologically speaking, without the protection of his patron saint. Furthermore, the prisoner is sometimes dependent for his very life on the whims and caprices of the prison administration and on the prison guards (8). Nor does the prisoner trust his fellow inmates, as he believes that in the prison it is each man for himself.

However, the person's need for love, affection, and closeness to a living thing is as strong in prison as elsewhere, and is clearly manifested in the loving care lavished on whatever animal life strays into prison. Animals and insects that are usually despised and considered vermin outside of prison are cherished by the prisoners. Recently 22 inmates of a county jail brought suit

207

against the warden and the county sheriff because their pet mouse had been "assassinated" by prison guards.

Surprisingly little has appeared in professional writings about the importance of pets for the preservation of the mental health of prisoners. The theme has occurred frequently in literature, however, particularly in poetry.

It is quite possible that the possession of pets makes life in prison sufficiently tolerable so that individuals can survive long terms of imprisonment with less deterioration when they have a pet they can call their own. Pets in prisons become their owners' friends, protectors, confessors, masters, and slaves. The pets offer companionship and love. Because of the time prisoners have at their disposal, they have been able to tame and train mice, rats, sparrows, and wrens, which when properly taught exhibit unusual intelligence (4).

Many dogs come to Sing Sing, for example. They are not turned away but thrive under the affection and care lavished on them by the prisoners, who may even deprive themselves of little tidbits which are so precious in prison in order to offer them to their pets (3).

The extent to which prisoners can go in their love for their pets is illustrated in an incident related by Warden Lawes (4), in which a murderer who was very fond of his little mongrel dog risked his own life to save it when it was being run over by a prison truck. Later he took good care of the injured animal by putting a splint on its broken leg.

Another prisoner made a splint for a chicken which had lost its leg, and nurtured it very carefully thereafter. One convict found an English sparrow with a broken wing, which he fed and took care of until it could fly, at which point it was released. The bird stayed near the prison for about two weeks and then visited the prison several times a week for a few months until it finally flew away. One of the inmates reported: "Many of us grieved when the bird finally failed to return (3, p. 11).

Rags, a small mongrel dog, appeared in Sing Sing Prison in 1929. The dog became a favorite of the prisoners, who felt cheered whenever the animal appeared. Rags had a remarkable ability to sense the mood of the prisoners. Whenever she came upon a lonely, isolated convict, she would spend time with the man, trying to distract him and lead him toward other prisoners until the inmate became part of a group and his gloom was dispelled.

One time, Rags saved the life of a convict who was planning to commit suicide.

> "That dog saved my life," the inmate explained later. "When I didn't get that pardon I figured no one gave a damn about me and I had had enough. I was planning on hanging myself with a sheet. That dog never gave me a chance. Every time I got out of my bunk, Rags would growl soft-like, and I knew if I went ahead she would bark and bring the cellblock guard on the run. I figured that if the dog thought that much about me, I'd better give myself another chance. So I finally rolled over and went to sleep." (3, p. 23).

It is reported that during the Wars of the Roses, Sir Henry Wyatt was imprisoned in the Tower of London. A cat found her way into his cell and owing to its devotion Wyatt was able to survive the tortures he was forced to undergo. When Sir Henry was released from prison, he had the cat's portrait painted with the following inscription:

> "This Knight with hunger, cold and care neere starvd, pincht, pined away,
> A sillie Beast did feed, heate, cheere with dyett, warmth & play" (3, p. 9).

When the Duke of Norfolk was imprisoned by Elizabeth I, his cat found her way to his cell and stayed with him for eight months until he was beheaded (3).

Because of the love the prisoners have for their pets, they become involved in the diagnosis and treatment of their charges when the latter fall ill, and some of them become authorities in this field (2).

"Robert Stroud, the 'Bird Man of Alcatraz,' helped keep his sanity during the 26 years he spent in solitary confinement at Leavenworth Penitentiary, before being transferred to Alcatraz in 1942, by breeding and raising canaries in his cell for sale in the open market. Stroud became an authority on bird diseases, and bird lovers whose pets had died mailed the bodies to him for postmortem diagnosis, not knowing that he was in prison. When his birds were taken away from him because conducting a business in prison was deemed to be a violation of Federal law, he fell into a depressed state. He was subsequently transferred to Alcatraz and later to the Federal Medical Center in Springfield, Missouri where he died a few years later."*

It is desirable that pets be introduced into prisons whenever and wherever possible, and that each inmate who wishes to have a pet of his own be permitted to acquire one. There is little an inmate can do on his own initiative. Having a pet can give him some sense of mastery over his own life by providing him with opportunities to make certain decisions and be responsible for the welfare of another living creature.

In a few forward-looking prisons in the world, attempts are being made to use pets in rehabilitating the inmates and in helping them to maintain outside contacts. The French SPA takes care of the pets of an inmate, occasionally visits him, and writes to him about his pet (7).

In many prisons, however, permitting inmates to own pets is considered as indulging or coddling them. The fact that pets can help to preserve the mental health of the prisoners and thus make it easier for the prison administration to maintain discipline is overlooked. The time that hangs so heavy on the hands of the inmates, creating boredom and a sense of futility which can lead to disruptive activities, may be directed into socially productive channels by utilizing pets in recreational and educational programs.

PETS IN TRAINING SCHOOLS FOR DELINQUENT CHILDREN

We have made some inquiry into the role played by pets in schools for delinquent children (5). Research has repeatedly demonstrated that most children placed in training schools do not seem to benefit from the experience. The question arises, why are there so many failures?

Many socially disturbed children are confined to institutions because of their continual defiance of authority and their antisocial activities, such as stealing, denial of misdeeds, truancy, and aggressiveness. Most of these children have never had a consistenly firm and kind authority figure and therefore have

*Personal communication, 10/19/71. Austin MacCormick, former Assistant Director of the United States Bureau of Prisons.

deficient superegos and low frustration tolerance. When frustrated, they become aggressive toward their peers, the authority figures at hand, or both. Counter-aggression, repression, and punitive confinement are frequently the disciplinary measures employed by training school personnel. The result is no therapeutic progress, and in many cases personality deterioration occurs. Some of our training schools were characterized by Joseph P. Rowan, an expert on delinquency, in his testimony before a U.S. Senate Committee in 1969 as "crime hatcheries where children are tutored in crime if they are not assaulted by other inmates or the guards first" (6).

It is well known that separation from the family, no matter how therapeutically justifiable this may be, is often traumatic for the socially maladjusted or so-called "delinquent" child. When a child is committed to a training school, he is exposed to many new experiences and to workers who may not be too sympathetic to his plight. Then, too, we must consider what placement in a training school might mean to a child. We need not fool ourselves into thinking that just because we believe a training school is therapeutic, the child accepts it in this spirit. We must remember that the child brought to a training school comes there after having been exposed to various therapeutic and not-so-therapeutic agencies of the government, and after having been committed by the court. The child who has been threatened with "jail" as a last resort now feels that the threat has become reality and that he is confined in a type of prison. This gives rise, in certain children, to profound self-devaluation and depression. The child feels that a great injustice has been done, that he has been unjustifiably condemned by society. His despair and sense of loss may be deepened by a final indignity: the things he treasures most, his few personal possessions, are taken away from him.

In this situation, it is important that the child have someone or something he can relate to and confide in, something non-condemnatory, something he can consider his own, to love and protect — and be protected by. For want of the requisite human companionship and friendship, an animal can often meet this need. In fact, it has been observed that institutionalized children frequently attach themselves to living things that are available in residential schools — to dogs, cats, or even mice. As indicated in the previous chapter, we have found that pets in many instances serve a therapeutic function in residential centers for the care of children with various handicaps. We undertook to learn whether this resource is also utilized by training schools serving delinquent children.

The purpose of our inquiry was mainly exploratory. We sought to determine what provision is being made in training schools for the use of animals in farm programs and for the use of domestic animals specifically as pets for the children.

One hundred and twelve of the 150 children's training schools in the continental United States to which we sent questionnaires responded to our inquiry. This represents about 36 percent of the total number of such schools in this country. The population of each school ranges anywhere from 10 to 1000 children, the median number being 125.

Thirty-eight of the 112 schools (34%) replied that they had work programs involving farm animals. The median number of children in these schools was 200. The farm animals included those shown in Table IX. Poultry was also used in farm

TABLE IX

Animal	Number of Schools
Hogs	24
Milk cows	19
Beef cows	12
Horses	9
Cattle	5
Ponies	5
Sheep	5

Taken from B. M. Levinson (5, p. 477).

TABLE X

Animal	Number of Schools
Chickens	11
Turkeys	2
Ducks	2
Pheasants	1

Taken from B. M. Levinson (5, p. 477).

programs, as the figures in Table X indicate.

There were some interesting comments on how the farm programs were conducted.

> Our best animal program is the one using horses. Each of the 20 boys is assigned a colt to care for, train, etc. When the horses are old enough, the boys ride them. No one but the boy assigned does anything with or to his horse.
>
> On a volunteer basis about 800 pheasant chickens are raised for the state wildlife commission.

There is a negative relationship between having a farm program and allowing the children to have pets of their own. Only nine (24%) of the schools having farm programs permitted the children to have pets, compared with 41 percent for all the training schools (see Table XI). The following are characteristic comments:

> We have 2 horses and 15 rabbits, and 1 dog which belongs to all the boys. We do not have individual pets, but try and teach responsibility by letting the boys share in taking care of the animals.
>
> Association of boys and pets appears to be mutually beneficial.

Forty-six of the 112 schools (41%) permit the children to own pets. These pets include the animals shown in Table XI. It may be noted that, in training schools as elsewhere, dogs are the most popular pets and cats rank second.

We asked who took care of the pets. Twenty of the 45 schools

TABLE XI

Pet	Number of Schools
Dog	45
Cat	35
Fish	28
Bird	26
Hamster	13
Rabbit	11
Chipmunk	1
Deer	1
Snake	1
White rat	1

Taken from B. M. Levinson (5, p. 478).

that responded to this question indicated that the individual child cared for his own pet. In the other 25 schools, children and staff members cooperate in caring for the pets.

In reply to a question about where pets (both individually-owned and school-owned) were kept, 29 of the 51 schools that chose to answer stated that the pets were kept in the children's living quarters, in 8 they were kept in classrooms, and in 14 they were kept elsewhere on the grounds.

We wondered if in some schools children were permitted to play with pets belonging either to the school or to staff members. Sixty-one of the 93 (65.5%) schools that responded indicated that they did have pets available on this basis, the pets including those shown in Table XII.

We attempted to ascertain the staff-to-child ratio in the various schools in order to determine whether there might be a relationship between this ratio and the schools' attitude toward permitting the children to have pets. One hundred and eight schools supplied an answer to this question. (We must note however that each school, of necessity, used its own criterion as to what constitutes a staff member, and these criteria may vary widely among the schools.) The figures in Table XIII summarize the findings.

There seems to be a curvilinear relationship between staff-to-child ratio and the ownership of pets. The data also indicated that the school census does not influence pet ownership: some schools having a large census permit pets whereas others with a small census do not.

TABLE XII

Pet	Number of Schools
Dog	51
Cat	20
Birds	12
Fish	12
Rabbit	5
Hamster	4
Horse	3
Donkey	1

Taken from B. M. Levinson (5, p. 478).

TABLE XIII

Staff-to-Child Ratio	Percent of Schools Permitting Pets
2:1	25
1:1	33
1:2	39
1:3	41
1:4	33
1:5	29

Taken from B. M. Levinson (5, p.479).

We asked whether or not those who replied to our questionnaire believed that owning pets would be helpful to the children in their setting. Thirty-two of the 80 schools (39%) from which we received responses to this question gave a positive answer. Twenty-nine of these indicated that it was not possible to permit the children to have pets, because of federal regulations (4 schools) or because of practical considerations (25 schools), such as financial problems, staffing, and health problems.

Here are some of the comments that this question elicited:

I feel that the use of pets on a selective basis can be very therapeutic in a residential setting. It is not practical here to have pets on an unlimited or unconditional basis. There are 21 staff houses, 4 apartment buildings, and house parent apartments in each of our 15 cottages. Many of these employees have dogs and cats that come on the campus, and the boys play with them. There are also a number of cats that stay around the farm barns, and the boys feed and play with them. The Fish and Game Department (a state agency) has talked with us about the possibility of our making provisions to house and care for small "wild" animals for therapeutic purposes. This possibility is being explored now.

At the risk of sounding contradictory . . . our rules do not permit the boys to have pets, but there are pets available on the campus belonging to the staff and with which the boys come into contact. There is occasionally a stray cat which is sometimes "adopted" on an informal basis by a group.

Some of the schools have had negative experiences in the use of pets. The following are characteristic comments:

> A problem we have encountered is the abuse of pets when they are on the grounds. Our staff has been on guard against such an abuse.
>
> Ours is an emotionally disturbed, aggressive population. We have tried allowing children to have their own pets, but could not cope with the problem of pet neglect, cruelty, and perversion. Some children are affectionate and responsible with pets, and are sickened and angered by the cruelty of others to pets.
>
> We have had more than six dogs, all of which met an unfortunate end at the hands of the boys. I live on the property, and I have a dog, but I keep her in my yard.
>
> We have no pets and do not propose to have any.
>
> At one point we allowed a certain number of cottages to rear a cottage pet — a dog or a cat. We found that too many of these animals were being hurt or destroyed and, of course, quickly stopped the practice of allowing pets.

Our findings, though supplying some answers to specific questions regarding the use of pets in training schools, suggest some interesting problems as well. We may note for instance the tremendous range in the number of children cared for in these schools. Inevitably the thought arises that no matter how many individual cottages a training school may have, the larger such an institution is, the more impersonal the handling of the children is bound to be, and the greater will be the insistence on rules and regulations. The bureaucratic load may become overwhelming.

This of course has implications for the therapeutic efficacy of the institution. There were references in the responses to our questionnaires to the children's attacking pets as an expression of their aggressiveness. On whom or what do such children vent their aggression when there are no pets on the scene? Surely a wholesome means of expressing aggression should be provided, through play or other types of therapy. We can envisage a progression of different types of therapy that would finally enable a child to treat a pet as a desirable companion rather than the victim of his hostility. And even though some children cannot be trusted with pets, certainly there are others within the same setting who could benefit from their use and who should not be deprived of them.

It seems to us that in most of the schools in which pets are allowed, their presence is incidental rather than planned, so that the therapeutic potential of pets is not realized by either the schools or the children.

Of course it must be granted that there are certain difficulties in having pets in training schools: they entail extra work, extra staff, veterinary supervision, insurance against damage, and added expense. Further, they may disturb the routine of residential settings. But is this all bad? Routines, we believe, should occasionally be disturbed, since such disturbance may well produce beneficial results. Getting away from regimented living can be considered a positive good in many cases.

Although we have no data to indicate that pets are actually considered "therapeutic" in the training schools we polled, we have cited evidence (see Chapter 8, p. 178) that they have proved useful in other types of residential schools. It seems to us that this "tool" should be employed more systematically in correctional institutions, so that living in such surroundings can be made as emotionally rich and educational as possible.

SUMMARY

Pets are perhaps more needed in correctional institutions than in any other type of institution. Children who have been removed from their homes and placed in what is supposedly a rehabilitative facility but is often a bleak, punitive setting where their needs receive little attention feel isolated, abandoned, and angry. The companionship and affection of a pet and an opportunity to be responsible for its well being can help promote emotional growth even when other conditions are not propitious.

Imprisoned adults, too, crave the warmth brought into their grim lives by animals, as shown by the care inmates frequently lavish on any living creature that shares their isolation, from mice to stray dogs. Caring for these animals gives prisoners some opportunity for autonomy and for taking charge in a situation where self-direction is in very short supply.

Unfortunately, allowing prisoners to have pets is considered undesirable coddling in those institutions where punishment rather than rehabilitation is the guiding philosophy. This attitude is somewhat less prevalent in correctional facilities for children, where farm work is sometimes included in the program of activities, or the staff's pets are available for limited contact, but by and large pets are not looked upon as a rehabilitative resource to be used in well-defined programs.

REFERENCES

1. Byron, G. G. Lord: The prisoner of Chillon. In Snyder, F. B., and Martin, R. G. (Eds.): A Book of English Literature. New York, Macmillan, 1928.
2. Gaddis, T. E.: The Birdman of Alcatraz. New York, Random House, 1955.
3. Gaddis, V., and M.: The Strange World of Animals and Pets. New York, Cowles, 1970.
4. Lawes, L. E.: Life and Death in Sing Sing. New York, Doubleday, Doran & Co., 1928.
5. Levinson, B. M.: Household pets in training schools. Psychol Rep, 28:475-481, 1971.
6. Report of the Joint Commission on Mental Health in Children: Crisis in Child Mental Health: Challenge for the 1970's. New York, Harper & Row, 1970.
7. Szasz, K.: Petishism. Pets and Their People in the Western World. New York, Holt, Rinehart and Winston, 1968.
8. Wolf, M.: Prison. London, Eyre & Spottiswoode, 1967.

Chapter Ten

EPILOGUE

A Dream

I creep in the parched desert
And find a sparkling fountain;
I put my head into its living waters
And it turns into a dazzling flower —
Blooming in forbidding beauty
And covering me with a radiant glow.
I stretch my hand and it moves
Scattering its incense in the air.
I run and ah!
It's within my grasp . . .
It turns into Sirius . . . the dog star.
I, a child
Try to reach the stars . . .
Sirius is so near.
I run to the nearest hill
My reach is always too short.
Wait till I am a grown man!
Now, I am old and bent with years
No more running to the hill and mountain top —
Yet, a warm, steady, life-giving glow
Reaches me from Sirius . . . the unattainable.
I collect
White iridescent and evanescent starbeams
For my trip home to
Sirius the dog star.

ANIMALS are a symbol of the rehumanization of society to the extent that they are allowed to function as members of the animal world, rather than as four-footed humans whose very nature is denied, and are permitted to bring their owners into that world of life, impulse, and love. The very fact that animals are introduced with such difficulty into caretaking and correctional institutions and are regarded by so many individuals as burdens and sources of disorder indicates how far our social structure has

219

strayed from a recognition of human needs and desires. Scientific investigation into the significance and use of pets for both children and adults has been very sparse. L. Carmichael's compendious "Manual of Child Psychology" (1), for example, nowhere even mentions the word "pet," while a thorough search of the psychological literature by this writer has not uncovered a single scientific article on the subject of animals in correctional institutions.

If pets are to be used as aids in upgrading the quality of life, particularly in highly urbanized societies, those holders of power − whether on a family or national level − who would disregard human needs in favor of an orderly, mechanized world must be brought to regard animals as necessary to the functioning of society, even as necessary evils if nothing more. Those prison wardens, for example, who care nothing about the emotional distress of the isolated, angry inmates in their charge and who would not, on that account, agree to the introduction of pets into their domain for the benefit of the prisoners might agree to let pets be kept if they were convinced that prisoner morale would thereby improve to such an extent that rebellious behavior and rioting would be diminished significantly. Nursing home administrators who see their functions primarily as ensuring orderly surroundings for orderly, i.e. docile, patients might not throw up their hands in horror at the idea of patients having pets, if they were persuaded that fewer demands for attention would be made on their overburdened staff and that deterioration of patient health would decline so that the staff could more adequately handle its tasks.

Unfortunately, some of those institutions − residential schools, nursing homes, etc. − which have tried to integrate pets into their facilities have encountered strong bureaucratic resistance from governmental agencies under whose jurisdiction they operate. Anxiety over sanitation problems seems to preclude, for the latter, a consideration of the over-all needs − emotional and physical − of the populations of these institutions. Similarly, a concern for ecology and the quality of the environment has been translated in some urban communities into an attack on dogs as possible disease carriers through their feces, when the major sources of pollution have in actuality been automobiles, industrial wastes, and ever-increasing quantities of garbage resulting from unrestricted use of disposable paper, plastic, and metal products.

Moreover, while recognizing the demoralizing effects of living in squalid, overcrowded surroundings under poverty conditions that lead to apathy and sometimes violence, officials charged with ameliorating these conditions often deny decent public housing to the poor who have sought to bring some comfort into their lives by acquiring pets. Thus those who most need the stimulation, emotional security, and protection provided by a faithful animal are the ones most frequently denied this resource.

Even when a matter of housing is not involved, the poor often cannot afford pets. Although stray animals can be picked up and abandoned ones acquired at no cost from such agencies as the A.S.P.C.A., the money required to feed such animals as dogs and cats, provide for their care when sick, and procure the necessary license can place pets in the luxury class for marginal families. Welfare officials would probably be horrified at the idea of providing an additional subsidy to allow for pet ownership by families receiving public assistance, yet who needs an affectionate animal to share his life more than a child with few, if any, toys and books, living in depressing surroundings, attending often inadequate schools, a constant witness to incidents of crime and drug addiction?

Schools in large urban communities are facing an unprecedented crisis at present and are being forced to reevaluate their philosophy, curriculum, methods, and personnel training and selection. Very little of this scrutiny however has led to a consideration of using animals for study, play, and training in responsibility and empathy.

In order to bring the opponents of pet ownership to relax their stance and to see animals as acceptable and even desirable participants in our social order, the efforts of those who know what benefits and pleasures derive from close association with animals must be directed toward resolving the problems which pet ownership does entail, particularly in an institutional setting, but also in crowded urban areas where sanitation and traffic conditions are already unsatisfactory. If those who believe pets are a real need for human beings in this day and age can show the way toward maximizing the advantages and minimizing the disadvantages of keeping pets in the home or in an institution, reluctant and even hostile individuals and groups may be won over. Interested individuals and organizations — lay and professional — must exert pressure upon appropriate governmental authorities and create a favorable climate of opinion among the general public so that animals can come to be regarded as a valuable resource rather than as a nuisance.

It is certainly worth the effort to bring about this change in attitude, for while it is quite possible that animals can do without man, it is much less likely that man can do without animals.

REFERENCE

1. Mussen, P.H. (Ed.): Carmichael's Manual of Child Psychology, 3rd ed. New York, Wiley, 1970, Vols. I and II.

INDEX

A

Abilities, 9, 48, 67, 69, 70, 79, 85, 111
  of child, 39, 182, 183
  of pet, 208
  reading, 77
Activities, 51, 83, 99, 109, 110, 170,
    191, 193, 199, 204, 205
  antisocial, 210
  of children, 39, 48, 50, 51, 146
  competitive, 70
  disruptive, 210
  fantasied, 140
  play, 7, 44, 49, 126
  sexual, 16, 20, 106
Adamic, Louis, 26, 30
Adolescents, 57, 67, 72, 73, 77, 78, 113,
    182
  and animals, 71-72, 76
Adulthood, 67, 71, 175
Adults
  aggressions of, 202
  apathetic, 175
  and children, 140
  emotions of, 180
  hostile, 175
  and the pet, 76, 83-95, 115, 129-132,
    150-153
  schizoid, 151
Affections, 38, 51, 52, 54, 55, 89, 90,
    94, 98, 99, 102, 104, 105, 108,
    118, 121, 151, 152, 195
  need for, 193, 207
  and pet, 129, 139, 143, 177, 208, 217,
    221
Aged, 97-111, 114, 131, 164, 171
  pets in nursing homes for, 192-205
Agents, 40
  therapeutic, pets as, 36, 136, 154,
    155, 215
Aggressions, 21, 26, 45, 55, 69, 70, 90,
    99, 119, 120, 126

  of adults, 202
  of animals, 18, 69, 70
  of child, 183, 211, 216
Aides, pets as psychotherapeutic aides,
    4, 36, 67-69, 139, 141, 142, 154,
    155, 166, 177, 183-204, 207-218,
    220
Alexander, L., 76, 79, 166, 173
Alienation, 4, 5, 28, 34, 87, 100, 139,
    157, 171
American Air Force Convalescent Cen-
    ter, 136
Ames, L. B. 15, 16, 17, 30, 39, 44, 45,
    46, 72, 73, 74, 79, 81, 126, 134
Amphibians, 60, 61
Anger, 16, 42, 55, 56, 91, 120, 121,
    127, 146, 147, 148, 170, 217
Animal Association Test, 18; *see also*
    Tests
Animals
  aggressive, 18, 69, 70
  behavior of, 11, 13, 28, 94, 95, 141,
    145
  domesticated, 11, 12, 18, 27, 74, 99,
    136, 161, 212
  fears of, 17, 44, 68, 90, 93, 132, 147,
    178, 200
  hunting, 11, 12
  kingdom of, 6-14, 29, 30, 50, 119,
    178, 182, 219
  in modern life, 26-28
  symbolism, 14-23, *see also* Symbolism
  wild, 10, 17, 27, 28, 29
Antelyes, Dr. J., 109, 110, 111, 164,
    165, 166, 172, 173
Anthony, J. E., 34, 79
Anthony, S., 51, 79, 133
Anthropology, 15, 19
Anxieties, 29, 41, 42, 44, 53, 70, 79, 95,
    110, 114, 115, 120, 126, 127,
    168, 169, 170, 179, 185, 199, 220
  "free-floating," 9

223

inner, 7
separation, 48, 122, 191-192
Anxiety-provoking, 178, 179
Apathy, 196, 198, 199, 221
Apell, R. J., 73, 74, 81
Ardrey, R., 70, 79
Armstead, W. W., 172, 173
Art, 15, 29
    prehistoric, 15
    primitive, 22-23
Arthur, B., 113, 133
Aschaffenburg, H., 150, 159
A.S.P.C.A., 91, 142, 221
Attitudes, 37, 67, 68, 69, 73, 83, 85, 89,
        106, 107, 158, 195, 196, 202,
        204, 214, 222
    emotional, 162
    toward pets, 99, 178, 182, 202
    toward self, 179
Auden, W. H., 83
Austin, A., 139, 159
Autism, 184
    fantasies of, 198
Aymar, B., 15, 30

B

Bastian, J., 9, 30
Battered children, 34
Bears, 17, 22, 27, 44, 45, 46, 72, 74, 75,
        94
"Beauty and the Beast," 20
Behaviors, 37, 41, 92, 117, 127, 132,
        141, 175, 195, 220
    aggressive, 185
    of animals, 11, 13, 28, 94, 95, 141,
        145
    of children, 50, 68, 122, 137, 138,
        174
    disorders, 137
    human, 28, 92, 94, 166, 168, 170, 172
    pet's, 42, 68, 92, 132, 133, 144, 157
    of plants, 13, 14
    species-specific, 11
Bender, L., 44, 79, 126, 133
Bennett, N., 192, 205
Bereavement, 104, 120, 131
    experience, 113-117, 128
    pain of, 196
    and the pet, 113-133

Bergmann, T., 119, 133
Berman, M., 102, 111
Bertos de Gasztold, C., 161, 173
Bible, 107
Birch, H. G., 40, 82
"Bird Man of Alcatraz," 209
Birds, 16, 18, 29, 44, 60, 61, 74, 75,
        110, 177
    uses of birds in institutions, 199, 200,
        208, 209, 213, 224
    uses of birds in psychotherapy, 144,
        155
Birth, 7, 37, 38, 39, 85
Bishop, N., 7, 30
Blase, B., 38, 82
Blenden, D. C., 162, 173
Boverman, H., 38, 80
Bowlby, J., 39, 41, 79
Brain-injured children, 185
Brain syndrome, chronic, 185
Brill, A. A., 119, 133
British Kennel Club, 24
Browne, C. E., 123, 134
Browning, E., 136, 160
Browning, R., 83, 95, 97, 111
Bucke, W. F., 25, 30
Bullis, G. E., 126, 134
Burlingham, D. T., 180, 205
Burmeister, E., 175, 205
Buss, A. H., 18, 30
Byron, G. G., 130, 131, 134, 207, 218

C

Calden, G., 18, 32
Callender, W. M., 82, 175, 206
Camuti, L. J., 76, 79, 166, 173
Cann, M. A., 37, 79
Carlson, C. E., 38, 80
Carmichael, L., 220, 222
Caron, Dr. Herbert S., 200, 201, 205
Cats, 19, 27, 44, 46, 53, 60, 61, 74, 75,
        76, 110
    uses of cats in institutions, 177, 178,
        194, 209, 211, 213, 214, 215, 216
    uses of cats in psychotherapy, 137,
        144, 154, 155
Cattell, J. P., 113, 114, 134
Cave of the Trois Frères, 23
Cawein, M. J., 8, 30

Centers
  day care, pets in, 191-192, 204
  rehabilitation, 94, 182
  residential treatment, 158
Chess, S., 40, 82
Child
  development, 34-79, 175
  ego of, 139, 179
  needs of, 141, 149, 174, 178, 182
  responsibilities, 35, 46-48, 71, 121,
    138, 190, 213, 221
Childhood, 5, 16, 40, 97, 98
  early, 41-43, 169
  problems of, 99
  regression to, 193
Children
  battered, 34
  behavior of, 50, 68, 122, 137, 138,
    174
  brain-injured, 185
  culturally underpriviledged, 137
  delinquent, use of pets with, 210-217
  emotionally disturbed, 121, 136-138,
    139, 140, 143, 146, 149, 158,
    171, 179, 183, 184, 185, 216
  exceptional, 137, 175-181, 204, *see
    also* Exceptional children
  institutionalized, 175, 178, 211
  mentally retarded, 182, 191, *see also*
    Mentally retarded, children
  schizophrenic, 139, 148, 150, 184
Children's Apperception Test, 17, *see
  also* Tests
Children's Psychiatric Hospital, 149
Chukovskii, K, 43, 79, 117, 118, 134
"Cinderella," 19
Civilization, 4, 9, 27, 39, 47, 94
Clayton, F. W., 162, 173
Clinics
  mental hygiene, 171
  psychiatric, 171
Closeness, 179
  emotional, 4
  needs for, 207
  physical, 139
Cognitive development, 42, 191
Coleman, J. C., 39, 79
Communication, 37, 38, 105, 139, 140,
    149, 157, 194
  nonverbal, 102

symbolic, 8
tactile, 39
Community, 36, 47, 69, 99, 180
  estrangement from, 4
  reactions, 5
  social systems, 5
  transitional, 34
  urban, 220, 221
Companions
  animal, 41, 43-46, 71, 88, 98, 103,
    122, 138, 149, 157, 168, 171,
    178, 179, 191, 195, 197, 208,
    211, 216, 217
  fantasy, 43-46
  human, 87, 88, 102, 211
Concerns, 7, 8
Conflicts, 56, 70, 198
  coping with, 5
  oedipal, 16
  preoedipal, 16
Conscience, development of, 48
Consciousness, 15, 108
Contact, 5, 39
  with animals, 192, 202
  human, 40, 139, 154, 159
  loss of, 8, 196
  physical, 38, 39, 40, 45, 139, 159, 179
Cook, E., 20, 30
Coping, 5, 70, 78, 103, 113, 115, 117
  with death of pet, 128, 129, 169
  mechanisms, 140
Cowper, W., 88, 95
Cows, 75, 189, 190, 212
Creativity, 43
Crisis, urban, 34
Cucuel, J. P. E., 27, 28, 31
Culture, 7-14, 15, 17, 18, 19, 24, 25, 26,
    35, 36, 114, 137
  American, 194
  development of, 50
  hunting, 119
  Oriental, 194
  primitive, 16, 22
  youth, 70, 110
Cumming, E., 100, 112
Curtis, G. H., 14, 32

D

Dale-Green, P., 15, 30

D'Amato, G., 174, 205
David, H. P., 18, 30
Day Care Centers, pets in, 191-192, 204
Daydreams, 16, 170, *see also* Dreams
Deafness, 105, 106, 107, 196
Death, 10, 13, 34, 67, 68, 78, 87, 97, 100,
    108, 110, 113, 114, 115, 116, 194
  and the child, 117-122
  fear of, 99, 114, 118, 122, 132, 198
  of parent, 117, 120, 121, 122, 123,
    126
  of pet, 122-132, 169
  trauma, 115, 129
  wish, 26, 51, 120, 196
Defense
  primitive, 98
  psychological, 128
  structures, 98
Dembeck, N. H., 12, 30
Dempewolff, R., 93, 95
Denenberg, V. H., 38, 80
Dependence, 46, 47, 72, 78, 86, 88, 98,
    99, 107, 159
  needs for, 165, 199
Depressions, 41, 103, 104, 105, 107,
    120, 121, 150, 151, 178, 198,
    199, 211
Des Lauriers, A. M., 38, 80
Despair, 4, 99, 151, 211
Deutsch, M., 70, 80
Development
  child, 34-79, 175
  cognitive, 42, 191
  of conscience, 48
  cultural, 50
  ego, 179
  emotional, 39, 83, 191, 204
  human, 70
  intellectual, 174
  mental, 174
  personality, 78
  of the race, 8
  social, 50
Developmental tasks, 36, 49, 67, 113
  at birth, 37-41
  of early childhood, 41-43
Dietz, Florence A., 3, 30
Di Leo, J. H., 7, 23, 30
Directory for Exceptional Children, 176,
    205

Dishon, C., 150, 160
Disorders
  behavior, 137
  emotional, 38, 171, 172, 180
  mental, 172
  physical, 180
Distress, 36, 71, 169
  emotional, 34, 220
Disturbed
  ego-disturbed child, 139
  emotionally disturbed children, 121,
    136, 138, 139, 140, 143, 146,
    149, 158, 171, 179, 183, 184,
    185, 216
  emotionally disturbed family, 138
  home, 77, 171
  socially disturbed children, 210
Dogs, 19, 46, 52, 57, 62, 63, 67, 72, 74,
    75, 76, 99, 101
  as companions, 44, 48, 49, 108, 168,
    191
  disturbed, 77, 157
  uses of dogs in institutions, 171, 175,
    177, 194, 208, 209, 211, 213,
    214, 215, 216
  uses of dogs in psychotherapy, 137,
    140, 141, 144, 149, 150, 154,
    155, 159
  "Seeing-Heart," 40, 171
Dolnihow, P. J., 7, 30
Dorn, R. C., 162, 173
Draguns, J. G. J., 39, 80
Dreams, 10, 15-17, 29, 42, 98, 120, 127
  daydreams, 16, 170
  nightmares, 17, 55, 118, 126, 141,
    179
  symbols, 15, 16
Drives, 15, 21, 37, 70
  destructive, 68
  sexual, 107
  species-specific, 8
  unconscious, 15, 21, 73
Drug addiction, 221
Dubos, R. J., 8, 30, 37, 80
Duclos, M., 109, 112
Durkee, A., 18, 30

E

Ecological awareness, 13, 220

Edgecombe Rehabilitation Center, 94
Ego, 40, 50, 78, 87, 139, 200, 202, 203, 204
  of child, 139, 179
  development, 179
  ego-disturbed child, 139, 179
  gratification, 121
  mastery, 194
Egocentric, 42, 120
Egypt, 19, 24, 27
Egyptians, ancient, 23
Elephants, 19, 72, 74, 75, 94
Ellul, J., 5, 30
Emotional
  adjustment, 183
  attitudes, 162
  breakdown, 77
  closeness, 4
  development, 39, 83, 191, 204
  disorders, 38, 171, 172, 180
  distress, 34, 220
  entanglements, 159
  growth, 217
  health, 172
  needs, 34, 44, 77, 110, 180, 194, 204, 220
  problems, 103, 155, 172, 191
  relationships, 111, 195, 204
  status, 115, 220
  strength, 6, 29
  stress, 85
  support, 48
  symbiosis, 164
  ties, 7
  trauma, 174
Emotionally disturbed
  children, 121, 136, 138, 139, 140, 143, 146, 149, 158, 171, 179, 183, 184, 185, 216
  family, 138
Emotions, 9, 16, 28, 35, 37, 89, 102, 108, 115, 121, 123, 128, 180
Empathy, 9, 221
Encounter groups, 5
Erikson, E. H., 26, 30, 39, 40, 79, 80, 95
Estrangement of man, 4-6
Europe, 19
Evernden, J. F., 14, 32
Evolution, 6, 8, 10, 11, 29
Exceptional children, 137, 175-181, 204

Existential problems, 10
Experimental Day Center and School, 181-183

F

Fairy tales, 19, 20, 34, 43, 117
  role of animals in, 15, 21
Family, 4, 23, 26, 48, 71, 88, 89, 107, 119, 141, 157, 161, 162, 170
  dynamics, 121
  emotionally disturbed, 138
  pathology, 77
  relationships, 163
  separation from, 192, 193, 211
Fanshel, D., 97, 112
Fantasy, 51, 87, 119, 120, 121, 126, 128, 145, 146, 163, 192
  activity, 40
  autistic, 198
  companions, 43-46
  of children, 144, 145, 170
  pet as object of, 43, 68
  unconscious, 123
  world, 77, 90, 122, 139, 169
Farquhar, A., 88, 96
Fate, 6, 36, 114, 120
Fathers, 18, 21, 23, 45, 84, 91, 104, 119, 146, 147, 149
Fears, 19, 20, 38, 40, 42, 76, 77, 85, 87, 88, 103, 115, 120, 121, 126, 128, 130, 131, 139, 140, 141, 142, 144, 148, 165, 179, 195, 198
  of animals, 17, 44, 68, 90, 93, 132, 147, 178, 200
  of death, 99, 114, 118, 122, 132, 198
  of desertion, 18, 129, 153, 170, 195
  of failure, 193
  unconscious, 16
Federal Medical Center, 210
Feifel, H., 115, 134
Fertility rites, 12
Finch, Dr. Stuart, 150
Finney, J. C., 181, 205
Fish, 62, 63, 74, 75, 94, 110, 144, 155, 177, 199, 200, 213, 214
Fisk, F., 121, 134
Folk tales, 15, 19-22, 43
Foote, N. N., 52, 80
Fox, R. B., 13, 30
Foxes, 17, 22, 44, 56, 74, 75

Frederick the Great, 88
Freedman, D. G., 38, 80
Freedman, N., 38, 80
Freud, A., 119, 133, 180, 205
Freud, S., 20, 30, 69, 80, 108, 112, 119,
    134
Friendships, 24, 97, 100, 101, 103, 114,
    131, 132, 159, 193, 195
  of child, 44, 45, 69, 121, 180, 182,
    191
  with pets, 5, 30, 42, 47, 50, 168, 191,
    194, 211
Fromm, E., 15, 31
Fry, F. L., 27, 28, 31
Funerals, 122, 123, 124, 127, 130

G

Gaddis, M., 132, 134, 208, 209, 218
Gaddis, T. E., 209, 218
Gaddis, V., 132, 134, 208, 209, 218
Gaitz, C. M., 193, 205
Galbraith, K., 5, 31
Garai, J. E., 43, 80
Gautier, J., 129, 134
Gay, W. I., 171, 173
Geber, M., 80, 175, 205
Generations, 4, 8, 34
Gessell, A. L., 123, 134
Gibran, K. V., 34, 80
Giffin, K., 193, 194, 205
Gill, W. S., 18, 31
Giraffes, 72, 75, 94
Goals, 36, 83, 110
Goldfarb, A. I., 108, 112
Goldfarb, W., 18, 31
Goldfried, M. R., 18, 31
Goldsmith, W., 7, 31
Goodal, V. M., 32
Gores, S., 181, 205
"Grass Snake, The," 19
Greece, 27
Greylag Goose, 11
Grimm, Wilhelm, 19, 31
Grollman, E. A., 127, 134
Grusec, J., 85, 96
Guilt, 6, 19, 51, 108, 114, 120, 121,
    123, 126, 127, 130, 168
Guinea Pigs, 62, 63
Gutheil, E. A., 16, 31

H

Habitat, natural, 28
Hacker, S. L., 193, 205
Haley, E. M., 39, 80
Hall, G. S., 123, 134
Hallowell, I. A., 22, 23, 31
Hammer, E. F., 17, 23, 31, 80
Hamsters, 64, 78, 155, 177, 213, 214
Hardy, T., 14, 31
Harlow, H. F., 37, 80
Hartley, E. L., 15, 17, 31
Hasselmeyer, E. G., 38, 80
Hatred, 20, 42, 55, 69
Havighurst, R. J., 36, 80
Haworth, M. R. 17, 31, 80
Hays, H. R., 31
Health, 86, 105, 106, 109, 168
  emotional, 172
  mental, 36, 37, 44, 99, 140, 162, 165,
    193
  physical, 162, 193, 205
  problems, 178, 215
Hebb, D. O., 38, 81
Hediger, H., 14, 28, 31, 50, 81, 94, 95,
    96
Heiman, M., 122, 134
Helfer, R. E., 34, 81
Henry, J., 194, 205
Hess, E. H., 11, 31, 37, 81
Heuscher, J. E., 19, 21, 31
Hilgard, J. R., 121, 134
Homes, 13, 34, 35, 78, 91, 99, 105, 106,
    110, 115, 137, 183, 192
  for aged, 192-205
  broken, 137
  disturbed, 77, 171,
  foster, 175
  pets in the, 157, 158, 159, 192-204,
    220, 222
Homosexuals, 19, 168
Horses, 16, 17, 19, 22, 25, 46, 72, 73,
    75, 78, 153, 155, 161, 177, 212,
    213, 214
Hostility, 20, 42, 70, 114, 139, 147,
    175, 216
Housman, A. E., VII
Huizinga, J., 7, 31
Hunger, 8, 37
Hunt, M., 20, 32

Huxley, J., 7, 32
Hyde, W. W., 115, 134

I

Identification, 26, 48, 76, 99, 100, 110,
 121, 145, 146, 147, 199
Identity, 5, 76, 175, 194, 196
 developing a sense of, 49-50
 "negative," 26
Iles, G., 32, 81
Ilg, F. L., 73, 74, 81, 126, 134
Image
 body, 39
 infantile, 53
 self, 48, 111, *see also* Self, image
Immaturity, 7, 115
Independence, 78, 144
 developing, 50-51
 need for, 199
India, 19
Infantilism, 53, 148, 190
Infants, 37, 38, 39, 40, 53, 70, 85, 86,
 95, 175
Inhelder, B., 117, 120, 134
Insects, 13, 47, 64, 177, 207
Insecurity, 70, 115, 141
Institutions, 136, 177, 178, 180, 194,
 203, 220, 221, 222
 caretaking, pets in 174-204, 219
 correctional, pets in, 207-218, 219,
 220
Intelligence, 11, 77, 78, 138, 181, 191
 development of, 174
Intelligence Quotient (I.Q.), 181, 184
 WISC, 73
Intrapsychic dynamics and individual, 5
Isaacs, Susan, 67, 68, 69, 81, 122, 127,
 134
Isolation, 4, 76, 87, 119, 157, 168, 217

J

Jacksonville State Hospital, 153
Jayne, A. W., 15, 32
Jensen, A. E., 118, 119, 134
Jersild, A. T., 119, 134
Johnson, Lyndon, 76
Joseph, R., 99, 101, 112, 130, 134
Joys, 69, 118, 148, 169, 196

of pet ownership, 53-66, 165

K

Kaplan, H. K., 18, 32
Kastenbaum, R., 131, 134
Kemme, M. L., 113, 133
Kempe, H. C., 34, 81
Kent, D. P., 100, 112
Killian, E. C., 192, 205
Kilmer, M. M., 196, 199, 205
Kirk, S. A., 182, 205
Kissell, S., 18, 31
Koupernik, C., 34, 79
Kroeberb, A. L. 11, 32
Krutzmann, W. G. A., 86, 96, 108, 112,
 162, 165, 173
Kutner, B., 97, 112

L

Landauer, T. K., 175, 206
Langdon, S. H., 12, 32
Langer, T. S., 97, 112
Language, 8, 9, 28, 29, 37, 165, 178
 "silent language," 38
Latency period, pets during, 49-51
Lawes, L. E., 207, 208, 218
Lawrence, E., 191, 205
Leach, M., 15, 22, 32
Leach, R. E., 15, 22, 32
Leach, W. W., 12, 18, 30
Leakey, L. S. B., 14, 32
Learned, J., 15, 30, 39, 44, 45, 46, 79,
 126, 134
Learning, pets as aides to, 67-69
Levinson, B. M., 9, 11, 32, 39, 53, 57,
 76, 81, 97, 112, 122, 134, 136,
 142, 143, 144, 154, 160, 162,
 173, 175, 176, 177, 181, 182,
 193, 197, 206, 210, 212, 213,
 214, 215, 218
Lévi-Strauss, C., 10, 14, 15, 24, 32
Levy, R. A., 17, 32
Levy, S., 17, 32
Lewis, N. D. C., 15, 17, 32
Life, 7, 34, 67, 110, 115, 118, 126, 180,
 204, 219, 220
 loss of interest in, 196
 philosophy of, 99

problems of, 114, 169, 200
Lions, 72, 73, 74, 75, 94
Lipton, R. C., 174, 206
Llama, 186, 187, 189
Loneliness, 5, 72, 89, 100, 101, 102, 104, 105, 119, 120, 129, 196
Lorenz, K. Z., 11, 32, 70, 81, 131, 134
Love, 6, 20, 28, 37, 42, 51, 55, 56, 69, 71, 103, 159, 195, 219
  needs, 86, 87, 100, 140, 207
  objects, 35, 51-53, 103, 178, 180, 195
  for pets, 85, 102, 108, 121, 129, 208, 209
  of pets, 111, 121, 204, 207, 208
Lowie, L. C. 98, 102, 104, 105, 106, 110, 112, 116, 117, 131, 134

M

MacCormick, Austin, 210
Manual of Child Psychology, 220, 222
Marcuse, H., 6, 32
Maslow, A. H., 83, 96
Maternal instincts, 55
Maturity, 6, 7, 51, 57, 95, 138, 140
May, R., 15, 32
McCulloch, J. A., 19, 32
McDowell, A. S., 14, 32
Meerloo, J. A. M., 114, 134
Mental
  development, 174
  disorders, 172
Mental health, 36, 37, 44, 99, 140, 162, 165, 193
Mental hygiene, 11, 36, 115, 122, 171, 172, 207
  clinics, 171
  teams, 162, 168, 172
Mental illness, 11, 36, 136, 170
Mentally retarded
  adolescents, 182
  adults, 182
  children, 182, 191
  and pet fairs and dramatics, 181, 183-191
  school for 181-183
Métraux, R. W., 17, 30, 72, 79
Mexico, 27
Mice, 75, 177, 208, 211, 217
  white, 65, 66, 177, *see also* White mice

Mitchell, M., 117, 118, 122, 123, 124, 126, 129, 134
Money management and pets, 70-71
Monkeys, 11, 27, 72, 186, 187, 188, 189, 190
Montagu, A. M. F., 10, 11, 32
Morris, D., 53, 73, 74, 81, 99, 112, 134
Mothers, 18, 19, 21, 23, 37, 40, 84, 85, 87, 89, 91, 95, 170
  and child, 7, 37, 38, 39, 41, 46, 48, 86, 117, 192
Motivation, 11
Mourning, 103, 114, 115, 127, 128, 130
Mumford, L., 5, 32
Munthe, Dr. A., 107, 112, 132, 133, 134
Mussen, P. H., 220, 222
Mutations, 10, 11
Mythology, 15, 16, 19, 20, 21, 22, 23, 107, 118

N

Nagy, M., 126, 134
National Institute of Mental Health, 35
Nature, 5, 6, 8, 9, 10, 11, 13, 27, 28, 29, 42, 68, 87, 94, 99, 114, 117, 122, 202
Needs, 6, 7, 8, 27, 28, 35, 36, 37, 40, 71, 83, 97, 111, 121, 217, 222
  of child, 141, 149, 174, 178, 182
  dependency, 165, 199
  emotional, 36, 44, 77, 110, 180, 194, 204, 220
  idiosyncratic, 39
  for independence, 199
  love, 86, 87, 100, 140, 207
  of pet, 50, 55, 70, 109, 141
  physical, 27, 110, 141, 180, 220
  psychological, 78, 180, 193, 203
  regressive, 138, 199
  satisfaction of, 193, 194
Negrito life, 13
Neurotic, 54, 77, 157, 162
New York State Psycholgoical Association, 153-154
Newman, M. F., 121, 134
Nightmares, 17, 55, 118, 126, 141, 179
Nixon, Richard, 76
Nonliterate peoples, 23
North Americans Indians, 19

O

Objects, 14, 41, 72, 89, 98, 194
  displacement, 157
  of fantasy, pet as, 43, 68
  inanimate, 19, 39
  love, 35, 51-53, 103, 178, 180, 195;
    see also Love, objects
  "transitional," 9, 40
Obsessive thoughts, 18
Oedipal
  conflicts, 16
  myths, 21, 22
  problems, 19
  relationship, 163
Old age
  and pets, 97-111
  withdrawal syndrom of, 192
Orchard Gables, Sanitarium, 203
Overs, R. P., 183, 206

P

Pandas, 72, 94
Parenthood, preparation for, 84-85, 95
Parent-surrogates, 4
Parents, 4, 26, 78, 91, 106, 157, 171,
    179, 183
  death of, 117, 120, 121, 122, 123,
    126
  relationships with 40, 51, 77, 113, 172
Parrish, H. M., 162, 173
Patients, conditions of, 18, 94, 128, 137,
    138, 140, 141, 144, 150, 153,
    157, 158, 192-204, 220
Peer groups, 7, 69
Peers, 26, 36, 44, 47, 48, 49, 69, 70, 78,
    139, 179
Perlman, E. A., 46, 47, 81, 191, 206
Persia, 27
Personality, 100, 102, 192, 211
  of child, 50, 137
  development, 78
  dynamics, 162
  traits, 18, 54, 76
Pets
  as aides, psychotherapeutic, 4, 36,
    67-69, 136, 139, 141, 142, 154,
    155, 166, 183-204, 207-218, 220
  behavior of, 42, 68, 92, 132, 144, 157

  and bereavement, 113-133
  and child development, 34-79
  as child substitute, 86-87
  death of, 122-132, 169
  needs of, 50, 55, 70, 109, 141
  ownership of, 53-66, 71, 78, 176, 214,
    215, 221
  responsibilities for, 46-48, 54, 56, 79,
    95, 141, 182, 192, 200, 201, 202,
    204, 210, 217
  value of, 157, 182
Pfeiffer, E., 112
Phenomenon, 9, 15, 16, 44, 115
Phillips, L., 18, 33, 39, 80
Phobia, school, 77, 144
Physical
  activity, 109
  closeness, 139
  contact, 38, 39, 40, 45, 139, 159, 179
  disorders, 180
  hazards, 155
  health, 162, 193, 205
  illness, 170
  needs, 27, 110, 141, 180, 220
  problems, 9, 10, 103
Physically handicapped, 137, 140, 157,
    199
Piaget, A., 78, 81
Piaget, J., 42, 81, 117, 120, 134
Pitcher, E. G., 72, 81, 119, 126, 135
Plants, 10, 13, 14, 67, 68, 117
Play, 7, 43, 46, 49, 50, 78, 123, 126,
    146, 175, 180
  imaginative, 44, 140
  with pet, 136, 138, 139, 183, 214,
    221
  role playing, 46, 77, 106, 146
  sex, 73, 77
  therapy, 216
"Pleasure principle," 41
Pleasures, 38, 97, 177, 196, 200, 221
Polt, J. M., 37, 81
Preadolescence, 69
Prelinger, 72, 81, 119, 126, 135
Preliterate man, 13, 118
Prenatal
  period, 95
  stress, 85-86
Preoedipal conflicts, 16
Primates, 7, 72, 94

Primitive
  art, 22-23
  culture, 16, 22
  defenses, 98
  man, 9, 10, 11, 12, 14, 16, 22, 23, 29, 36
  societies, 194
Prisoners, 207, 208, 209, 210, 217, 220
Prisons, 211
  Alcatraz, 209
  Leavenworth, 209
  pets in, 207-210
  Sing Sing, 208, 209
  Tower of London, 209
Problems, 10, 18, 19, 36, 43, 57, 69, 70, 97, 99, 111, 137, 156, 162, 193, 197, 200, 216, 221
  childhood, 99
  emotional, 103, 155, 172, 191
  existential, 10
  financial, 215
  of health, 178, 215
  of life, 114, 169, 200
  oedipal, 19
  physical, 9, 10, 103
  sanitation, 220
  social, 9, 40, 70
Provence, S., 174, 206
Psyche, 15
Psychoanalysis, 15, 21
  theory of, 15
Psychodynamics, 24, 156
Psychogenic, 163
Psychological
  assessment, 182
  characteristics, 25
  defenses, 128
  examination, 137
  functions, 39
  mechanisms, 20, 25
  needs, 78, 180, 193, 203
  processes, 20
  problems, 9
  regression and pet, 76-78
  shock, 28
  strengths, 18
  weaknesses, 18
Psychomotor, 175
Psychophysiological ailments of animals, 162

Psychotherapeutic aide, pet as, 4, 36, 67-69, 136, 141, 142, 154, 155, 166, 183-204, 207-218, 220
Psychotherapy, 36, 156, 158
  and animals, 136-159
  pet-oriented child psychotherapy, 119, 144
Psychotic, 138, 144
Punishments, 42, 119, 122, 123, 127, 141, 145, 211, 217
Pygmies, 12, 13

Q

Quaytman, A., 144, 160

R

Rabbits, 18, 22, 35, 65, 66, 75, 127, 177, 178, 192, 213, 214
Rappaport, Dov, 203, 206
Rappaport, Eva, 203, 206
Rationalizations, 10
Rats, 73, 83, 89, 122, 177, 208, 213
Reality, 4, 8, 9, 42, 43, 44, 50, 87, 95, 105, 111, 118, 121, 126, 127, 128, 129, 130, 139, 169, 196, 198, 204, 211
Reality-oriented, 179
"Reality principle," 41
"Red Riding Hood," 21
Regression, 16, 98
  to childhood, 193
  needs of, 138, 199
  psychological regression and pet, 76-78
Reichel-Dolmatoff, G., 20, 33
Relationships, 5, 11, 19, 42, 48, 52, 54, 57, 78, 79, 87, 90, 95, 114, 131, 168, 178, 195, 200, 202, 213
  between child and parent, 40, 51, 77, 113, 172
  emotional, 111, 195, 204
  family, 163
  between man and animals, 6-14, 15, 21, 52, 54, 89, 95, 99, 102, 110, 161, 162, 166, 197, 202, 204
  oedipal, 163
  symbiotic, 6
  therapeutic, 146, 158

Religion, 6, 15, 35
Rensch, B., 12, 33
Report of the Joint Commission on Mental Health in Children, 81, 211, 218
Repression, 8, 211
Resentment, 55, 179
Residential
  schools, pets in, 171, 175-181, 183, 204, 211, 212, 217, 220
  settings, 137, 174, 175, 178, 179, 197, 215, 217
  treatment, 149, 158, 180
Responsibility, 47, 52, 71, 84, 105, 157, 159, 169, 178
  of children, 35, 46-48, 51, 71, 121, 138, 190, 213, 221
  for pets, 46-48, 54, 56, 79, 95, 141, 182, 192, 200, 201, 202, 204, 210, 217
Retirement, 99, 100, 111, 196
Rheingold, H. L., 38, 81
Ribble, M. A., 38, 81
Rice, B., 99, 112, 130, 135
Roheim, G., 10, 16, 20, 33
Role, 73, 99, 100, 106, 158, 161, 170, 172, 179, 183, 194
  of pet, 15, 101, 115, 141, 157, 159, 175, 176, 179, 191, 210
  playing, 46, 77, 106, 146
Romans, 25
Roosevelt, F. D., 76, 130
Rorschach, the, 17, 18, 39, 72 *see also* Tests
Rosenberg, I. H., 18, 33
Rowan, Joseph P., 211
Rubin, Dr. S., 144, 160

S

Samuels, H. R., 38, 81
Saunders, Blanche, 76, 82
Schaefer, C. E., 43, 82
Schaffer, H. R., 82, 174, 175, 206
Schilder, P., 126, 133, 135
Schildkrout, M., 128, 135
Schizophrenia
  adult, 151
  child, 139, 148, 150, 184
School Readiness Tests, 73, *see also* Tests

Schools, 48-49, 69, 77, 78, 137, 158, 169, 192, 221
  for the blind, 176, 177
  for the deaf, 176, 177
  for delinquent children, 204, 210-217
  for the emotionally disturbed, 176, 177, 204
  for the mentally retarded, 176, 177, 181-183, 204
  for the socially maladjusted, 176, 177
  phobia of, 77, 144
  residential, pets in, 171, 175-181, 183, 204, 211, 212, 217, 220
Schwalb, G., 93, 96
Schwartz, A. A., 18, 33
Searles, H. F., 40, 82, 84, 96, 114, 135
Security, 9, 41, 49, 51, 71, 79, 94, 98, 99, 118, 140, 142, 150, 169, 194, 200, 221
"Seeing-Heart" dogs, 40, 171
Self, 5, 40, 41, 46, 49, 69, 97, 196
  acceptance of, 26
  actualizing, 67
  concept, 25, 43, 97, 102, 106, 111, 145, 178, 181
  control, 139
  defeating, 67
  denial of, 26
  devaluation, 211
  direction, 217
  enhancement of, 25-26, 97
  esteem, 26
  fulfillment, 20, 83
  image, 48, 111
  inner, 5, 29, 76
  protection, 70
  regard, 181
  rejection of, 26
  respect, 194
  supporting, 181, 192
  worth, 43, 181
Sensitivity, 5, 9
Sensory contact exercises, 5
Separation
  anxieties, 48, 191-192
  from family, 192, 193, 211
Sex, 19, 20, 70, 71, 73, 90, 110, 199
  activities, 16, 20, 106
  drives, 107
  education, 67, 178

play, 73, 77
Shames, C., 15, 17, 31
Shaw, G. B., 86, 96
Shomer, R. R., 94, 96
Siblings, 7, 44, 70, 92, 117
Sloan, A., 88, 96
Smith, J. C., 18, 33
Snakes, 16, 19, 44, 47, 65, 66, 73, 75, 177, 185, 213
Social
  adjustment, 183
  behavior, 175
  development, 50
  interaction, 175
  life, 144
  needs, 78, 110
  problems, 9, 40, 70
  responsibilities, 99
  situations, 70
  skills, 47
  solutions, 36
  stimulation, 174
Socially disturbed children, 210, 211
Society, 4, 20, 28, 36, 108, 109, 174, 181, 194, 211
  American, 34
  "future-oriented," 100
  primitive, 194
  rehumanization of, 219
  technological, 4, 36
  urbanized, 220
Solkoff, N., 38, 82
Solutions, 5, 36, 203
"Sorcerer," 23, 108
Sorrows, 108, 110, 114, 118
  of pet ownership, 53-66
Soul, 6, 8, 123, 194
South American forest Indians, 11
Speck, R. V., 162, 173
Sperling, O. E., 44, 82
Status, 69, 100, 111
  emotional, 115, 200
  symbol, 27
Stekel, W., 16, 33, 100, 102, 112
Stimulation, 38, 175, 179, 221
  of curiosity, 199
  intellectual, 191
  sensory, 37, 38, 175
  social, 175
  visual, 185

Storr, A., 70, 82
Stovall, A., 58, 82
Strengths, 49, 115, 129, 143, 158, 183
  decline of, 193
  emotional, 6, 29
  psychological, 18
Stresses, 29, 39, 72, 95, 172, 175
  complex, 4
  emotional, 85
  prenatal, 85-86
Sundaran, S., 48, 71, 82
Suomi, S. J., 37, 80
Superego, 211
Superstition, 35
Symbolism, 8, 9, 14-23, 27, 51, 110, 165, 199, 219
Szasz, K., 99, 112, 135, 210, 218

T

Tasks, 46, 47, 79, 95, 100, 179, 220
  developmental, 36, 37-43, 49, 67, 113
  domestic, 183
  Technology, 6, 9
"Teddy Bear Syndrome," 165
Temper, 67
Tensions, 7, 70, 78, 85, 95, 115, 137, 162, 164
Tests
  Animal Association Test, 18
  Children's Apperception Test, 17
  drawing, 17
  Rorschach, 17, 39, 72
  School Readiness Test, 73
Theory, psychoanalytic, 15
Therapeutic, 115, 137, 138, 140, 146, 157, 180, 200, 211, 212, 216, 217
  agents, 36, 136, 154, 155, 215
  relationship, 146, 158
  setting, 201, 202, 204
  technique, 158
  value of pets, 182
Therapy, 77, 78, 156, 157, 159, 178, 179
  group, 159
  nude, 5
  occupational, 193
  play, 216
  "primal scream," 5
  touch, 157

use of pets in, 139, 140, 141, 142, 155, 156
Thirst, 8, 37
Thomas, A., 40, 82
Thomas, Dylan, 111, 112
Thompson, S., 19, 21, 22, 33
Thompson, W. R., 85, 96
Tigers, 72, 73, 74, 75, 94, 185
Tillich, P., 114, 135
Togo, A. M., 97, 112
Tolstoy, Leo, 19
Tools, 94, 177, 204, 217
Totems, 19, 93, 95, 98
Touch, 39, 68, 151
therapy, 157
Toynbee, J. M. C., 25, 33
Toys, 38, 52, 68, 84, 221
Traits, personality, 18, 54, 76
Trauma, 23, 53, 113, 115, 121, 122, 129, 174, 175, 211
Treatment
of animals, 163, 164, 166, 209
philosophy of, 158, 178, 201
residential, 148, 149, 158, 180
setting, 302
team, 175
use of pets in, 136, 137, 139, 144, 145, 150-154
Trust, 39, 40, 41, 79, 120, 139, 140, 148
Turnbull, C., 13, 33
Tursiops truncatus, 14
Turtles, 65, 66, 94, 103, 155, 177, 185, 192
Tylor, E. B., 10, 33

U

Unconscious:
drives, 15, 21, 73
fantasies, 123
fear, 16
minds, 15
thinking, 98
wishes, death, 120

V

Values, 4, 22, 26, 95

of pets, 157, 182
Van Krevelen, D. A., 15, 18, 33
Veterans Administration Hospital, Cleveland, Ohio, 200
Veterinarian, 86, 108, 109, 143, 192
as "therapist," 161-172
Vogel, B. F., 44, 79

W

Walker, R. N., 17, 30, 72, 79
Walpole, Horace, 87
Weaknesses, 158
psychological, 18
Wechsler, J. A., 129, 130, 135
Weintraub, D., 38, 82
Welch, M., 58, 60-66, 82
White mice, 65, 66, 177, *see also* Mice, white
Whiting, J. W. M., 175, 206
Winnicott, D. W., 14, 33, 40, 76, 82
Wolf, M., 207, 218
Wolff, K., 193, 206
Wolves, 17, 21, 44
Woodlanders, The, 14, 31
World, 4, 5, 8, 25, 28, 29, 39, 42, 78, 86, 97, 99, 106, 115, 141
animal, 29, 50, 119, 182, 219
external, 35
fantasy, 77, 90, 122, 139, 169
impersonal, 35
inner, 9, 15
man's estrangement from, 4-6
mechanized, 220
outside, 40, 71
real, 140, 204
Wyatt, Sir Henry, 209

Y

Yaffe, S., 38, 82
York Retreat, the, 136

Z

Zeuner, F. E., 12, 15, 25, 33
Zoos, 28, 29, 50, 72, 73, 74, 94, 95
Staten Island Zoo, 185
Zurhorst, C. 27, 33